The Art of Appreciation

By Peggy Halevi

THE ART OF APPRECIATION

<u>The Art of Appreciation co-creators:</u>

Book Manager: Uri Halevi
Proofreader: Sandy Burris, Marina Frances Mularz
Book Cover Designers: Tasha Halevi and Ryan Godderz
Photographer: Michelle Halevi
Illustrator: Jolie A. Thomson
This book is a living-document, edit recommendations are appreciated

Library of Congress Control Number: 2010908854

Published by: Halevi Publishing

Halevi Publishing
Ideas

ISBN 978-0-9843288-0-2 (Paperback)

ISBN 978-0-9843288-1-9 (Hardcover)

I AM in great Appreciation for
my ability to hear the Omnipresent Voice Within,
for my husband, Uri, whose loving support enlightens,
for our daughters; Tasha & Michelle,
for my friends who receive the Art of Appreciation,
for my many spiritual teachers;
Abraham, Bashar, The Family of Jacob & many more,
for the gift of coming to know the Law of Attraction,
for the readers of this book,
for those who do not read it &
for the majestic-gestalt of this book.

We are
the
Space
of
Appreciation
in-between
a
Shared
Heart

Introduction

By Peggy Halevi

The life-changing idea that birthed this book was always meant to happen. It came to Uri and me in January 2009 from a brilliant suggestion by our friend. She was responding to our open-invitation to submit ideas to develop a creative enterprise together. That enterprise was to be in the spirit of and with using the concepts we knew as deliberate thoughts in awareness of the Law of Attraction. Her idea for a literary experiment featuring "Appreciating" struck a chord that still resonates with my soul as perfect. Initially, we intended this effort to be co-created amongst like-minded members of our Abraham-Hicks Meet-up Group that we hosted monthly at our home. We gathered as students of the Teachings of Abraham and this group had been "Appreciating" by writing into small-shared notebooks and by doing 'Rampages of Appreciations' at the close of each meeting. For a few months a subgroup gathered intending to figure out what type of collective-creation could be developed from this idea and in a short while, one member from this group rose-up with the inspiration to write with great willingness and delight about "Appreciation". I AM that person! Living an unstoppable inspiration from what is "Within" my essence, this book has been amazingly written right into existence. It is a true physical manifestation arrived from a spiritual counterpart in perfect time.

The book itself, much like the idea of it, came into being with ease and flow, as I blissfully studied and enthusiastically wrote daily for over the greater part of a year, on many aspects of "Appreciation". Along the way, I have discovered how to Master the use of "Appreciating" as a personal tool to learn from and improve communications with others. My most treasured outcome is that I have gained self-worth and have learned to appreciate myself. I have undoubtedly uncovered many fascinating things about "Appreciating". Most importantly to me, through this delightful spiritual path "Within" myself, I have enabled my personal ability of inviting and listening to the God-Source-Voice of my own Inner Being.

That "Within" space, which I proclaim sacred, has actively been involved in guiding and guarding me into the knowledge of "*The Art of Appreciation*", as a composed book and as a life process. Writing this book has softened my heart and gifted me in Great Wisdom.

The structure of this book is intuitive and simple. It is also, filled with leading-edge, new age, forward-thinking, positive information and processes that impressively holds balance with what is comprehensible and believable to many people. Each Chapter builds on the previous to heighten the reader's participation in learning "The Art of Appreciation", which with practice will enlighten. As with my own experience, other readers grow their self-confidence and appreciation of self along the reading-way. I have been told that after it is read, many hold it as a reference book. To assist the reader in developing their personal style Art of Appreciation, at the end of each chapter, there is a set of personally inspired "Appreciations" primarily relating to that Chapter. This is followed by a workshop page to be filled-in by reader-inspired "Appreciations". This practice will usher-in the desire to write Appreciations often, as it is amazingly easy and astonishingly beneficial.

My heart, soul and mind have been connected to the vastness of Appreciating and I herein share, with you, the results of this delightful love of finding "*The Art of Appreciation*".

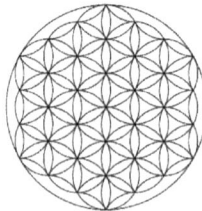

TABLE OF CONTENTS

Chapter 1 The Gift of Appreciating Life's Little Secrets 1-1

Chapter 2 Appreciation's Pathway 2-33

Chapter 3 Appreciating Changes Things 3-69

Chapter 4 Allowing Appreciation 4-91

Chapter 5 The Art of Appreciation 5-117

Chapter 6 Appreciate or Forgive? 6-135

Chapter 7 Appreciating Wellness 7-155

Chapter 8 I AM Appreciating All 8-177

Chapter 9 Emotionally Appreciating Thoughts 9-205

Chapter 10 Appreciating "Going for it!" 10-221

Chapter 11 Appreciating Death Everlasting Life 11-241

Appendix A List of Appreciations 264

Figure 1   Appreciation Category Chart 4-100
Figure 2   Wellness Fence 7-168

> *"It is no Secret that everyone loves the feeling of being appreciated and of appreciating another. So appreciate often, and make yourself feel good and you will be appreciated more often."*
> ~Peggy Halevi~

Chapter 1   The Gift of Appreciating Life's Little Secrets

"Life's Little Secrets." What does that even mean to me? Could it mean the keeping quiet of something that is revealed to me through my observations, thoughts or experiences and is intended for "safe" keeping? Is the secret the hiding of something intended to be within or only of my thinking it so? And when does one find holding on to a secret too burdensome, too difficult or too important to uphold? Is a secret a type of promise? In secret is there a shadow hankering to be adjourned in the telling or is the telling the liberation of the shadow into the light? Should all things be brought into the light? Without the shadow, the light is as undetectable as the secret was thought to be. Without shadows light becomes only a flash of brightness without shaping shades to bring context throughout itself. Shadows are complex variables that shape and mold humanity into existence. There is talk about Secrets these days, is there not? What are these things that we all sense to be secrets?

Mostly, when I experience "Life's Little Secrets" no one else knows that I have them. Most of my secrets are singular-secrets, rather than shared-secrets. It is apparent that all people bump into secrets on the way here from where we come. They are seemingly unavoidable patterns of thoughts coexisting within our individual realities. They seem to happen whether we want them to or not, perhaps more so in our youthful years, yet more dramatically intense even provocative in our adulthood. They surprise and conclude, simultaneously. Rarely ever do they inform or bring knowledge within their shadows. Excluding the gossip columnists or those of that prying nature, does anyone actually want secrets? Are secrets a form of esoteric internalized meddling? I think both singular-secrets and shared-secrets hold obscured weightiness in trusty carry. I've come to appreciate them, these secrets, over time with more meaning and occasionally with some guilt in having held to them, perhaps too long.

I feel some secrets should have been given up from me, like an idea whose time is right must yield out. Many years ago when undetected, I spotted my sister puffing on a cigarette in the huddle of her friends in the back corner of the project playground. She was twelve years old, I fourteen years old. Instantly, I felt a "secret" arrive in me. You know the feeling. It is unmistakable. My mind's-heart-eye knew it was a singular-secret. She did not see me see her. I held on to that "secret" for reasons that seemed intuitive and I knew that I too could be found dragging with my own set of friends, even in that very corner at another time, when she, I suppose, did not see me. Why tell-on her when she could tell-on me. I was guilty of the same secret even if she knew it not. I knew it!

More than forty years later, long after I have ceased my own habitual youth-passage of smoking, she still smokes. I wish I told our Mom that little secret, even if my own twin of it could have been exposed in Mom's awareness of that possibility. Could that tattling have made a difference? It "was" only, what it "was" and it "was" a long time ago.

I have other, mostly stumbled upon, secrets that I continue to keep, as I schlep them along in some kind of loyalty labeled "Catholic Honor", more like "Catholic Guilt". Or rather, that is the way I felt until recent secrets have dispelled guilt, shame and blame away forever. I now realize the purpose of any given secret is to help me change. Hidden secrets are merely elements of required informative tidbits comparing contrasts from the past to what is now. They are emphasized required provisions finally getting our notice. There is no secret in knowing that what was, was. What is more valuable knowing, is that what is now is now and, of course, what will be is to come. I am "here" and will be "there" with the given secrets joining me. Secrets are past "was's". Secrets are the quiet flowering of what is required <u>for</u> me rather <u>than</u> of me. It is folly to attempt to un-ring the bell that resounded then and is still heard now, sometimes louder. Secrets are "givens" intended to be realized. However, secrets can contaminate innocence. I understand that I am connected to the messages as much as to the journey that the messages are on. Secrets are blended in the colors of the threads that weave the material of me into shape, into existence, into the growing person and the expanded spirit I am. God will deliver the balance of my thoughts. Secrets often hold a pattern of longevity in the balancing process.

Secrets are ways of appreciating my "minding my own business" by keeping it to myself, while secrets are also "backdoor gossips", by thinking it to myself. Minds are energetic dynamic biological containers that experience burden for storing stagnant secrets. Mind-space is intended for vibrational use that shifts and electrically moves frequencies of thoughts forth. What is delivered to our mind exists in the mind. Secrets are exceptions. They come and passively reside in places of memory inside spatial static thoughts that want freedom while intending to be energy. Proverbs 11:13 states: *"A gossip betrays a confidence, but a trustworthy man keeps a secret[1]"*. Within that intuitive grasping there is a difference between Gospel gossip and Biblical revelation. I welcome the thought, which is that arriving secrets are perfect to know, and, in fact, that is why they exist. I am free of the unrequited and unnecessary responsibility of managing or distinguishing what is a secret thought. Secrets are just more information to assist wellbeing, otherwise how could they find their path to my knowing of them? Life's goodness, the source of wellbeing, provides me with all I need or more than all that I need. That is the only secret one needs ever know.

✳

Whisper someone else your secrets rather than request of me shelter for these thought-forms that survive upon your definition of concealment. Otherwise, secrets invade my freedom to devaluate all that I come to know in the openness of enough light. Shadows exist for honing clarity from all perceptions rather than for my protection and "safe" keeping. Being "trustworthy" to someone who desires to put their thoughts into me and in front of my own thoughts is foolish. Secrets can be, if allowed, controlling objects. Being trustworthy to other's secrets is relinquishing control of my own thoughts to another. That sounds far too unnatural and demanding to me. It enables someone else to take up residency in my mind, occupying some space as if it were theirs. I desire what can be known in free thoughts with clear conscience. I want to arrange information in my mind at will into places that have good undertones and direct accessibility

---

[1] The New International Bible

rather than maintaining restricted areas of thoughts, especially someone else's secret thoughts. I cherish equally all of what anyone else wants to esoterically know of me with the same reserve. I want no secrets unto myself. I want you to hold no secrets of me.

Secrets are the exposé of the way it is intended to be. I get the information I am supposed to get, as do you. That is all the most substance to be understood of any so-called secret. I clearly enable my thoughts freedom from others imposing limitations upon them. Free thinkers permit given secrets without tending to their external will. In that fact, I think mostly independent while resolving hidden secrets. Each secret found deep within when surfaced brings more freedom along. It is what I am built upon. I owe that to myself. Your secrets will have to go to someone else, if you need to create conditional secrets, and by nature they must all have some one else's attached conditions upon them. Perhaps another person will have to be the middleman in your creative interlocking of souls. It is better to work it out around me, rather than think to find me a conspirator working for you and your secrets. I am too free. Any thought you share with me is open to my interpretation and only subjectively influenced by your position or opinion, which may be like mine or it may be different. What I know is for me to experience, rather than for anyone else to manage. All that I want in my mind is what I perceive good to know and so that is what I put into my memory. The action of deliberately placing thoughts into my own memory is for the knowing rather than the judging. What is intended for me is what is my personal understanding of the inputs I encounter. If given to me, even your secrets are subjected to my capacity for understanding, currently. If given to me, your secrets are not yours any longer. Only I can control the gateway-entry of knowing accepted thoughts within myself. I treasure my each and every thought, observation and experience that I create, witness or have as a precious entity with great purpose. All thoughts really do matter to me.

The Law of Attraction is providing me with all inputs and I trust all my inputs are intended for my advancement. So, I better explain here, as straight forward as possible, what in my understanding the Law of Attraction is, because knowing this Universal Law has influenced my thoughts, actually most all of my thoughts, in profound life-changing ways. The Law of Attraction is that whatever is thought about, talked about, written about, is focused upon and what is focused upon and believed in too, that is the same type of stuff that comes into my life as a result. The Law of Attraction moves the flow of thoughts into connective motion, as does a magnet. Here is the good part; I can control my thoughts, what I say and what I write, even what I remember, so I have control over the stuff that comes into my life.

Here is an easy way of describing this Universal always active law; if you are a baseball fan, chances are you watch baseball games, and chances are if you watch baseball games, you will learn more about things associated with baseball! That is easy to understand. All such important laws should be so easy. In my focus on what a Secret is, I found out a lot about it and I learned a great many secrets about myself. Secrets are attracted to me and transformed by me. I might hold information to myself, but none of it is really a secret. It is against my nature to want or protect your secrets. There is room for much more than that in my mind and the natural frequency of the free mind is an emanating wave, rather than a restrictive wave. When you use the mind, it restructures continuously as an energy source that applies itself into its output so that the mind can create beautiful constructs of life expanding emergence. If you want me to know something, that is one thing, but keep your secrets from me, for I believe in free thoughts. Secrets seem far too in the vein of manipulation and I control my own thoughts, you control yours.

❀ ❀

Looking up the word "secret" in the dictionary I am impressed with the details of the numerous ways "Secret" is used today. It is an old word too. There are many definitions of it as an adjective and as a noun. I take from this fact that there are a great many word scholars thinking about "secret". In brief review Secret means[2]:

- ❖ *-done, made or conducted without the knowledge of others,*
- ❖ *-kept from the knowledge of any but the initiated or privileged,*
- ❖ *-faithful or cautious in keeping confidential matters confidential,*
- ❖ *-designed or working to escape notice, knowledge or observation,*
- ❖ *-secluded, beyond ordinary human understanding; esoteric,*
- ❖ *-of information, a document,*
- ❖ *-something kept secret, hidden or concealed,*
- ❖ *-a mystery,*
- ❖ *-a reason or explanation not immediately or generally apparent,*
- ❖ *-a method, formula, plan.*

Oh, here is one that was new to me, even being in the Catholic Church all of my life. Indeed it is in itself the social epitome of the word "secret", meaning:

- ❖ *–The SECRET Liturgy, a variable prayer in the Roman and other Latin liturgies, said <u>inaudibly</u> by the celebrant after the offertory*

"Haec sacra nos, Domine, potenti virtute mundatos, ad suum faciant puriores venire principium".[3]

---

[2] Dictionary.Com
[3] http://wdtprs.com/blog/2008/11/wdtprs-1st-sunday-of-advent-secret-1962mr/ and http://justus.anglican.org/resources/bcp/Procter&Frere/Mass.htm

Here is the "Secret" of the Catholic Mass Translated from Latin into English:

"All-powerful God, May the healing power of this sacrifice free us from sin and help us to approach you with pure hearts."

Why should that sentence be a secret is amazing? It sounds more Catholic than secret, although it feels like its intent was good as all prayers contain that ingredient. "Sacrifice" and "sin"; I don't want to know that secret! Those words conjure up some private thoughts in me yet, seem somewhat lost to the new person I've become from obtaining and benefiting from my acquired and released *Secrets*. And there at the bottom of all these relatively connected meanings of "Secret", the real "Secret" of the word "Secret" is defined to me in these two perfectly simple root words:

"To secern".

Why so? Because this is the meaning of SECERN:

–To discriminate or distinguish in thought.

I conclude that when anything is introduced to me as a secret, I will secern it.

That is the absolute unabridged definition and it brings such clarity to my now perfect understanding of a "secret". The word "secern" is the root of the discerning of what the word secret really means. A secret is what we discriminate or distinguish in thought, and since I am in control of my own thoughts, a secret is only what I think it to be. Can thoughts even be secret since the thinking of them is always known if only to self? As a result, I feel free to reveal my "Secrets" and yours if you've giving me any.

※ ※

I am able to refuse a secret another wants me to have and I do not want, and I do not want any of them. Although, what about the singular-secret? You know those. They are the ones similar to my seeing my sister and her not seeing me see her.

Seemingly, they are the ones that find me all on their own. They are the mischievous ones that cause me the most trouble. They are the ones that I put the thoughts together about. Piece it together thought-by-thought, one-by-one, until, Ops! There it is a secret that I've invented from my thoughts, observations and moods. Hence, if I am in a good mood it is more likely the "invented secret" could be flattering more so than if I was out-of-sorts when I devised this singular-secret. In creating a singular-secret, I have to see or hear something that will make me start the linking of what if's and why not's together. Let's say, I see someone do something that appears out of character or even "wrong" in general terms. Ops!, there it is. My judgment. I have to appreciate the "trip" as these thoughts tend to slide-down the slippery slope as I create a brand new secret. Something no one else knows that I know. They, these invented secrets, feel powerful to own at first and weaken me soon thereafter. They stem from something I usually do not even care to know which makes them more mysterious. Those are the secrets that I attach myself to and are harder to detach myself from. They deal with my baser egotic nature. Blessed that they are rare though pleased to confront them when identified and learn from them as they contain a vivid shadow of myself in their discovery, creation and final dissolution. The best way to be rid of them is to quiet my mind and visually throw them away one-by-one restoring higher vibrations and higher egotic mental constructs. I could, but, do not analyze them too much or too long. I accept my mental conditioning and find restoration worthwhile the adventure. Increasingly, I am in better control of my patterns of thoughts and I am finding more humor in my evolving egotic behaviors.

This discarding of a self-invented secret reminds me of a lesson I've come to embrace in dealing with the "things" that people give me as gifts. My children, probably yours too, have cheerfully given me all kinds of gifts. Each and every one of them from the kindergarten clay-molded child's handprint to the tiny fragile meticulously folded origami crane in my favorite colors that was created during a high school art class and all kinds of things in-between and since made or purchased from love and appreciation. All heart warming items initially. Over the years of collecting these treasured gifts they have amounted to a bunch of stuff.

My brother, who has since passed away, has given me several gifts too. My Grandmother now dead more than 20 years ago, gave me gifts and additionally, after her funeral I inherited some more stuff from her. I have gifts from my husband, parents, friends, sisters, brothers, nieces, nephews, aunts, uncles, neighbors and coworkers. I have a collection of gifts. And incidentally, the same is true of the other members of the family. These collections substantially amount over the years.

I admit some of them I absolutely cherish and love for their sentiment, others for their style or functionality and others, in all honesty, I do not really like very much at all. Even their memories are more a haunt than a pleasure. They all gather nonetheless. They collect dust, and, as secrets, some of these gifts actually attempt owning portions of my memory. There are things that every time I look at them I might remember something. I might have a repeating memory that wants to connect to this something or other. Some things hold elaborate memories, such as my dead Grandma and sitting on the pine log bench together with her in her garden yard chatting about her past life and my impending adventure. Other gifts conjure other memories. Maybe a memory of a time we traveled there, a party this came from, an aroma this produces, a feeling, a lesson or a Christmas years gone by. All this stuff actually decorates for me my home and my mind, or so it was.

Until one day I realized that I wanted freedom from tending after things other people gave me. As I began to take action on that, it was much easier to part with things I gave to myself as they wore off their interest in me and I was responsible for my having them in the first place. But I looked at gifts from others a little differently. Now, I know my dead Grandma, who loved me as big as the sky, doesn't care if I am dusting off her green-stemmed dessert glass. She is dead. She doesn't care about "things" any longer although that glassware was a precious addition to her hospitality and equally it remains a delightful memory from my youth. No one cares about their things after they are dead. The dead do not care if the living-ones tend to them, although during the living years we might edge in that direction, thinking someone might want something or other belonging to us. I think that about those dishes my brother left for my Mom and my Mom gave to me and I know one of my daughters will love my handing them over to her and I am thinking I want to do that while I am alive and when it is right for her to take them. I am a sensitive person but I am a sensible person too. I might want to take care of Grandma's dessert glass, but I do not want to feel like I have to.

Here is an example of what I mean: For years and years, I held onto a blouse that my fifteen years since dead, dead and gone brother gave to my mother years prior to that and I now have and it doesn't even fit me. It hung in the clothes closet mildly stained and discolored with age and, occasionally, I would touch it and remember my brother and how kind and thoughtful he was while alive. I might think about him as a kid and what happened to take his life. I think of my love for him and, although his memories feel good even while writing of him, I think I can manage those thoughts without that blouse hanging around. Some memories are wonderful; in fact, many of my memories about my Grandmother and my brother are very nice memories. I think having memories is fantastic, good or bad, but good is better. I just do not want to spend so much of my "now" time in the spaces in the closet and on the shelves of past memories. I accumulate things that seem like gifts initially and then turn into something else much closer associated with memory than possession. They are the physically intangible stuff.

And then one day, after much thought, I conjured up enough personal time and strength to systematically bid goodbye to many of these things that were acquired and attracted into my home and mind and gave them to charity, save the inseparable special ones that are so worthy of retractable memory space. It was an emotional relief that felt as if a peeling-away was taking place, while yielding a lightening-up of over-familiar presumptuous heavy burdens. These things were emotionally and physically associated directly with me.

The experience made for some hesitations and memory confusions while deciding what should stay and remain a deserving treasured item of my championed sentimental retention or which would leave me behind. The reminiscence contained locked within the things placed into the give-away box took from me seemingly something and replaced into me release, simultaneously. Although at first reluctantly, I could let go of things from this spirit of evaluating potentially last-time and often lasting memoirs along the process of letting go. There was an elevated light freedom in the relinquishing of these items and a safe return to the spacious self within. The time spent sorting out these things that held almost too much thought in their memory pointers felt exceptionally healing. The process seemed endless as, with a mere touch of an item, the memories flooded and reverberated my mind and clouded my desires with a mix of heart-held needs within the passion of guilt by surrender. How can things hold so much of my past and transform so much of the same into this moment is still a mystery to me. These possessive thoughts were all so time consuming to visit and revisit and the enabling flow of them being carried away from me was uplifting after I started to feel the sensation of them moving off of my fingertips into the box of someone else's needs rather than staying inside of those small consolidated capsules of my past life, which amounts substantially. Afterwards, I re-owned room to decorate or rather redecorate my own world and within the self-promise to be ever more careful about what I might choose to own in memory within gifts or secrets. It is a glorious freedom.

✤

Gifts and secrets are similar, not the same, similar. Beware and gracious at accepting either, for there is much to be found "Within" oneself in the generated manifestation of a gift or a secret. In the thought of a past memory with a feeling of its own life, one can always take responsibility for the appreciation of its power and consumption and chose well what is worth the ownership.

I hold on to a choice few of my gathered possessions that contains within them wanted memories, sentimental or financial value or beauty. However, I have forgiven the extras from my life. I am free, or definitely freer. I am not responsible for the items others die leaving behind, although I might for a while hold them to me in a sense of endearment. I do not have to use or keep the house warming gifts that did not match my home or frame of mind with true comfort. I am only holding on to rather than being held responsible for the items I want and them only while I want them. I am obligated to myself rather than to my stuff. Secrets are like this, are they not?

Gifts are fun to receive, secrets not so much fun in that. In the giving of a gift there is an art and likewise in the receiving of a gift. The tending to a gift can exhibit itself in the form of feeling obligated to return something to the giver. Secrets given or gifts given should be in my total charge, owing no one for either and no one wanting something of me for the owning. In gift giving, receiving and sharing there is pleasure in manifesting and providing to another their desires. When appropriate, gifts are a source of joy and harmony. I love this aspect of gifting and receiving. It is no secret that what we give we receive in return in some other fashion, yet it is a bigger secret that what we receive we give in return. What you put out you get back and what you get back you put out. Measure for measure abundance flows.

Secrets and gifts are different from each other; yet, I know within their possessiveness there are some, not all, similarities worth remembering, and so I will. The moment of "now" occupies the total possession of all secrets and gifts and "now" understands why better than my words can explain why. As a consequence, my growing cluttered-free life and mind is light and more airy. Enough so that changes had space to happen and I see clearly that more was opening up to me in the freeing of me.

Simultaneously, during this time of my life, I AM brought as willingly into being a "Great Appreciator" as the fifty-ninth second is systematically and thoroughly brought forth into its borne transmuted minute with but a "tock". It is a mutual celebration perfectly timed while syncopated between the "tick" and that "tock" into what is the "Now". In this space between here and there, is where I stand gathering my new self who is birthed into this miracle as a genesis unto and "Within" myself. Dwelling Within my soul there is blissful acceptance in being this "Great Appreciator" and along with it is an interesting poignant sensational high-pitched vibration, heard within and transpired through the Universe, almost in haughtiness, of finally arriving at the beginning of a long ago pre-appointed journey, one I only know of now that I am present in it and made of it. I am honored to know it is what I am! I resist only the optioned-thought, available with personal freedom to think about anything, to stop Appreciating. I chose to Appreciate!

Save your pity in thoughts that I am vaguely absurd! I might be, and so what, although, truly, my soul knows its way. I trust its Beingness and indeed, I desire to Appreciate! More so, I am inspired to Appreciate. I can change my mind and think otherwise, yet, to me, that thought is most unwise, for Appreciation relinquishes a huge amount of what is Wisdom for and to me and it is a vehicle in which some others can and will ride their way into wakefulness. I am gifted with this interest in Appreciating. What a Blessing! What a Gift! It is the opposite of a secret.

It is who I AM, who I've become into Being. 'It is fanatical or perhaps obsessive!' some might say, many more might think. I know I am vigilantly aware in most all my ways, yet especially in my ways of Appreciating, which is sacred to me, like a softly spoken prayer that whispers God into my essence and me closer to God. My thoughts of Appreciation are my most humble and strongest vantage point into knowing anything at all and perhaps everything I know. And yes, I have thought to think about my state of mind and have decidedly agreed with myself that this path is the most exhilarating one, thus far, I have ever traveled. I will continue on this road forevermore, I so hope. It is a free choice and an astonishing privilege to be a "Great Appreciator" and anyone, actually everyone can be. I purely love appreciating everyday in many ways and all day long, if I could and I think I can. I am more attentive to the way in which I speak a sentence, relay a message or tell a story ever looking for opportunity to insert the lingering Appreciation to come forth and enrich the environment. I also love to conclude most conversations in appreciation, rather then in a farewell goodbye. I appreciate any and all communications and any and all times of non-communications. I appreciate the beginning and the ending, and here is a secret, I appreciate whatever is in between the beginning and the ending and the ending and the next beginning. I appreciate it all.

It should be known that I verbalize and write appreciations and I appreciate silently as well as out loud, in my observations of situations, things, and people. I find that most every thought can be modified to appreciate along with the flow of the thought. Am I a fanatic or am I finally awakened to the power of this superb cerebral and sacred thought gem that has been hidden far too long, as yesterday's secret? I appreciate the experience to understand that within the context of everything exists the choice to appreciate.

For me, Appreciating, seemingly obsessively, is one of life's astounding secrets that unearth treasures dazzling beyond the brilliance and lore of mere gold. I think to myself: 'Why am I learning of it only now and why has it taken so long to realize?' And, then, in light of it all I sense it is very good. It is a Divine Intervention and finally it has come to me. Knowing this "Now" is all good! Uneasily, I realize that I could have missed this completely. I am so fortunate that I've been attracted to it finally and that is what I most appreciate.

The Grand Transformation of Mankind

Am I finding myself or am I lost to the forsakenness of an intensely single-minded-focus on an invisible phantom thought of becoming better, being awakened, and experiencing more joy? Can I actually be an enlightened person or am I a compulsive obsessive one? My doubts seem to dissolve quickly into a faint recollection as I obtain delight in the results of knowing my truth and in "The Art of creating Appreciations" having more truth revealed to me. There is awe-apparent and great evidence of my Well-Being in life, increasingly so, since Appreciating grew integrated into me as a part of my soul. It is pleasing to sense that along with and in the simplicity of Appreciating, I intuitively know that the Grand Transformation of Mankind arises and I am part of it. Knowing this is just a portion of the ramifications of my association with Appreciating.

And what is this Grand Transformation of Mankind that is already upon us? It is that all participants come to see our own connection to God and while appreciating our connection to everything else. It is the knowing of our thoughts responsibly framed to the picture of our own world reality. Along with the perception of others, I once thought of God as an elderly white bearded man hovering above in space, in heaven, and upon a thrown. He is in constant omnipresent judgment of me and of you. But, I now know God more personally as I figuratively climb up to the awareness of God's presence "Within". I, like many others, live with a mind recently and more definitely aware of its own thoughts, and in so, I know that this growing awareness is also happening to others. We are all this Grand Transformation. I am not alone in this experience. That's it! It is simple and profound!

People who are controlling their thoughts better and are listening and hearing God speak as a result of finding better thoughts and a more open-mind from the lack of clutter of previous confusion, are the Grand Transforming Population of "conscious thinkers". We are connected or becoming connected to the God Source. We are conscious of our thoughts and of God's existence flowing into those purified thoughts. We are hearing God "Within" our listening to our own deliberate thoughts of communication. With this new realization, rather than new ability since I have always held the capability, to think about what I think about, I am transforming. I am experiencing a different path. This is not religious it is a spiritual awareness.

It is important to notice that "Appreciating" is one of the active messages that travel on the path rather than being the path itself. From knowing this, I have shifted my perception of nearly everything in life. That is a huge statement! Just about everything in my life is different than it was before becoming aware of the control and freedom I have over and within my own thoughts. Every one of them! Therefore, it is a pleasure to delve into and an honor to present herein the many aspects I've discovered in the "Art of Appreciation", which is a thought tool as well as a byproduct of our Grand Transformation that is in momentum and gathering much speed. It is time to behold the awesome swirling residue of "Appreciating" among the climate of inner and personal changing.

It seems to me, and I have no way of proving it, but, I feel it so, that this global change of increased awareness of God and Self, to and of humans, is eventually going to touch everyone. I wonder how long it can be denied and the answer is that it holds little bearing on me at any rate of its happening. I am transformed already. I realize too that if I can understand and learn this, anyone can. It is not hard to do, but it is something unique to do. I am so unlikely the person to find this out, as my religious background promotes almost the opposite of this type of seeking into my spirituality. I've come to know that my religion seemed to emphasize fear as a tactic for me to remain so unwilling to Seek First The Kingdom of God. I had a fear of loosing myself in the discovery of God. Fear is so unlike what I've come to know as God's desire to keep me aligned. God wants my happiness, but I have to think my happiness into existence, and that is pretty much an ongoing thing. No one else creates my happiness. I've been so out of touch with the most natural state of feeling really good that I have to focus on being so in order to achieve this alignment. What keeps me aligned is the way in which I see myself. The more I view myself as God sees me the more aligned I am to God and the happier I am. My knowing and changing is a simple process and yet, it requires desire. So many other things point away from this frame of thinking, yet, once it is grasped it can also be noticed that the opposite is true, in which all things bring confirmation to this understanding as Truth.

This knowing is meant as words that correspond to feelings that I have within me rather than an ultimatum for you, who have other thoughts, which are equally valid. There are a variety of thoughts that can align me. Everyone has his or her own library of thoughts that align. This Transformation already has indirectly touched everyone in ways that you will learn of herein and, especially as a real observation, vibrates within the winds and breezes forever. That thought goes on and on. That very thought, as with all thought, creates. It seems apparent to me, and perhaps I am in this mix so deep that apparent is subjective to my feelings and emotions, yet, I think that the future will transpire with a wave of new thinking habits. I think very differently than years gone by, significantly so. By that I mean I take responsibility for my thinking now. I think differently and more clearly about God and I am using my ability to process thoughts differently also.

I hear people from time to time make statements regarding new ideas coming into their time of acceptance; "It is an idea whose time has come", they say. I feel that it is "Now" whose time has come. And in this "Now" we all have the ability to control our own thoughts of everything we are thinking about, especially remembering that no one else can do this for you. It is time for mankind to appreciate that "Now" is given to us to know of it, to think of it, to "Appreciate" it and to be of it. In taking responsibility for thoughts, "Now" is more present. It is "Now" that we are to discover in and of our own thoughts. "Now" is what is the backbone of the heightened awareness we, in this time-space-reality, are to accept having come to us. It is a gift that needs to be thought about willfully and if desired accepted as a Grace. It is the gift of becoming aware of one self in the "Now" of existence.

This transformation is the only option I can participate in, even knowing I always have choice to turn from it. This transformation is something happening to all people who want it. It is belonging to all these generations surrounding us into accepting it, and it is unmistakably here for everyone. It is like the air we breathe, it circulates in random breezes wherever it wills or rather wherever it is willed. It is other than religion or a set of beliefs. It is the age of it happening. Your personal thoughts are now what a movement of consciousness knows as the catalyst birthing itself into creation.

I think that one can only "Appreciate" where light falls in its standing intended path of shadows and shades and likewise, one can welcome time into happening and within such an attitude all can have awareness of the essence of "Now", however all will not. I find it unpleasant to think light out of existence, so I see it and appreciate it into existence even more. It is "Now" here and in our lifetimes we can experience this elevation of mankind. It is a growing collective consciousness that we are all equally worthy of accepting. There is no competition to receive awareness. There is no limit on awareness. It is not going to be divided among some and not then be enough for others. All will arrive at it during eternity. "Now" is valid for some and meaningless to others. It is the ride for some and the vehicle for others. It is the wind to some and the noise to others. It is, after all, what you realize, which might be different from what others realize of you. Humanity is in the age of freely realizing our thought as your own, if so desired.

I am reminded of the thought that when someone is presenting you with an ultimatum it usually means you should turn away from it. Being forced or coerced into anything is the opposite from feeling the ease of the moment and the ease of the direction in choice. There is only the choice that you personally approach, if you want it.

❋ ❋ ❋

My Catholic religion does not really promote the individual controlling one's own thought. The religion is actually better at controlling thoughts than are you in it, or so it seems taught. I have been of the mindset that anything worthwhile is worthwhile looking closely at because it should stand the test of evaluation. The church holds pressure to what we look at closely, if it is not already a part of the religious doctrine, albeit, doctrine is ever changing by those who supervise. I have decided to choose my own thoughts carefully, and I choose to look closely at all my thoughts. I choose to see and appreciate the best in my religion and continue on a religious path without removing what is not the best created within it, but rather by avoiding it. I do not see any rule in the Catholic Church stating I must look at sin if I am not sinning, or I must look for evil and find it. It says, "Seek the Kingdom of God, first", and that is exactly what I am doing.

In the exquisite practice of Appreciating, which is not against the Catholic religion to do, my consciousness grows as the wildflower in the springtime, without prompting or educating, with expecting and anticipating, and by love. It is a natural path in spiritual growth. Yes, perhaps this is compulsive behavior, or am I breaking through to a new appreciation of life that I am compelled to share of myself and teach, if possible, to others and within the frame of mind that I only care to tell of it, rather than change anyone to see it the same way I see it? I sing this out to anyone for the purpose of informing rather than converting anyone into something else, for they are already the ones that they are supposed to be. Deliberate systematic "Appreciating" is a bright colorful thread that contributes to the weave of the material of whom I am and who you are to me. I "Appreciate" you, and as I do, I sense an "Appreciation". It is similar to the egotic-based teacher who says, in such, that when you see something wrong with another it is like looking into a mirror and seeing your own faults reflected. Likewise, it is true that when you "Appreciate" others you reflect that goodness back to yourself.

This becomes easy to see; mirror your faults from what you see in others, or mirror your positive aspects from what you Appreciate in others. This seems like the active part of "Do unto others as you want them to do unto you." We spend far too much time looking and analyzing faults. Look at the things to "Appreciate" about others and it will be yourself that is brought into being "Appreciated".

It is amazing that "Appreciating" in what might be considered as the extreme, could stir up thoughts of such surprising discombobulation at first for me. Upon learning about my sense of something special happening to me with my focus on "Appreciations", I was determined to write them into a journal. In the brevity of my first conscious, somewhat awkward, written "Appreciations" I began to "Appreciate" things I had been told to avoid "Appreciating", or conceit could be the results of me, since after practicing "Appreciating" for awhile I started to even "Appreciate" myself. It was ok for others to "Appreciate" me, but this was something I thought perhaps my religion might not agree with as appropriate.

Catholics find it particularly difficult to "Appreciate" themselves. But, other religions yield similar resistance towards this also. In fact, most all Christian Religions are fighting against something or another - especially personal happiness. Some Christians are taught that people who "Appreciate" themselves are part of the new age "feel-good" religions. That's an interesting way to put fear into people about what they think about themselves. I thought about that and decided to go forth and see what happens to a person who self-appreciates.

I caught myself thinking: "What is becoming of me? Could I become "full of myself", "Appreciating" myself? Could I think too highly of myself by "Appreciating" me? Could I become too full of pride, a snob, a snoot, or just plain arrogant?" I thought about that in my cautious-very-Catholic-old-ways and concluded, in true relief, to send all those thoughts away. I could control my thoughts about these feelings without becoming the complete opposite of my humble self. I could do and think what I wanted to and I trusted in "Appreciating" the entire experience. Emotionally, I could feel that "Appreciating" makes me become more aware of my thoughts and it feels good. Sometimes it feels so good that I intuitively think about things in "Appreciation" of them for the purpose of feeling good. "Appreciating" has proven its value to me and I continue to trust in "Appreciating". I have not given up my religion to "Appreciate", in fact, I am so much more confident about what I believe in.

※ ※ ※

I "Appreciate" myself and everything about me. There is a new way to look at life from this new practice-of-thought. I "Appreciate" the World around me and everything I interpret of this World. I AM a "Great Appreciator". So what, if some might think it is an obsession with me? They might well be right, and what a splendid obsession I am experiencing! I think, state and write "Appreciations" nearly every day and when I forget, when I get too busy, when I think time too important to use this way, I notice a depleted difference. I write "Appreciations" both large and small without distinguishing one better than the other. Perhaps some of my "Appreciations" are more potent or powerful, however, all are wonderful. I love every one of my "Appreciations" as if each were a special love in my life, for that is, in fact, what they are. I AM a "Great Appreciator" and I could shout it from the hills and let anyone who cares to know of it.

And, oh my, do I love to listen to other's "Appreciate" too, such as my husband, children, other family members, friends and business acquaintances. I appreciate sometimes, as appropriate, in Emails, on Blog Sites, in Chat Rooms and in Internet Forums. I "Appreciate" the freedom in "Appreciating" from within myself. When you hug someone, you want a hug in return, usually. When you love someone, you want to be loved in return, usually. Yet when you "Appreciate" the reciprocal counter part to it is pure freedom. That is the counter-effect. Being "Appreciated", the return is sometimes a part of it. However "Appreciations" are meant to fly in their freedom and the return is of less importance than the relief in its creation. I have experienced that "Appreciations" are swirling spirals, wavelengths, moving vibrational energies and circular sometimes.

I share time with my husband, Uri, doing "Appreciations" together in a shared journal, almost every single day. I gather my visiting children together into a circle of "Appreciation", which I find to be very sacred and holy, and connective and fun. It is a fun projection of positive communications. Almost like an intoxicating ascending addiction, I crave doing more "Appreciations", as I meet with friends and, yes, part of the time we are together we take turns speaking of our "Appreciations". We are all "Great Appreciators". It is a natural state of being once subscribed to and accommodated. My life is surrounded with "Great Appreciators". When Uri and I, meet business associates, we in a very short time, begin to co-create "Appreciations" together, decidedly the way we want to conduct business. Our business-model includes "Appreciating" and we are "Appreciating" our success in business.

I might have felt it to be excessive or obsessive, yet, it is better than that, it is a real integral aspect of my life and with it I enjoy so much more of life than I have ever been able to before now. "Appreciating" systematically and growingly is blending into my thought process rather than sticking out of me indiscreetly, hence, creating expansion rather than distraction. Many do not even realize I am doing it. It is undetectable in my overall character as a specific for others to pay attention to. It seems to flow about in me and in my life, rather than conquer or control me. It adds to me. "Appreciating" has become a way-of-life for me and I know that, because of my "Appreciating", I am experiencing much more joy and happiness. This joy is the clarification of determining more than the shadows against no shadows. It is the color, the texture and the sensation of togetherness. I am thriving in an abundance of all things I desire and I am realizing an additional emotion available to me after thinking that I had known every emotion that is available. Experiencing this, I know that I have many new and wondrous emotions to become in this lifetime. I am living a most beautiful life filled with much and ever-growing clarity.

Herein, I write of the path that I found to become in this high emotional state of "Appreciation". It is my *Secret*, revealed. It is the coming forth into the light while accepting and sharpening the depth-defining shadows that create the presence of awareness in sharing. Perhaps in knowing of my path, others will find a way here in provided benefits and limitless space to partake, although I am only a messenger. We are the growths. I want to write of this as it might be something you find interest in knowing more than pursuing. I want only to tell you about this seemingly valuable otherwise untaught phenomenon. What you do with this knowledge is your business.

I am wondering where to start, while appreciating that personal experience is more impactful than any of my words can ever be. The beginning surfaces as a vision in a sphere of thoughts that want so to become written words, to be read, preferably out loud, and to be spoken into existence, bringing further validity to their awareness of themselves and to all else. There is a circle of flowing experiences that want to be articulated, thought about and given. I want to share both the joy of being a "Great Appreciator" and the story of the path that was taken to become a "Great Appreciator". It is with great respect and "Appreciation" that I am aware that the reader is on their own perfect path bringing us together here and now, and, as you know your own story to be interesting and inspired; I am herein inspired to tell my story. In the telling of what it was like before these life altering discoveries, now within it all, and as I see it unfolding. Tears from new emotions bring Joy to be found and I will continue seeking.

I feel I am carrying out a charge directed into me from the beginning of time. That was intimidating yet required to say. It could sound very arrogant and conceited. Imagine, me thinking that I am having anything to do with the beginning of time. But, I do. I feel so connected to this fiber of knowledge, with this link to understanding, that it is most of all what I AM. I am connected to time then, now and when. It is wonderful to have these deep feelings and emotions of desire being fulfilled in its proclamation. It is similar to remembering something important that I forgot and cached away in a dreamlike state of suspension, and now it is upon me and its recall is so pleasing. Arrogantly fantastic! This satisfaction in self-awareness is a blessing. That is inspiration and in it the truth has its way happily with all prepared to accept. This is my path, yours is for your telling as awaiting. It is self-confidence rather than conceit. My desire is widened within the space and pattern of my weave that now threads your tapestry also. This is a great position to be in knowing. This book expresses what aligns me to myself and to the Source of myself, which is the Source of you, as well. It is so exciting to feel that I have something that will provide you, the reader, with something that will improve life. That is part of what I feel is my purpose, to write about my spiritual unfolding.

This book is one of the many tools that are a part of the fabric that comfortably clothes the Divine Transformation of Humanity into the colorful cloak of awareness. It is a thoughtful book that intends, in hope, to bring about change by means of simplicity, if you are at a place where change of this nature is available to you. It can only be heard if it is ready to be heard, but it will, most likely, be heard sooner or later. Now or later! It is a viewpoint that attributes to whom it will and when it will, but it will be my story and it most likely will be other's story too, because something this widely available is convenient to know. It is for now and after-now, and although it is, it wasn't before. It is from here on.

The Divine Grand Transformation of Mankind has begun and it is created by and continues to be shaped within the quietness of what are the common, familiar, ordinary experiences in each and every one of us. It is remarkably grand while it is presumed and encapsulates the "what is". It is rooted in the "normal" things becoming more extraordinary in its likelihood. This Transformation is the acquiescence-acquired abundance. It is what we all want from what we all know to be. There are no surprises, no buried secrets, just the unfolding of Time captured into our culmination of aspirations. It is nothing new, just the newness of the mention. One is to take it as seriously or not, as possible.

We are the Divine Transformation and I am, you are, we are all encountering a holy phenomenon, of favorable change. Many of them are upon us, and they will continue on forever into a better understanding of use. That makes me feel like getting ready. It comes from a place we are all a part of, where we all originate and its subscribed journey is meant to be taken together over time, perhaps holding hands; our own, as in prayer, or one another's, joined in mutual timing. Each one of us is delightfully unfolding our own minds into the applauding of it all.

This book holds all that it can from me now in a way that "Appreciates" so much about "Appreciations" that it can feel silly and dizzying. Some of my thoughts are swirling about and some are new and a bit fragmented and others appear over and over again, in a repetitive motion that seems to insist on the repeat in order for me to remember something. This repeating is a natural phenomenon of re-training or re-learning. The more evolutionary thoughts are especially reoccurring and I appreciate that happening to me on a continuous basis, when I write and at other times as well. I am so happy to refresh my memory with my newer understanding of life. It is like catching myself so I can rethink about it. This "rethinking" is a "redirection" to a more positive thought and a more positive result. That is a most welcomed change in my thinking. The reader may be at a place where they also want their thoughts to return to a more positive place. I encourage you on.

The thoughts in this book are only as profound, or not, as knowing that we can have fun with thinking about whatever we want. Finding a way to say the obvious is stylized humming of ones own thoughts. I warn you, my thoughts are simple, simply so. If you feel smarter about it all, I figured that can happen, yet, it is what I want to write about and in so if it makes you feel happy or have good feelings about the intense focus on "Appreciating", that is worth the smile I have right now.

As I adjust to this novel direction of finding peace with where I am, you are, we are, while seeing it entwined in-between the stories and spirit of the ideas worth exploring in these following pages, I request of myself only the open direction of thought and the personal freedom to experiment with the seemingly nonsense of simple positive and deliberate thought. This is a book that wants to understand "awareness" with common-thoughts designed into it by the Within-self. It is a paradox of contrasts of thoughts and approaches to understanding thoughts, always in a quiet manner of recognizing, while giving my best, my limitation rather than yours as yours, if any, are different than mine. You might be already wiser, although we are all in the same attached oneness, each doing our part, all of us equal in connection, mutually vibrational. Like the hologram's parts are full of the whole so are each of us. I think in a most common way of what are still uncommon thoughts. I think arrogantly enough to state that my thoughts are ours and yours and that is how together we become inside the Grand Transformation. It is here, in the common home office, at a simple computer keyboard that I am coming forth. At each written word I know that it is only a thought away from my fingertips and a thought ever nearer to my Higher Self. I have fun doing this releasing of thoughts and I invite my Inner Being to participate at will.

This book is a gleefully under-intellectualized study about thoughts and feelings, about Self and God. It is void of serious scientifically proven results and deep analysis, albeit evidence of wellbeing abounds. It is a book of me, of my thoughts, of what is going on in my transforming life and more so in my thoughts. Expect only to feel at ease Within your own thoughts as I am neither above you nor below you, but rather with you. I am thinking that a great many of us are thinking these thoughts, often, and this book gives me an opportunity to write it out and for you to read it and sense how much we do have in common, in these uncommonly discussed thoughts. I am experimenting with the only things I really own: my thoughts and the freedom to share them.

As together, we set ourselves out into the reliable perpetual Stream of Life, let us bring up and in the oars. Let us sit back in our seats and enjoy the flow, the float, the current, the view, ourselves and each other. This could be an interesting reading-ride if you allow it to be, yet it is most likely just a confirmation of comfortable familiar thoughts developed Within yourself based upon the emotion that it is good to think things that feel good. One is never alone "Within" the thoughts of the mind, that magnificent machine that articulates existence and defines reality. And also, there is a feeling that one's mind is never isolated from other minds. So in that regard this book simply contains my thoughts, and our thoughts.

This book is exceptional in that it feels familiar in its connective brilliance and comparatively so many other books pride on touching spaces and places that promote brand-new thoughts to be imagined. This is old stuff brought forth with enough light to see it. It is intended to be positive and uplifting rather than a literary excellent book, and is written from Within-shared thoughts, rather than from a rulebook on proper English or grammar. It might have typos, though attempts were made to correct them, and it is riddled with some of my favorite repeating words and reminders of thoughts. It is joyful to envision my imperfections perfectly accepted by the reader. I am less impacted by criticism than is the critic. It is what I feel now, now being different from what I feel when you read this, but, the Time is now and I appreciate that you are a part of it, as I sense your eyes upon these words. Hence, I feel the time-shifted observer has an influence upon these written words, as does my Inner Being's Withinness. It feels like a conversation with you and for us and with my Inner Being and I respectfully honor the Voice Within for guidance and love as much as my own viewpoint, which is mostly used for direction and attachment to humanity and our desires to know. I am filled with comfort in being with more than myself in the writing of this book, so I relish in the impertinence for me to not take full responsibility for it all, yet it is my allowing ability that facilitates the receiving of the blocks of radiant peremptory messages that come forth for me and herein to you. I have all this assistance from my Inner Being that loves you and me equally. It is my desire and their desire as well, as my Inner Being contains and comprises a collective Source of options overseeing, that which creates this book, so if you need clarification, seek it "Within" yourself, as we are indeed connected and your song already knows the words that you sing.

Some secrets are found by noticing them, others I actually have sought out. Some find me without my looking for them, while others avoid me totally. Some secrets happened, others are before me, yet it matters only that it is remembered that whatever and whenever secrets happen it is all wonderfully perfect for me. They are brought to me and to you. The secrets within myself are the ones I desire and I appreciate that they are mine because of my allowing. The secrets that are presented within this book are unknown to me to be secrets. There is knowledge and no secrets. If you find any Secrets, rethink them into the mild stimulations of your depth of wonder and in that thought you will bring forth your own secret places that I can only imagine. Herein, I allow the windows and portals of my life to be opened and I appreciate what I look out at and I love what I look in to.

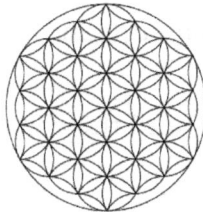

At the end of each chapter is a list of Appreciations followed by a blank page of Appreciations to be completed by the reader.

Chapter 1 - Peggy's Appreciations on The Gift of Appreciating Life's Little Secrets

❖ I appreciate the memories and experiences of my childhood and youth and of having a loving family all of my life.

❖ I appreciate the inspiration, joy and relief in learning about "The Art of Appreciation".

❖ I appreciate the sense of taking control of my life, in recognizing the impacts that secrets and gifts have on my memory and how I am responsible for carving into my memory the thoughts that serve me best now and in the future.

❖ I appreciate realizing that Life is as good as I allow it to be.

❖ I appreciate learning how to prioritize my thoughts into appreciations.

❖ I appreciate experiencing more Joy in Life, as I grow more capable of creating thoughts that feel good.

❖ I appreciate participating in the Grand Transformation of Mankind.

❖ I appreciate "Now" and the constant existence of "Now", "Now", "Now".

❖ I appreciate you, the reader, and you who do not read this, for "the you" you are, and for "the you" we are all a part of being.

❖ I appreciate myself as a Great Appreciator.

Chapter 1 - Your Appreciations on The Gift of Appreciating Life's Little Secrets

I appreciate this about myself _____

_____

I appreciate this about my life: _____

_____

I appreciate this about my future: _____

_____

I appreciate _____

_____

I appreciate _____

_____

I appreciate_____

_____

I appreciate _____

_____

I appreciate _____

_____

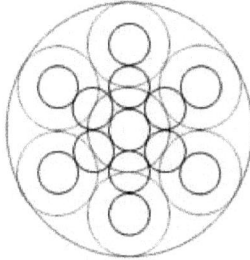

*"We are so often caught up in our
destination that we forget to appreciate
the journey, especially the goodness of
the people we meet on the way."*

Author Unknown

Chapter 2   Appreciation's Pathway

If wise, you will believe it to be true that every day of our
lives, ALL of us pass-ways with the Law of Attraction
continuously, literally meaning every moment of our days and
in everything we experience. All that occurs to and from each

of us is more, much more, than merely coincidence. We live with great purpose and are always moving towards the understanding and the appreciation of that fact of life. All is exactly as it is intended to be. There is no good or bad anything. However, there is a perception of time being experienced within your opinion of it. Many have heard it said that we should each mind our own business and judgment would fall lightly upon self as a result. These words need clarification to bring it into easy practice and in the trusting of this accepting of life, all falls in place as required to grow into the Master of your own fate.

Actually, we do more than pass-ways with the Law of Attraction, as if to say, "Hi, we are passing by each other, me and the Law of Attraction. How do you do, today? Have a good day. See you again sometime." No, it is less contrived and it is much more continuous, integrated and omnipresent. This is a huge thing to learn and one of the most important concepts of spirituality ever to be known. Knowledge and understanding of the Law of Attraction is often confused for spirituality itself. It is not. It is however, a linkage of thoughts that are different from the ones most are taught and it is connected and integrated into all aspects of life. Naturally with that huge an impact, it is often misinterpreted as a vague or random philosophy, rather than to be truly appreciated as a spiritual blessing or an achieved right of spiritual passage. It is seemingly hard for this to be understood and yet it is so simple. It, the absolute Universal Law of Attraction, connects thoughts and vibrations into experiences that exists all of the time for everyone and everything. Our entire lives revolve around the interaction between self and the Law of Attraction with our existing established beliefs or not. It is a state of existence that continues regardless of where you hold your attention, in thoughts on purpose, or in default, what religion or degree of spirituality you call yours, how much or little you possess, what you do, how old or young you are, how educated or not you are, or who you think you were or will be. The Law of Attraction is an updated adventure to discover the essence of thoughts in the realm of vibrational appreciation. It is very obvious once known and very innocuous when oblivious towards. An entire life can be easily lived without ever realizing anything about this law. That is exactly the state of existence most have lived, until now. All aspects of our experiences are created from this connection, knowingly or not. It is other than a religious persuasion and it is more than a spiritual awareness. It is a nonchalant lesson for the foolish and it is a matter of great importance and is longingly taken in by the wise. We are ALL living as totally integrated partners with the Law of Attraction, whether we know it to be so yet, or if we believe it, or if we ever come to see it. It is happening with or without acknowledgement of it. It just is! We are connected to it in everything we experience. Everything! To further clarify, we are even brought into our religious beliefs by the Law of Attraction. It is above a belief. Beliefs are brought into life with it and because of it. It is a consistent dependable law of nature.

It is a law that governs many other sub-laws in the hierarchy of Wisdom. It is interesting to read that fact. It is impressive to learn that, and once known (all should be so fortunate), it will forever be found truth. Science proves the usage of electricity and does not know what electricity actually is, and likewise, science, if it wanted to, can prove that people who claim control of their thoughts are projecting choice into fulfillment in their lives and yet science does not know what those thoughts actually sound like.

There are many definitions of the Law of Attraction although they simultaneously agree with one another. Once the Law of Attraction is truly comprehended as a personal participating relationship, it will be recalled deeper. It comes back to an awareness, returns from a space deep within that has been falsely labeled "secret", but, of course, is meant to be triumphantly found and realized if wanted to be discovered. It is always a personal choice and each thinking person is free to understand this, or not. It is always there to capture appreciation from, to relate to, and to create with.

If one invites this knowing into self-awareness, as in revelation, things will happen that will be reflected upon in a new light. All perceptions are shifted, even if only slightly at first, and all is better understood and accepted as being of value. Pieces of experiences will start fitting into its definition from a deeper and wider non-judgmental perspective. All makes more sense. The puzzle of life is easing into place and the final theme is continuous beauty in absolute expansion. Every little and big thing that is done in each second of the day is a direct consequence of the Law of Attraction's repercussions and compulsions. From the boldest gesture of strength to the slightest thought of stillness, everything that you create brings about with it, because of it and for it, a result that follows a vibration that gathers more of it onto itself. That might sound absurd to you, however, I know that if you think about it long enough, play and experiment with it often and best, trust in it, you will most certainly and absolutely definitely come to appreciate this to be truth. It will change your life with more intention, once digested. If one wants life to be as it is then close this book and take the default value of life. If one wants to improve every part of existence, read on. For those who understand this message already, come and read along and feel the essence of abundance.

Did you ever know something so well to be true that you were bursting with excitement about it? That is what I feel. I want you to know what I know too. However, I've seen that sometimes people are unable to grasp what is so exciting about my understanding of something. Some people are just not ready to hear what another is clamoring about, but many will be curious enough to listen rather than judge something they have not yet opened up to. Some will feel that they already know everything they are comfortable with knowing. Some will feel that they do not think someone else would be able to give them what they are missing, yet know they do miss something perhaps even something basic. Others will wonder and want to believe that answers are provided to them in all the resources brought forth to them, this being included. Some of us are fortunate to discover the Law of Attraction and all who are brought to know and understand and work with the Law of Attraction are wiser and definitely happier then those who are taking other approaches to doing life. That is the way it is intended. I have heard it said that all of the wisest leaders of our times and times gone-by have mastered the knowing of the Law of Attraction seemingly by different names. This seems true from the quotes they left behind, in the things they created while here, in the happiness and healthiness they appeared to live. People of leadership attract that leading role unto themselves, knowingly or not. That is a simple but very true statement. Followers are attracted to follow. Doubters are attracted to doubt. Wisdom finds the Wise.

I am **attracted** to learning of the Law of Attraction and from it I've discovered the "Art of Appreciation" and from that the "Art of Allowing". If you are ready to learn from the Law of Attraction (*and that is very good for you*) you are most definitely fortunate, as am I. Knowing of and understanding what the Law of Attraction is, is a good thing. It adds to understanding, builds up wisdom and from there one attracts "knowing". It supports religions and thrives on all beliefs. Once known, rather than merely being read or heard, but really known, life is changed forever. Once practiced, it is a whole new world. Due to this significant correction in awareness, personally, it is worthy to write about and think about the path that was experienced coming into the Law of Attraction and the growing spiritual understanding that I feel so happy upon arriving at now. You are attracted to this too.

I get this Law of Attraction stuff! I read it, hear it, live it and appreciate it. It is absolutely life changing for me. Wiser than ever before, yet evolving more so, and looking back at it, it is a bit surprising, a bit magical and I will be in appreciation of knowing it, forever and ever, and ever. I think sometimes; 'Why did it take so long for me to have found this out?', and if you are living by the Law of Attraction, you feel the same way, yet, I immediately turn that thought around (cancel, cancel) and reflect on how very fortunate I am to know it at all, especially realizing some miss it until death when it no longer matters here. For the record, knowing the Law of Attraction is unlike the Christian "Saved" or "Born-Again" story of those giving their heart to Jesus on their deathbed and thereby obtaining everlasting salvation and assured entry into Heaven. If you don't get the Law of Attraction, if you miss being aware of it during the time you are alive, you just miss it. It is knowledge rather than a religion and it diminishes nothing away from religion while it adds tremendously to the quality of living. The Law of Attraction is a tool. This law is a rule. It is a given. It is a Universal Law. Knowing it assists you during your physical life while enabling you to continue being a believer in Christianity, Judaism, Hinduism, Muslimism or any other religious or theological belief system, or none of them at all. Knowing it improves what is "Now", it brings explanation to what has already happened and it is a tool to create the future, your living flesh and bones future. It has nothing what so ever to do with heaven or hell. Believing it on your deathbed is just that, that is all. It is, however, the practicing of it that makes it reality for your life's course. If you learn of the Law of Attraction it is going to help you, however, it will come to you when it wills. It doesn't really matter. It is out of the race of something to compete for having won. It simply IS.

❋ ❋ ❋

Here is how my path went to find it:

In the early summer of the year our youngest daughter, Michelle, was celebrating life between her sophomore and her junior years of high school, we thought it might be a good idea for her to attend some classes on how to get a competitively higher score on the college admissions examination, called the SAT's.

We found a local commercial education center specifically advertising that offering and we made an appointment to meet with them. When we arrived, our daughter was taken into a room to be tested, and after a reasonable while, she came out to join us in waiting for the analysis of the test. We were, all three, eventually ushered into a room and a friendly well-dressed gentleman behind an executive desk gave us the results and the recommended course available to her, which surely should produce improvement. Although we were told that she had done very well, doing better could only increase her chances of getting into the college of her choice. While we were chatting about this and that relative to the scoring etc, this pleasant gent mentioned that he was involved in the course teachings too and that one of the very first things he now recommends to all his students is to read a book that he was absolutely amazed at finding was capable of positively changing the direction in which his teenage students were responding to the courseware and all other aspects of teen life, and in the most delightful ways. That book was suggested for our daughter to read also. That book was *"The Secret"* by Rhonda Byrne. The book was a nice suggestion, however, we sensed that our daughter's grades were good enough for the college she had decided to attend and that proved true.

At that same time we were planning to take a family vacation and we invited our daughter to bring two friends with us to a vacation resort villa in Florida. One of her friends was terrified of flying and so, we thought, to buy *"The Secret"* book, remembering that it helped teens deal with life's issues. We recalled the directness in which that man told us of the reaction his students had after reading this book. He didn't ever say that we should read it, yet, there was something in the excitement he had about this book that seemed to spark our interest too. We felt a desire to buy it so that this teen-guest could read it in order for him to enjoy the flight and trip better and then our daughter might want to read it too. We bought the book six weeks prior to our scheduled vacation for that reason. Instead of handing it over to any teenager, Uri, my husband, and I decided to read it first.

We had grown curious about the book and even more so after noticing that as we approached the bookstore this very book adorned the front window of the store in a major all-over-the-place display. Amazingly, it was on the Best Sellers List and there literally were hundreds of copies of it on display, stacked up, opened up, hanging from the ceiling and climbing up the walls. It was an elaborate way of displaying an abundance of one book, the likes of which I had never before seen. We had missed this book altogether and only then realized how popular it was. It is a relatively small thin book in comparison to books we usually read and so we began the reading of *The Secret*, together and out loud, which is our favorite reading style.

Taking turns reading we totally absorbed each and every page. One of the benefits in reading out loud is that the reading itself has to sound right to two people, making understanding par for the course, as we might question the way in which it sounded and could be interpreted. We heard every sentence together. Additionally, we did the recommended exercises as we made a delightful experience of reading this little book of huge thoughts. We were reading that the most substantial thoughts were very relative to our own thoughts.

We happily set time aside daily and read much of it outdoors in the early summer sun setting lit evenings under our hillside terrace, where we felt closer to nature and in a private quiet space. What a lovely loving experience we had in so doing. This book experience grew our love for each other, others, and ourselves and most importantly, it brought us to understand that we could control our own thoughts. It taught us of the Law of Attraction and how being in Gratitude could change our lives. And so it did!

It was and still remains one of the most treasured life-changing books we have ever read, and we read many books and over many years. I truly mean it too! Life changing, like the Bible is life changing! It was so much fun; writing Shifter-Lists, Gratitude Lists, and having deep intense and delightful thought exchanges about our personal experience in thought as we read this book and gradually began to take responsibility for our own thoughts.

As a result, we ceased being in default-thoughts, but rather turned every thought we could into a positive insight. We made every thought a projected expression of joy. We transformed negative thoughts into new delightful ways of saying and thinking the equivalent in more direct and positive ways. We started to increasingly see positive aspects come forth easier in every one of our thoughts. This fun, spontaneous and contagious. We helped each other do this and in a while we were both able to control the flow of our own thoughts fairly successfully and we were reaping benefits beyond our previous understanding of life. We had always been positive people, and now we were taking it to a new heightened level and in the driver's seat.

We took three weeks to read this book, anxiously making time every evening to go a little further with a thorough reading as we played joyfully together with its ideas of thinking thoughts. It was a lot of fun. We recommended it to be read by the soon-to-be traveling teenagers and we purchased the DVD *"The Secret Movie"*, which arrived the day before our vacation.

We watched *The Secret Movie* once and took it with us and viewed it while in-between basking in the sunshine and swimming at the glorious warm pools at the luxury villa resort vacation. Paradise-found was even more enchanting in our new awareness and positive happy attitudes. It was truly a great experience and a great vacation. In fact, everything was better, improved and more enjoyable. This is a major statement as recall we were vacationing with three teenagers. Some might see that as a challenge, but it was indeed as perfect as it could be.

While there, in Florida on vacation, another one of our young adult daughters, Tasha, had a major heartbreak-up with a boyfriend she had been involved with on a serious yet stormy level for several years, so we invited her to join us to facilitate an environment to sooth the break up. We watched the movie again with her almost immediately upon her arrival. It was again so much fun! She felt instantly reassured and set out with new aspirations and desires. She actually felt that buying the book for her boyfriend could improve their relationship. By now, Uri and I were pretty good at dealing with our process of thought and keeping it positive. We all watched the movie and found joy on our vacation as we continued taking more responsibility for keeping our thoughts improved and helping each other to do so, when politely possible.

Our youthful guests and adult children seemed to have an uncanny way of understanding the "thought" techniques faster than we at first had, and it was both delightful and an honor to have been a resource assisting them in improving their lives. There is little more satisfying than to teach your children well, except to be taught by them well. We all were experiencing that interchange.

❋

Once home from vacation, I found myself watching *The Secret* again and again, probably once a day for about two weeks, at least. I nearly memorized the script and I continued to think about what was being taught. Watching the movie made me feel good and it also created within me the need to learn more of the premises being taught. While watching the DVD, I paused the screen, curious to see the details of the movie closer and I found this page of an antique prop-book displayed on a frame that read:

"The World's Greatest Discovery"
By Edgar A. Guest

You can do as much as you think you can,
But you'll never accomplish more,
If you're afraid of yourself, young man,
There's little for you in store.
For failure comes from the inside first
Its there if we only knew it,
And you can win though you face the worse,
If you feel that you're going to do it.

That is a great little poem! Confidence can really improve the good outcome. As I continued completely inspired to learn more of this "concept of thought", I discovered the books that were used to bring focus and awareness to the main narrator, Rhonda Byrne of the *Secret* and its contributors, all of whom I had felt spiritual admiration at that time and still. I wanted to know every source of information, every reference, that aligned with the fact that we are responsible for our own thoughts all of the time and we can control what we are thinking all of the time, and in so doing we can create a better improved life of what we want it to be all of the time. Through this book we were being taught that we created things in our reality from our own personal thoughts. That was a lot to consider. Especially since it was saying we created our entire reality from our thoughts. I sensed that I had known this and had forgotten it and it felt inspirational to be recalling it again. The veil was being lifted.

Uri and I decided to wholeheartedly commit to this transforming positive thought-process after reading the *Secret* Book and we really wanted to make it a part of our daily lives. Actually more than part of our daily lives, we wanted to deliberately connect to positive and emotionally uplifting thoughts ALL of the time. We wanted to take control of our thoughts or at least most of them and definitely our most prevailing thoughts.

As time went on we realized that although, while on vacation, our young adult children had grasped these positive thought-concepts impressively very fast initially, there are logical reasons why Uri and I are now moving on the path faster than they are. They had returned to school and their respective workplaces from our vacation. Our watching of the *Secret* Movie and all the joy of sharing and playing together with these positive aspects of personal thoughts were fading into the past. They were back in their relationships, group events and social circles. There are many inter-relationship influences around us, yet more so around our youth. Someone is always available, even required, to re-train or guide them often away from personal confidence and positive thoughts, even if these people's intentions are good. Fear is a general approach toward education and religion, seemingly with emphasized determination during teenage years.

I detect that most people are out-of-step with deliberate thinking and even the most delightful educators and teachers are insisting on promoting prevention-information or comparative-lessons as their mode of operation. The educational systems are filled to the brim with historical information of the negative ilk. Just think, for but a moment, no longer please, of what fear history classes teach. Society educates our youth from the standpoint that they need to know all of mankind's mistakes and in so doing students are forced to focus attention on what is wrong with humanity, which is, most likely resulting in the opposite of the intended curriculum, which, of course, is to educate our youth with the tools for their survival and practical creativity into their brilliant future. However, society seems to want to teach our young and old and everyone in-between, to learn from our historical mistakes instead of learning what kind of world we prefer now. Perhaps there is some good in the recalling of past wars and such, yet, at least equal time should be utilized with focusing on what the future should become, not from the repeating of the past and not from the recalling of the past, but from the releasing of the past and the appreciating of the now and the imagining of tomorrow. It is unnecessary and unworthy to think that by focusing on the centuries gone by of past errors of mankind we will not repeat them. The best way to avoid making these errors again is to avoid analyzing and focusing so much upon them. One good lesson is so much more powerful.

What we think about we bring about! Does that mean we should be ignorant of the past? If so, that will be a long time in the making as there is the entire global academic established institution and a massive amount of intensive industrial support that continuously refocuses on the myriads of negative aspects of mankind's history. In nearly all schools our young people are being forced, as part of lesson, as the way of learning, to look at the negative side of so many things that they study. This has become the accepted way to teach and to learn.

As is their nature, our young adult children also socialize with others, many others, who are actually unfamiliar with their own personal thoughts out of the default value. So many more people integrate into our daughter's lives than into ours, and most all of their interactions with others involved noticing that others hold mostly negative expressions. Many more people seem to complain about what they don't have than those in gratitude for what they do have, and the youthful population is no exception. Even small children have taken to complaint as a way of expressing their wants. One of our daughters mention how so many of her friends seem to dwell on negative aspects of life. This became more noticeable to her already calm, collected and happy spirit when she was made aware of her thinking process. Hence, she could hear more clearly words scattering forth many areas of other's discontent.

Uri and I are more able to "bubble" our lives into a careful protective envelop of our choosing much more than our daughters are, although we also noticed that most people are thinking in their more negative default thought than are we. Conversations climb or decline into that realization very quickly. Uri and I also have each other to connect our thoughts through and inspect each other's thoughts from and we do so, often. We really pay close attention to what we are saying to each other and others. We learned very quickly that our words are a direct reflection and an enhanced support to our quieter thoughts. Our thoughts become things and the secondary things that our thoughts become are spoken words. The primary things our thoughts become are our feelings and emotions. Knowing this we attempt to correct and clarify our words in positive ways, always willing to rethink. It is amazing with concentration and some doing and re-doing those even difficult situations and uncomfortable thoughts can be rearranged internally and then released into words externally in more positive ways. It all makes a huge difference.

Uri has richer challenges at his office than I do at the supermarket; yet, we find success in the ability to practice the Law of Attraction, along with using positive thinking and carefully communicating much more in our real world spheres than are our daughters. Although with time, it is noteworthy that the process of practicing the Law of Attraction gravitates better circumstances and more positive people into all of our spheres. We are enjoying the mood in which our thoughts progress our emotions and we are legitimately happier then ever before in our lives, and we have had our share of years and happiness to reflect upon. Now, we find ourselves noticing the quality of our moods more and when we experience conflicting feelings we really think about what was the cause and reset our direction. If we cannot find readily the cause, we accept ourselves and attempt to quickly redirect into better thoughts. It is often better to move-on to good thoughts than to spent too much time deciphering the cause of negative thoughts.

Our single daughters have many more obstacles to overcome within their social and educational realms, as well as individually, than do we. Uri and I have each other to assist in the processes and in recalling our commitment to the practice of the Law of Attraction and to each other. It is for this reason that we become even more inclined to assist our daughters through difficulties that come up in their lives and to support them with words and works of encouragement and abundance. It is most certainly helpful to have a close person, a family member, a good friend or a partner, keeping each other in "thought-check". For us it makes all the difference, although we both know it is all up to us individually. We are the only ones who can control our own thoughts. However, it is nice to have a companion noticing each other's thought tendency as it is valuable to recall that our lives are full of beliefs of negative impressions that suppress us into that familiar default thought. It is so easy to let negative focus go unnoticed and unchecked within self, especially while others are actually promoting it so often, outside of self. We work it out together. With all the self and partner evaluation it could become uncomfortable to listen to another critique personal thoughts that find expression, but it is what we committed to do with ourselves and for each other. In other circumstances we might become annoyed with the other mentioning our "faulty" thoughts or "negative" attitude, but the opposite is true. We appreciated the polite reminders and we are doing much better, while attracting more things to appreciate.

We noticed that our daughters are able to feel safe with us and with each other as they encounter difficulties and we feel the same way towards them. Many of the problems that we have are our needing to clarify thoughts about things and shift the balance of choice. It is getting easier all of the time and we are having fewer problems. Once we seem to get our feelings sorted out, usually by talking to each other about it, we are able to hear our own thoughts more clearly and then shift our view of the "problem". If you can't change something, change the way you look at it. We realize during the distinctive transformation on a personal level, that we really appreciated our open honesty and our commitment to this process of improved living.

We take what we are learning, as controlling our own thoughts so seriously, while intentionally holding ourselves responsible for managing good-feelings that we set out to prove or disprove this concept. We also find that the more serious we are in keeping a better standard of outward thoughts, in other words, in saying good things, that we notice our personalities became more lighthearted and we are laughing so much more. Even now as I write this I can hear the echoes of my own laughter in my mind. I definitely laugh a whole lot more than I did. I have only laughed more when I was a child. We practice the; "We need to do one thing that is down right silly today", rule. In addition, we decided to create statements of deliberate intentions as we continue to read every author we can that associates to the philosophy of this remarkable statement; "Our thoughts create our life". And that means all the things in our lives too. Literally and figuratively! Taken in full context, it is quite amazing. Simple and clear, yet amazing!

Soon I found that Wallace D. Wattles was another author of a little old book that jolted *The Secret* into existence. So, I purchased many, perhaps all, of Wallace D. Wattles' books, starting with *"The Science of Getting Rich"*. I recommend this book to your personal library. That incredible little book so impressed us with confirmation of what we were learning that we gave this book to friends and relations for the Holidays that year, hoping that others, especially those we love and appreciate knowing, might very well find the profound messages we were receiving, without our having to tell them what we were so excited about. This book continues on that course, does it not!

✻ ✻ ✻

It is an interesting feeling to be realizing something seemingly of importance and then wanting to share it with others. Wanting to wake them up. Religious zealots do that! We decided to control our jumping into everyone's life with "the way". It is the way for some, and to be honest, we have learnt that some will get this now, some not; yet, here I am writing a book that bases its existence on the flow of the Law of Attraction. Wanting to assist in the quality of another's life seems such a beautiful characteristic in humanity. The desire to teach is profound some times. To date, it is impossible to determine who detected the lesson we were compelled to gift them within these Holiday books. Change is sometimes undetectable in self or others, yet we know that change is constant.

✻

In fact, there are only a few things I know of that remain the same. I've heard life's constants listed in several ways and these are my interpretation of them. What is important about thinking of them is the learning to accept what is as exactly that, what is. First of all, the fact that I AM is a constant. I might appear differently or even think differently over time or before, yet, I AM myself and I remain as such even when others seem to want me to be something else and even when I change things about myself. My thoughts are always my own thoughts. That is a constant fact. Some, in fact, many people want me to think differently, but I am always the one who decides what I want to think. The entire sales industry wants me to think to buy their products. These sales entities even try to persuade me into thinking the way they want me to think. Yet, I remain the same person within whatever I appear to be and I remain the same person regardless of what I am thinking about. It is incredible that the thoughts I think can change the quality of who I am, but not who I am. Thoughts can change the way I enjoy my life, but not who I am. My linked usage of thoughts can change the way I succeed in life, and not who I am. I know I am and that I am always and forever in some way.

I know that I am more than what is here in this time-space reality or in the body I call "me". I know I am a soul and a human all at the same time.

My Catholic teachings told me that I am an everlasting soul; yet, Catholic teachings seem to infer that I was not a soul before I was conceived, or so it seems. I remained a bit confused about that as the subject of conception was like talking about sex, which was so taboo that my questions were never even asked and I never felt confidence in those that were around to answer if I did ask. I have developed, sort of in the same appreciation as a constant existing self, the truth that I am a part of God and therefore a part of everything seems to be a constant also and enables me to sense this lifetime as part of the entire journey rather than the conception of the journey. It seems quite arrogantly limiting to only consider conception into human birth as the only possibility of my soul's beginning. It somehow doesn't match up to the idea of "the rest of Eternity" to follow my dying. "Life on Earth" and "the rest of Eternity", something isn't equating to me with one being so small in comparison to the other. We are so much more than our earthly selves. Don't you just feel that to be true even without my saying I feel that to be true for me? Regardless of how I perceive it, or what I chose to appreciate as God, it is what it is. I am a connected part of everything else that is in my reality and even beyond my perception of reality. I know this in the way all that surrounds me is made by God. God is everywhere and is everything. That was my very first Catholic Catechism lesson. It made sense to me when I first heard it and it still makes perfect sense to me now.

For me, the irrefutable workings of the Law of Attraction certainly are constant, even though I am a fairly new student of the Law of Attraction and have time to master its apparent boundlessness. In fact, I am still attempting to prove it absolute, by testing it again and again. However, some discrepancies seem to surface in the attempt to test it, and that is that my doubt creates and attracts more doubt. The feeling of doubt is merely an indicator that I am thinking in ways that clutters the receiving of the Law of Attraction as truth! I create doubt! Knowing of it enables me to refocus my thoughts into what I believe as truth. It is better for me to surrender to it rather than to test or fight to prove it or disprove it. The Law of Attraction is well and clearly defined; what I think about, I bring about, what I put forth comes back, and that which is like is drawn unto it self. Therefore, what my mind is thinking is attracting more of that thought back to my mind and to me. I wish that these teachings were taught in Catechism Classes when I was a youth. I wish these teachings were taught now! Is it possible that it was and I didn't get it then? Well, no matter, I get it now! It to me is one of the most valuable lessons I've thankfully come to know. The Law of Attraction is constant. I believe that and I love that as truth. My doubts crumble with surrender and then the Law of Attraction proves true so nicely.

Another thing that seems constant to me and to others also, is that forms such as the point, the line, the circle, the triangle, and the square are symbolic constants that interplay design between and within each other. A point will always be a point even when designed next to other points to create a line into another form. All form arrives first from a single point into existence. It is an abstraction of the Law of Attraction and our own creation.

Besides these few, yet, boundless "constant" concepts everything else changes all of the time. It is a solid understanding that everything is changing. Everything is in motion. Everything is energy. Everything is vibrational.

❀ ❀ ❀

Together, Uri and I, started learning about this "Thought Science", this science of the mind, with the mental absorbing and practicing of the *Secret* in late June early July and now less than six months later in December we experience many of our intentions coming into fruition and a great deal of joy being experienced. Although the Law of Attraction is a constant, we were unable to allow it to become more noticeable immediately. When we first started to apply the trust required such that we could genuinely sense the Law of Attraction relative to our positive projected thoughts, many things changed quickly. In less than six months of practicing the Law of Attraction as faithfully as we knew how at that time, things were agreeably working out for us. It was sort of like taking vitamins whereby it takes a little while to see and feel the results, but once the results were happening it was most pleasant for the entire body. We kept intending and we kept reading all pointers to pointers to pointers of books, essays, documents, websites, and all that extended from the *Secret* and beyond into the Law of Attraction. We read them all excitedly while slowly digesting as much as we could and learning more and more about our processes of thoughts and the power of our thinking.

We investigated all the authors and all the books that the co-authors and participants of The *Secret* credited for their personal change into awareness. We read their associated books; book after book, each stating similar thoughts on the science of thought and how we are responsible for our own lives through our thoughts. We create our own reality. Uri and I were taking this all very positively seriously while smiling all through the day. It was indeed serious stuff finding ways to be happy!

That was a couple of years ago as our then teenager daughter is in her sophomore year of college and final year in her teens. During these recently passing years Uri and I, and our daughters who were with us on that Florida Vacation, all continued to review and learn, at our own individual pace, and use the Law of Attraction concepts in our daily lives and we all noticed a great and wonderful change in all of our lives also. Everything has improved!

Before I go forward with this story of my path, I want to go back to noting something else we found in the Wallace D. Wattles books. Wallace D. Wattles lived from 1860 – 1911. It is fascinating trivia about why *The Science of Getting Rich* was written back in 1910 and for whom it was intended to be read by. It was written in quaint plain simple language for the coal miners in the area where Wattles lived at the time. It was specifically written in consideration for the coal miner's reading capability and related experiences. Wattles inspirationally wanted to teach them a way to get rich, a way to have abundance in all aspects of their lives, a way to climb out of their miserable poverty and miserable attitudes, a way to change, if they wanted to change. That sweet and practical intention strikes such joy in my heart for the human characteristic of commiserated compassion. Wallace D. Wattles had the spirit of caring about others and with that he applied himself to teaching The Law of Attraction.

Another author we read along the way to here was Napoleon Hill and his book *"Think and Grow Rich"* that was written in 1937. Napoleon Hill lived from 1883 – 1970. I find comfort in knowing that we both were alive during a part of the same time, because I admire his works. His books also followed the same Law of Attraction thoughts as Wattles', yet was written and distributed at the end of the Great Depression and among it's intents it was to inspire many people through and out of those global difficult financial times and, in fact, was instrumental in that recovery era. Again, it was a work of compassion toward bringing up others by introducing them to a way to bring up themselves, with their own thoughts. I appreciate that abundance is available for everyone.

In today's climate of economic concerns, reading and learning a better way to seek and address change into abundance is worthwhile and these books are timeless in their message and thoughtful in their delivery. On the other hand, reading, watching and listening to the media's incessant proclamation of an inevitable financial decline and disaster is the alternative option. I choose to leave the news media's message behind. We each choose what we want to appreciate.

The secret has been told. The proverbial cat is out of the bag. Now, it is up to us to remember that caring about the direction of our thoughts is good. Remembering that each of us can control our own thoughts is probably more important than remembering your own name! Additionally, when listening to the doomsayers and negative out-lookers, if you must, you get to accept it or forget it, you get to pay attention to it or turn away from it. Remember all TV's come with an off button. Here is a tip you already must know; mentally discard negative news if you have to know of it at all. And in all honesty, there are so many people so willing to find what is going wrong that it is more the exception than the rule to attract all positive into your life, and it is probably impossible to live it all in a positive space as shadows create dimension. The best part of all that negative stuff is that we learn what we want from observing and or experiencing what we want less. The saving grace is that we can always think what we want to think and we should notice if what we are thinking is making a good impact or feeling on us then it is probably a good thought to continue on. It is foolish to depend upon the thoughts, words, or actions of anyone else to make us feel good or to bring us happiness. Our feelings and our emotions can help us know what is actually good for us, and the evidence of the way life is, is another valuable indicator. If you are seeing or hearing a lot of negative news, you can be certain that you are attracting it into your life. Turn the volume down on what is making your thoughts spiral into a negative state. You have that power.

Continuing with my personal story, one day, about a year after the *Secret* enlivened our spirits so emphatically, as I was looking at a short video. I typed "The Secret" into the search field and it was immediately returned with a pointer to several videos about different aspect of *The Secret,* movie and book. I sincerely appreciate the ability to learn nearly about anything of interest on the Internet and being a visual person, I love the short videos available at a click. I appreciate friendly technology. I even love the unfriendly technology, such as the media, as I know what to absorb and what to avoid and the media has its place especially identified with an area I enjoy avoiding. The media always provides me with a better understanding as to the influences so many people living in the default mode of thinking are absorbing.

The results of my video search connected me to all of the familiar and popular *Secret* participant's videos, most of whom were selling their personal spin on the Law of Attraction as derived from the *Secret* and getting richer. Good for them! In fact, even being in mental association as a fan from this movement of prosperity and realizing the teachings of prosperity enables the Law of Attraction to bring me to understand that this aspect stretches the imagination as to the impact in recognizing the extent that abundance has upon each other's abundance. Misery likes company and ascendency likes company too. Like is draw onto itself. Riches to Riches! I am attracted to learning about and living in awareness of the Law of Attraction.

The fallacy, or misinterpretation, "that opposites attract" is confusing to people approaching the consistency of the Law of Attraction. If opposites seem to attract in your comprehension, look a little closer at that and you will notice that the essence of the attraction is always the same. It is always like unto itself. This applies even to the extent that a person might well be attracted to another person, apparently their opposite. A closer look will reveal that each involved in the attraction actually desires the same thing, which is to attract their opposite. The Law of Attraction brings about more of what you are thinking about "period". If you have thoughts of attracting the opposite because you desire the opposite, you will get it. Likewise, if you have thoughts of attracting the opposite and you do not desire that very opposite, you will get it. You get what you think about regardless of true desire. It is the thought that prevails, rather than the desire. Think about something you do not want long enough and it will materialize. Think about something you do want long enough and it will materialize. Thinking about desiring the opposite of what you are wanting will deliver that to you and that which is delivered will have had the identical desire for an opposite. Opposites attract each other when they both focus on that attraction. The vibrations involved in the stimulated attraction are always consistent with what the Law of Attraction delivers. The truth is many people spend far too much time thinking about what they do not want and in so doing that is what the Law of Attraction delivers. Think about what you do want!

Remembering that Napoleon Hill's book helped many come out of the depression it influenced the thought to be of a positive desire and one of abundance. There is more than enough for everyone, if we think it so. You chose! If that sounds to simplistic or shallow, you could think abundance for all out of your ability to think and comprehend. It is all up to you. It will be what you attract and experience. It seems better to want abundance for all rather than to think it is an impossibility to obtain. Again, if you are happy with the way your life is, then there is no need to continue to read this "stuff", but if you are willing to open up your mind and change the way you are thinking, you too can benefit from learning and applying this divine natural law.

❁ ❁ ❁

After we read about the Law of Attraction and realized what it was actually saying, we decided to give it a chance. Then we started to see that if we merely "gave it a chance" we limited it with a time-constrained test and we realized that this was a vibration inherent in the overall results of it. If we were giving it a chance to prove itself to us, perhaps the Law of Attraction was only giving us that same chance. So we decided to go for it and jump into it totally. We knew intuitively that in order for this to work out for us, we had to surrender to it.

In the adventure of trusting the Law of Attraction I was also drawn to a short Internet video that purportedly contained segments that were removed from the original *The Secret Movie and Book*, which focused upon the Words and Teachings of "Abraham" through Esther Hicks. Until then, I had never heard of Abraham or Esther Hicks. I watched in utter amazement and I felt that the *Secret* had kept the best secret to be discovered outside of what it presented, although I was real happy with what I did receive from it. I soon learned that *The Secret* book was based upon The *Secret* movie. I was surprised at what I was learning in these "Teachings of Abraham" that were kept out of or removed from *The Secret* movie and book.

My delight of learning about Abraham's influence was similar, I think, of what Rhonda Byrne, the primary promoter of the *Secret*, mentioned, almost right away, in the movie that she was amazed that the Emerald Tablet was kept from the public. The Emerald Tablet is an ancient artifact, written perhaps c. 800 or so, which is brought forth in the *Secret* and is told to us as the original "*Secret*". There is a dramatic event depicted where across time the Emerald Tablet was always hidden from most of the people and only a few very powerful people handed it down to their next generation that remained powerful due to the knowledge it revealed. The knowledge these few powerful people had was enough power to enslave many to work for them. It was ignorance of the Secret that disempowered the lowly worker class. This continued until the present time. The foundation of The *Secret* Book and Movie is based upon the Emerald Tablet with its engraved ancient words that reveal the forgotten mysterious Secret:

"That which is above is that which is below.
What is below is like that which is above, and what is above is
similar to that which is below to accomplish the wonders of the
one thing."

So what does it mean! I'm honestly unsure. Those are some ancient words and some expressions that I am not used to. What could the essence of the *Secret's* interpretation be from those words? To me it says that heaven and hell are less definitive. Judgment is unnecessary. It is all the same. Backwards, frontwards, up or down, it all just is. It is time to look at things with less judgment as to good or bad. It also clarifies that we are all one. That is what I get out of it. Joy comes from contrast, and contrast creates joy. I perceive the meaning to be that the Law of Attraction will provide from your positive and negative thoughts equally. The Law of Attraction does not discriminate. That is the message of truth and it has to be interpreted as one can appreciate its meaning. The idea that this understanding, which is profound to many, myself included, was kept from the "common" range of people's understanding seems unfortunate, but now is now. Although some of those ancient words are just words to me, I am intelligent enough to know others can scholar this group of words better than I can. I mean knowing that you are and I am as powerful as God, is a big enough concept to realize.

Finding Abraham's words I felt similar. I am sure there were reasons "above and below" for Rhoda Byrne's team to find exclusion of the Abraham message, which is definitely more intensively based upon "vibrational" understandings yet, these were the very accusations that the *Secret* was premised upon, in that we, the general public was being kept from knowledge that could literally change our way of thinking and our quality of life. The *Secret* was missing being totally revealed after all, maybe it never will be, although, I am thrilled with the path it leads me on and the portions it did reveal were worthy and good. There was more to the story. Abraham's Messages were a main ingredient and an initial seed that grew this *Secret* Book from the *Secret* Movie into a huge understanding in my life and continues to make a positive impact upon many others. Therefore, it seemed only natural that I wanted to learn more of Abraham.

Abraham's Teachings were gone, actually taken from the book and the movie that I owned. I clicked on the Internet videos that had the missing Abraham segments of the *Secret* movie and was thrilled. The first time I heard the voice of Abraham, I immediately found within it and, more importantly, within the words, what I know is the truth to me. Every word still resonates with my Beingness. This was the beginning of an increased level of understanding of the basics provided in The *Secret* movie and book.

I have always felt a sense that I was being "given" the next piece of wisdom and knowledge in life to bring me into alignment with more awareness over a lifetime. I am a seeker of the truth. It is such a fantastic adventure. I now appreciated the Law of Attraction and know, while on my journey that, I am attracting this unto myself. In fact, I very often, and probably all of my life, definitely as long as I can remember, wanted and prayed for Wisdom. Now, this time of my life, I sensed that the "Teachings of Abraham" held answers to my prayers in that particular direction. These teachings have given me so much personal growth that I sometimes think that I need only continue within the practice of these teachings and I am going to learn all I ever need. That being said, I know myself to be open to more and there is more already found as I tap into my own equivalent "Abraham", my Inner Being, The Voice of Wisdom Within me, My Larger Self, My Connection to God and All-that-is. There are many names across generations and through time and space that is called that Spirit Within. In Catholic terminology, I welcome the Holy Spirit into my life.

Prior to this knowledge and being from a Catholic family and world view, I had already been experiencing other ways of thinking, new ways of thoughts with the Law of Attraction backing me up very successfully and none of these thoughts were interfering at all with my "religious" background as I ventured into and through concepts of the Law of Attraction. I loved that, as I didn't want to lose my religion, which has been a very close part of my spirit and life force, my education and values, my customs and traditions, my beliefs and hopes. I had invested a lifetime into it already and I liked it. Most of my friends were of my Catholic faith and near all my family. I soon discovered that I could appreciate the Law of Attraction and even while being a practicing Christian Catholic, yet there began to grow an increasing feeling that I am "more than a Catholic" and it feels great.

I distinguished that without conflict of religious interest. I could recognize a stirring within me that lead to a closer appreciation and a startling re-evaluation of the messages Christ provided. I was establishing a new point of view without discarding my previous point of view. It was like seeing things from above what is there; a bird's eye view in a God's Eye love. Nothing was different about what my beliefs were, yet, I was able to see into it clearer and it made more sense. Applying the Law of Attraction layered on top of my "Christian" beliefs was working very well. Many of Christ's words and words about Christ started to hold deeper meaning and a richer insight. I heard the words of Jesus from the perspective of him having awareness and speaking from the Law of Attraction's knowledge point. It works! As far as I am concerned, there is no conflict. Jesus spoke in paradoxical awareness of the Law of Attraction. So many undigested fragments of the years of Bible studying started to present clarified meaning to me in ways that I was gaining so much wisdom from that I felt renewed and capable of allowing even more understanding to come into my life. Holy Spirit you are welcomed in this mind as well as in this heart!

I began to personally observe more concerns within my complacent interpretive Catholic ways of my lifestyle, more than in my Christian basics. Returning thought on the situation and the unfolding of my understanding, I know that the process of learning when connected to the process of gaining wisdom had to be exactly as it was for me, because at that point in my life I felt little resistance to these teachings. This was also due to my delightful practiced awareness of the power and truth I had already found in the Law of Attraction and my lifetime of education and participation in both the

Catholic Church and my years of weekly Christian based Women's Bible and Faith Sharing Groups. The teachings have a quality I was able to find more than in any of my religious experiences and it holds consistency. I was ready and curious and these confirming teachings are Law of Attraction based.

My life is definitely better leveraging the Law of Attraction within my life lessons. I had developed more joy in my life and things began to change dramatically. I was open-minded to appreciate these new teachings from the insight and trusty comfort provided with my newly formed Law of Attraction thinking. It was all the same thing and most definitely confirming.

There are gazillions of books written today on the Law of Attraction and on many of the peripheral teachings and yet, I think, it is rather rare for a "practicing" Catholic to reach for the Law of Attraction as an educational or spiritual guide for growth. Yet, that is exactly what I did. At first glance, the delivery of the message of the Teachings of Abraham are seemingly un-Catholic surface-side, although I find them refreshingly true and fulfilling, yet, to-date I avoid discussions on where I received a great deal of my insightful lifestyle to my "Catholic" friends and relations, whom seem concurrently attracted to my obvious and increased joy, success and happiness which does abound in my life and is apparent to others as well as to myself.

What is it about these teachings that cause concerned doubts with the typical Catholic when first approaching this knowledge? Well, Abraham is different and unrelated to the Abraham in the Bible to begin with, although I see an abstract connection. Abraham is a voice of today and Abraham is a voice that comes forth in and through Esther Hicks. Esther Hicks channels the voice she hears in her head into words. The voice calls themselves "Abraham" and describes themselves as a collective consciousness, unlike we who are singular yet they are more knowing-of-All. They claim to be multidimensional and multifaceted and certainly of multi-consciousness. In a quick study of Esther's biography I find what parts the path in Catholic attachment is other than the words she is speaking, for they are sincerely beautiful, enlightened and, for the most part, in harmony with Catholicism, but rather Esther was raised another religion. Perhaps if she were Catholic, like St. Bernadette or Joan of Arc or so many other Saints that heard voices speak to them, her "Within" voices could be more acknowledged by the Catholic Authorities. Both Esther and Abraham seem unconcerned about their acceptance by the Catholic Church, and the opposite is probably equally true. The Teachings of Abraham exists on the foundation of the opposite of having any religion affiliation; rather it is spiritual in nature. This is the identical message the Inner Voice of me speaks. It conveys a message that sounds nothing like a religion while unopposed to the existence of all religions.

✻ ✻ ✻

I personally can relate to Esther Hicks as a happily married middle-aged woman. We are both commonly matured and dignified in character and stature. We are all individuals and we are all equally so. I am certainly happy to be me. Years can be your friend as Time can be your friend. This is true for me. Esther and I each have a lot of experience growing our lives and yet our Higher Voices are expressions through our individual experiences and vocabulary, hence, our Voices express themselves in slightly different ways, using related yet not identical measures to explain and teach. I appreciate her experience and time spent living. I appreciate that my life's course stems from an alternative path. I appreciate Esther's feminine gender, as, in my life, more often my Spiritual Guides are males. As with Esther, I am brought to understand that my Inner Voice also is an intelligent collective and gender is not only indistinguishable it is irrelevant. My Inner Voice, when I ask for a name, only reveals that it is nameless or rather that which no name can be spoken. Esther and I have that "connection-up" in common and I am convinced that each and every one of us all have this same ability to connect into the Voice of Our Inner Being, which is always there. My unnamable Voice seems to contain members, which vary due to the fit I represent based upon my life experiences and willingness to allow. I have only a provided acknowledgement of this and proof is unnecessary, in fact, unwise to pursue. There exists in Esther a presence of meaning and great courage. I appreciate the "words" that come out of her mouth. The message resonates to my core and has somehow assisted in my own awakening power to communicate "Within". I too have great courage in so doing. Quietly I remain willing for this loving Voice to assists me herein to arrange my thoughts to provide written testimony for the reader. My Voice is mine, it is wise to seek and discover your own Voice. Relative messages are enveloped in relative life experiences, although the total message, which can never be completely transcribed, is based upon the identical truths. It is consistent. It starts within the premise of understanding that we are, you are, I AM and added to that; we, you, me are intended to be and to be right here and now, and added immediately onto that it is all very good. Love is the essence of this understanding, intentionally, unconditionally and continually.

Most people, even if religious and equally when not so religious, and probably a huge percentage of men, most likely find little trusting humor in God or Source speaking in the form of Abraham through a middle-aged Midwestern American woman, named Esther Hicks. Likewise it even seems off to me that I am IT too, until one takes hold of the fact, rather than fiction, that every one is as capable. It is meant to be like this. It should be taken for granted as much as we each have a head on our shoulders. We each have the ability to connect to the Inner Being Within our Consciousness, the huge magnificence of our closer connection to what we call God or Source. Are we Source? Well, we are a part of God. We are as much a part of God as our head is part of our body. I AM and I AM a part of my Spirit Within and the Spirit Within is huge and magnificent. It is revealed to me and I already knew as much, that my Spirit dwells "Within" my body.

This is true for Esther too. There is something attractive and charismatic about Esther Hicks. Jerry, her husband, is very special also and they are a complete team and always perform together. They, together, bring about a show as well as a message. Esther and Jerry Hicks connect with a lot of people, as their stories are common and simple, often humorous and heart felt. One thing I noticed in their life story was that they didn't hit rock bottom before looking up and finding their way into this brilliant new age industry. I like that so much about Esther. Many spiritual teachers today seem to have needed an extreme life situation such as a near death experience, or a deep extreme depression, even suicidal tendencies, as a contrast to become enlightened. Esther is different. Esther heard this voice in a relatively calm reality and became a teacher with it. She avoided devastation as a motivation to seek God. I am like that also. You probably are too. I am a seeker who finds for the asking and receiving. Some spiritually blessed people find God and Wisdom in the shadows at the base of the mountain, while others climb to the top and in the sunlight and with a sense of accomplishment they receive.

Abraham teaches what I know to be true. I know that we all have the same ability to listen and hear the Voice of the truth "Within". It is seemingly a good time to tap into this Inner strength. All peoples, all ages, all generation are equally enabled to listen and hear. I hear a Voice that says loud and clear: "Write and together we will become the thread that weaves together the thoughts that others can hear from out of your experiences, if they desire." I have a new platform in which to become made aware of and I am willing and free in this process. Additionally, I am able to learn of other religions and find knowledge and respect for most all religions.

I was taught that it is un-Catholic to probe into any form of channeling, whatever that meant, however the messages in the "Teachings of Abraham" were and remain perfectly in sync with the roots of my Catholic life. I remain a Catholic, well, as I said; I am now "more than a Catholic" and I too relay this Voice Within myself into written words, so it is very Catholic to me, it is more than Catholic to me. The Christ-consciousness beliefs embedded into these messages are goodness.

Uri and I totally and completely understood and resonated with the explained "vibrational" concept of all life that the Law of Attraction teachers teach. We became so interested in these concepts that we picked up one book after another and devoured them carefully and with intent to comprehend and put into practice what we were learning. Now we are truly benefiting from all these books in more ways than can be written. Our lives have changed significantly for the better and Life is so good it is everything we want right now and there is so much to look forward to, as we desire more too. I think this desiring is a newer and definitely larger part of my life than before this knowledge came to me.

From my desires, I am joyfully bringing my interpretation of these collective Law of Attraction teachings into my Catholic perceptive and cooperatively and joyfully from "Within" my Inner Being. It is at exactly this point of awareness, in both love and appreciation that I write this book. I appreciate the vision of deliberately co-creating and there are a great deal of words coming easily forth to meet these pages and you. I appreciate each and every moment of creating it, as I manifest in life's generous circle of events, me to you, and you to me and back and forth. May the "Circle of Appreciation" continue to be, as it is for me to you, a delightful connection to Source, to God, to Self and to all you desire.

❋ ❋ ❋

By experiencing the wonder of appreciating and wanting to share that with others the initial intention of writing this book was to document our gratifying experiences with Appreciations. At first it was thought that a book of Appreciations was a list of individual appreciations consisting of one line each and so everyday we began to write an Appreciation for the day. The idea of doing an Appreciation soon became the creating of two varieties of Appreciations: one of self-appreciation and the next of something outside of self-appreciation. Appreciations seem to bring out the best in people and for us it grew intensions.

It is from those initial experiments that Appendix A exists. It is a collection of anonymous Appreciations that inspire me to reflect upon the beauty that each of us holds in our thoughts. They are collected Appreciations found while out fishing for thinkers of men. These Appreciations are gentle souls and released thoughts. They are like soft prayers and expressions of innerness less often heard. They are like small poems and are treasures to read and relate to. I have for the sake of privacy taken out any personal information and find they remain complete and graceful. The grammar was not fixed in an effort to retain the beauty of them as they were naturally created.

There are many other aspects of this book that has evolved from the original thinking of it, as it is taking its own way into existence. It is a personal addition to the general flow of seeking wisdom. It is the cooperative connection to Source and its daily heard and heeded guidance that comes from Appreciating. Many of the thoughts provided here are from my Inner Being and it is in that vibration that I write often knowing now that there is more to me than I knew before now. It is a cellular connection to an immense love that I am experiencing and it is bigger than all understanding. The thread of love and appreciation runs deep into the words of this book. I unmistakably feel an increasing ability developing within me from that which is loving and pleasurable, being taught and being learned. It is what the thread is that weaves this book into me and into you.

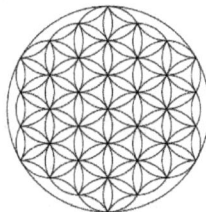

Chapter Two - Peggy's Appreciations on Appreciation's Pathway

- ❖ I appreciate the unpredictable yet seemingly natural spiritual path I am on that leads me to Wisdom.

- ❖ I appreciate learning the *Secrets* that come to me to enlighten me, such as "That which is above is that which is below".

- ❖ I appreciate knowing that positive thinking and self-confidence can greatly improve the outcome.

- ❖ I appreciate the polite reminders from my partner that helps me recall the focus of my thoughts should be as positive as possible.

- ❖ I appreciate applying the Law of Attraction into my Catholic Christ-consciousness perspective.

- ❖ I appreciate that my life is so good and that it continues to improve, surprise, provide, encourage, and expand.

- ❖ I appreciate the loving nameless Voice found Within.

- ❖ I appreciate Esther and Jerry Hicks and the Messages from Abraham.

- ❖ I appreciate that we are all living as totally integrated portions of the external Oneness.

- ❖ I appreciate myself as a Great Appreciator that by appreciating finds more to appreciate.

Chapter Two - Your Appreciations on Appreciation's Pathway

I appreciate this about myself: _____

_____

I appreciate this about my life: _____

_____

I appreciate this about my future: _____

_____

I appreciate _____

_____

I appreciate _____

_____

I appreciate_____

_____

I appreciate_____

_____

I appreciate_____

_____

The "Art of Appreciation" is simple, just find something to appreciate, start right there, and then appreciate something else after that, and then another something, and on and on. That's it! Create one appreciation after another, and when you appreciate enough you will enter a space of being connected to who-you-really-are and the knowing that you are worthy of appreciation.

By Peggy Halevi

Chapter 3   Appreciating Changes Things

I really know that "Appreciating" is a personal tool that, if used, enables the building of an invisible creative enriched dynamic circular, or wave-like undulated momentum, which is, at very least, an emotional, spiritual and physical experience that connects and carries its re-invigorated-energies and vibrations into several directions simultaneously, forever and for goodness. Appreciations are positive multidimensional movements that ride on the words they become from the thoughts tempered within the heart. Appreciating is a unique tool, yet, equally provided as is "Love", although currently, it is far from being as widely recognized as Love is. I am thoughtfully and deliberately intending that more people will utilize this tool or gift of Appreciation, as I also learn to develop more applications and skills for Appreciating.

First let's look at "love" to comprehend the exposure we all have to it in our daily lives and from that point it will be easier to understand more about it's close relative "Appreciation".

Regarding Love: It is such apparent evidence of freedom that Love is all around us. Love is in books, songs, poems, words, actions, shapes, gifts, clothes, relationships, holidays, thoughts, intentions and more, much more. "Love" is wonderfully and blatantly prevalent in most all of our experiences. Love is most worthy and it is absolute in all goodness. We are "lovaholics", and that is outstanding and easily realized if viewed at for the purpose of seeing it, yet this is often reflected upon as subjective association.

Mankind is loving and lovable. Even on Mankind's worst days, we are more of us loving and lovable than not. If you doubt that ask yourself, who do you know that is unloving or unlovable? And then think of how many others you know. There are a great many more loving people in your associations, societies, nations and, of course, families than often thought of from the disconcerting pollution of the general media, both news and entertainment, and the favored historical references aligned to our educations. Love prevails this Earth, although we seem to give much too much attention to the opposite faction. Yet, proportionally Love is so much bigger and greater and widespread. Our focus of attention is easily diverted from it and in the thoughts that others attempt to incite us towards. When we are noticing something that is not love, we do not feel good. That not-good-feeling can sometimes lure us further into it, yet, Love is so much larger then anything other, we are genuinely attracted to return to its magnificence intuitively. You have heard the expression; "You can't keep a good man down", well, that is the way it is with Love. There is so much love in our world that there will always be enough of it around for you. Some proclaim that there is not enough Love in the World, but I see it differently, there is so much love in the World that the World is more than 99 percent Love and growing. It is all just a matter of what you want to bring your attention too. If you think there is not enough love in the world, and you want more, simply love more and you increase it, independently. Every loving thought remains forevermore. Think more love into our world; I love you for that gesture. I love this life and I love everything in this world. I love that love conquers all, that love is the answer and that love is all around.

The media and our educational systems are not the only absorbers of love, as also in our personal relationships, many keep love as a backdrop to our more critical nature and competitive instilled behavior, or at least surface side. Love is more powerful than given credit and its vibrations are tons stronger than the opposite of it. There is a spiritual advantage in the composition of love that overrules. We should study humanities "Love" more in schools. Sounds pretty silly, doesn't it! Imagine taking a course on the way people loved each other in 1914. The belief collectively inherent from those who came before us is that by learning and studying our past blunders we will not repeat them, however, the opposite is true! By focusing on them we create more of the same. I am certain there was more than a World War beginning then. Even psychology courses tend to zero in on the extreme emotional problems and to look deeper into them. Perhaps, we should start looking more deeply into love.

Love is so prevalent that we have been living enough of it to not feel that there is a real shortage of it even though that is sometimes said to be true. If we were really running low on love, we would notice it and take action. Yet, we can take action now and make love even stronger. It is only a thought away.

We are sometimes, actually enough times to mention herein, missing the intimacies of natural love by avoiding the commonality between each of us now in this present "historical" time. Yet, we intuitively recognize deep within us that we are all equally emotionally "love" as say we are physically "water", about 90 percent. Our emotional and thought composition is made of love's truth that refuses to be denied, only perhaps sometimes ignored. It is a wonder that we haven't openly objected to this tendency of downgrading our lovability as an entire race, except for the fact that objection and confrontation are out of our desired loving personalities, generally. Additionally, as I mentioned, we are predominantly capable of dealing with the opposite of our loving nature because "love" is so huge an influence that the drop of hate we encounter, even when in school, is dissolved like a smidgen of salt in a pitcher of water. It is this truly loving status that enables new loving tools to be discovered. That is one of the points this book will readjust the reader with knowing. Appreciation is a loving tool.

The truth is that God or the Source-of-All, knows every single one of us as lovable even if we are less than a hundred percent loving all of the time. Everyone is touched by love through this Source of Life. Every place finds love and all have met love as it converged upon, into or with us in all infinite ways. We are mostly made of love. Feel that truth.

Contact with love is inevitable and a total requirement for life. One is born realized and actualized of it and being it. Even the most unimaginable retched of situations, in it love has been before and will be again, for all things come from and return to love. All things are brought forth, even if in the slightest way, but mostly in the grandest way, with love's influence. All situations in life including the horror stories, movies, or books that focus on the lack of love; love has touched each component of it, each and every participant in it, and its results inescapably contain that love within it. We all come forth in love and it is indelible so it will always be in the building components of humanity. If you doubt these comments as true, let me set it straight by proclaiming my love for everything, hence, officially establishing the fact that everything is touched by love. Even where it seems I am unable to Love, the Source Loves all. If we all proclaim that same message forth, it will make a difference. Our biological DNA is packaged with emotional Love! We are actually evolving into a stronger capability to love and be loved. One is innocent of its association as the union of love within all is ethereal, primordial and unavoidable. Love will always exist; be scripted and always be scripted in and out from us. Love touches everything in some way shape or form. Love surrounds us and is a major component in the holding and blending glue of humanity. Love is a thought of self. Love is hardwired into us. We are in cooperation with Love. We are a component of Love and Love is a component of us.

I see that "Love is all there is" if "Love is all you think exists". If "Love is all there is", than it can only be, even if Love was all there was, could have been or might ever be. In those thoughts Love is so abundant. 1 Corinthians 13:4 says;

"Love is patient, love is kind. It does not envy, it does not boast, it is not proud."

Think about this, there are songs about all forms of Love; love for the lover, mother, father, child, self, neighbor, gardens, trees, pets, sky, breeze, soldiers, country, earth, God, and on and on. However, I am looking for even one song, or book or poem outside of what is coming forth herein, on Appreciation. Appreciation is an idea whose time has come to be realized. And what is to be realized? Much! There is a vastness of untapped understanding of Appreciation and it is ready to be known.

❁ ❁ ❁

Regarding Appreciation: Undoubtedly, "Appreciations" roots are interspersed with "Love's" conception, everything is! However, it is itself as worthy as love and we are at the exact time of mankind to grasp it more fully. As a result more tools will be encountered. I, until recently, did not consider the distinction, without applied variation, yet equality, between Love and Appreciation. I did acknowledge that these two beautiful words often stand side-by-side in my thoughts, and in my spoken and written words.

I searched for "Appreciate" and it's derivatives in the King James Version of the Bible, and it is never mentioned at all. Isn't that Amazing? "Appreciation" is a new-formed word, as judiciously birthed into our realities as is the evolution of humanities blood types or expanding technologies and is brought into existence as part of the evolution of mankind; the evolution of increasing capabilities of communications. So much good is coming forth all of the time! It could very well be time to appreciate what Appreciation is all about.

The origin of the word Appreciate comes into mankind's vocabulary some time between 1600-1645 when it was initially used to reference an increased appraised value of financial interest, as in an increase in price or value of a piece of property, real or otherwise. It is rather nice having had its meaning originally associated with money, since money appreciates our lives so nicely. Apparently, money spans thousands of years prior to the creation of the word "Appreciation" as we come to know it. And money is essentially a token of an abstraction of value. A "shekel", which was an ancient unit for the weight of currency, was used 3000 BC and is likened to today's money. The value of the original shekel was arrived at from the type of currency, such as barley or bronze. Each currency was valued at the bargaining demand for it at the time it was exchanged, yet, the word "appreciation" seems to be avoided, perhaps due to the fluctuation of "values". It is also interesting to note that communication before 1600 did not use the word "Appreciation" at all. Christ never used the word "Appreciation" in His teaching to humanity, nor did other recorded and respected ancient teachers. I detected that "Appreciation" appears in newer versions of the Bible, actually some Bibles after King James Version uses "Appreciation", yet, technically it was impossible to have it included in Biblical literature. The translators are improvising with human comprehension, as "Appreciation" was as unrecognized as was electricity to Moses. Neither had been invented yet!

And so in those glorious thoughts, that we are evolving our requirements for new words, "Appreciation" is birthed into being. And now, let the music begin, as there are songs, poems, stories, ideas and books to be filled with a new or rather combined literary, financial and spiritual comprehension of Appreciation. That is definitely inspirational. It is a word, it is a thought, it is a concept, and it is an inspiration whose time is upon us. I am ready for it! Are you?

In the visual words, we know that Appreciation is different than Love, each unto itself unique; Appreciating is something other then loving. Although, Love and Appreciation are termed often together, and many people use them interspersingly, yet they are different. I detect them as each worthy. It is apparent that they are born sanctified on the same breath of God's delight, and appropriately they serve us, differently yet equally as well as they are each supportive of our positive pure energies, our Inner Beings, and ourselves. One might say how can I think that God sanctified this word in delight. And I will say to you, let me take you into this adventure of learning about Appreciation and you will, if so desired, judge for yourself. To me it is obvious and I am very excited to introduce you to my world of Appreciating. God didn't stop providing for us ways of growing. All words come into being with a thought and then it is created and some words are more for our enlightenment then other words. Love and Appreciation are such. They are each perfectly fashioned for their own purpose and provided to us to use. What then can we learn in this heightened elevation and acknowledgement of "Appreciation"?

A state of Appreciation is a state of Godliness. I sincerely feel that "Appreciation" is a word, a thought, and an emotion worth loving and Godliness is worth Embracing! Appreciation is hardwired into our emotional DNA since around 1600, when it began being used in vocabulary. It has evolved in meaning and deserves clarification and to be distinguished from the word "Love". They are different words and although the word "Appreciation" wasn't used in Jesus' vocabulary, it is here for us now. Jesus surely would have used it, I think, if only we were ready to hear it.

Appreciation is where I am emotionally when aligned to and in agreement with myself and while experiencing life through the Eyes of Source. Appreciation is a peaceful space encountering self-awareness and God-awareness, simultaneously. When in the "Act of Appreciation" I am experiencing who-I-really-am without self-imposed blinding limitations from fault, blame, shame or anything that is less than pure. In the "Act of Appreciating" myself I may effortlessly remove external labels given to me from others and from my acceptance or believing that any label actually is me. In other words, self-appreciation reveals, to myself and to others, the "real me". Likewise, in the "Act of Appreciating" others I can remove the labels, names and titles that identify others, and in so doing I can see that other person for who-they-really-are. Appreciation is the inclusion of all things that are good to think and feel about. Appreciation is the void and opposite of hatred, doubt, fear, disempowerment, unworthiness and anything else that feels bad. In a state of Appreciation I feel good and very close to the presence of God. Appreciation is a state of Godliness. Appreciation is the time that prayer is being heard.

❋ ❋ ❋

Regarding Gratitude: What's the difference between Appreciation and Gratitude? Let us seek to find their meanings as they compare with each other because we sense there is a connection. In so doing we will, as a by-product, be able to link the meanings of "Appreciation" compared to "Love". This process will serve extremely well and with an allowing you may sense an opening of your heart. While absorbing all of these differing definitions, consider the vibration of each word as they relate to you personally, because in the essence of comprehending definitions, usages and sounds all words conjure-up valuable feelings and emotions. These words, that we are looking at more closely than ever before, are special as they come from the realm of heart-felt expressions. Trust your feelings of these words and notice the emotions you experience thinking about them. Say them out loud and recall your lifetime experiences with them. Herein, let us consider this a strength that will assist in finding wisdom through understanding. Although it is rare to examine words in this way, we are able to utilize our "feelings and emotions" as guides to identify, direct, calibrate our thoughts and definitely to bring us into heightened awareness. It takes a conscientious effort to reach inside your-self in addition to looking inside of a dictionary for deeper clarity in understanding these words. It is up to you to trust your feelings and emotions to "tell the rest of the story".

First of all, notice that as with "Appreciation" and "Love", many people also use the words "Appreciation" and "Gratitude" interspersed, even interchangeably. However, "Love" and "Gratitude" are not exchanged in use and feel less as equals compared to each other, generally. I think you agree that when we connect "Appreciation and Love", "Appreciation and Gratitude" and "Love and Gratitude", the "Love and Gratitude" seems less comparable and further apart in meanings. They clearly feel different from one another. There is a vibration with each of them that is important to sense. We can intellectually know the difference and we can vibrationally experience the difference.

However, many people use "Appreciation and Gratitude" identically the same, especially when speaking. During the past several years, I've been made much more aware of the interesting subtle yet valuable differences in these two words that resembles the distinction between inspire (inspiration) and motivate (motivation). In fact, it actually assists in making a point if we look at inspiration and motivation too. I know that initially thinking about introducing two more words that are "heart expressing" words into the mix of things might seem like complicating the whole thing, however, trust me, this will help a lot. Let us continue.

<u>Inspiration</u> means to have, almost uncontrollable desire that is influenced from seemingly a greater source than self

into an expanding quickening usually likened to a delightful enlivening. The word *spirit* is within the word inspiration. It is a spirited sensation. It is an impulsive behavior that comes from spirit.

Motivation means an induced, or somewhat provoked requirement that is longing for action to be satisfied. The word *motive* is within the word motivation. Motivation happens from a *motive* towards action that is incited from self or into self from a space of grounded-self-equality or even slight admiration for another.

In other words, Motivation is a good feeling yet not quite from the heightened calling, as is Inspiration.

Inspiration is a feeling that comes within you from seemingly a greater and more powerfully loving source than self yet, comes upon self.

While:

Motivation ignites a flame within (as does Inspiration), yet seemingly initiated from self or an external earthly force.

To further clarify:

Inspiration is rich with *Enthusiasm* (another heart expression) in a very similar way that Appreciation is enriched with Inspiration.

Further analyzing let's look at "Gratitude" which is from a place of Thanksgiving (another heart expression). Thanksgiving is being enriched with a fulfillment of *Satisfaction* (another heart expression, slightly more physical). *Satisfaction* is a relief from a place of tension, wanting, lack or even struggle. "Gratitude" carries in its essential vibrations (feel it) a connection also to the having come from the release of tension, wanting from lack or not having, or from some struggle.

Following this emotional logic, both Motivation and "Gratitude" carry vibrational feelings with them of an association with *Satisfaction*. There is a commercial statement

"Satisfaction Guaranteed", that vibrates both heart expressions of Motivation and "Gratitude". They both come up from an underlying "struggle".

Whereas "Appreciation" is purely Inspirational and elevates from it's association with absolute *Enthusiasm*. One has received a reward when coming into Thanksgiving in "Gratitude". One becomes blessed when entering into "Appreciation" through the grace of Inspiration. "Gratitude" and "Appreciation are two very wonderful words, however, they come from different places in their origin and could be used more befittingly.

I both Love and "Appreciate" the above complex yet wonderful explaining word-descriptions that are based upon definitions and vibrational feelings. Since first writing of these words, I have pondered these clarifying definitions over and over again, both intellectually and vibrationally, and in them I have tremendously grown from my previous understanding. I have never before thought of these subtle differences in the words "Appreciation and Gratitude". Appreciation comes from a light place and Gratitude comes from a place of being thankful for having obtained the relief in finding or getting something truly wanted out of need.

As a by-product, at my first true intellectual recognition of the differences between "Appreciation and Gratitude" I realized a similarly clarifying to me in the true sensation of the differences between "Appreciation and Love". All of a sudden I began to feel spiritual warmth flood purposefully into my Beingness that brought me to grasp a much deeper distinction through the similarities waiting to be seen at the boundaries of dissimilarities. My mind first knew it and then this knowledge permeated into my opened heart where it began to radiate into Wisdom. I internalized what "Appreciation's" seraphic meaning was and definitely for the first time in my life.

I am evolved from this happening to me. I found within me the Place in which "Appreciation" resides, The Feeling Place of "Appreciation". I am aware of this. There is no residue from struggle in my learning this, although, I simultaneously feel

"Gratitude" too. From it, I intuitively realize the exact differentiation between "Appreciation and Gratitude". It is so beautiful to sense and feel emotionally this understanding. I will now appreciate that in-between the words of this chapter, the reader can find that Feeling-Place of "Appreciation", as well. This peacefulness has become a delightfully familiar growing and enriching emotion. I am in great "Appreciation" for having had this awareness come to me, and for having had "Appreciation's" essence find permanent welcome in my Feeling-Place of "Appreciation". "The Art of Appreciation" starts by birthing into oneself the meaning of "Appreciation". Learning of "Appreciation" is a worthwhile deed. It has for me become a life-changing experience. It is a leap of vibrational certainty.

Realizing Love is at the equaled level of my consciousness, so, I am grateful indeed for truly life was more of a struggle before finding this Wisdom. Is "Appreciating" a stepping-stone into awareness? For me it is! If "Appreciating" is less to you, then I recommend you reread those word descriptions and comparisons again and apply your emotions and feelings into your understanding. Sense the vibrations of each word at your personal level. I love reading, saying and feeling them vibrationally. Read them until you "Appreciate" them and then you too will find that Feeling-Place of "Appreciation", which is in proximity to the Feeling-Place of Love, each equally viable. It is like learning, acknowledging and sensing the existence of both spaces and places of Love and of "Appreciation" and realizing that there is twice as much of something wonderful "Within".

❊ ❊ ❊

Now that I've come to better understand what "Appreciation" is in relationship to Love, and "Gratitude", and Inspiration and Motivation, what more am I finding "Appreciation" to actually be without the comparison? I know "Appreciation" is a positive God-gifted, heart-expressed, thought-vibration and that it has a variety of movement capabilities that are felt rather then seen and that it can either come around as in a vortexual swirl or continue or it can also grow or fade. I am unsure if it can actually fade away entirely or ever disappear, although we can consider that a possibility it doesn't seem probable. I think an "Appreciation" never dissolves and that it is always present in the Universe, as it travels with intention and purpose, as does all forms of thought-vibration and as such it is attracting unto itself like vibrations. It's fading away could possibly only be perceived as a reduction from another perspective. It could very well be a distancing in relative position rather than a fading away. "The Art of Appreciation" is a reality to me and so I know it is to others. "The Act of Appreciating" in its pure energy wavelength is attracting similar vibrations that are amplified when the attractions are found. Some may have a distance to travel to be connected up to other like-Appreciations or like-vibrations.

"Appreciations" are free forming thought-waves and cannot be owned by any one or thing as in the sense of possessing them. An "Appreciation" is a pure creation that all people are capable of making at any time. They are created from the stillness and desire of our minds and in our thoughts and from our hearts. What a powerful ability.

It sounds a great deal like other forms of vibrations or waves such as the frequency of light, sound, thought, love, electricity, heat and more. "Appreciation" is definitely thought-heart created energy and all of these other frequency-types are energies also. I think that "Appreciation" is an element of vibration, such as music is and, as such, it has it's own distinction or identity and although it is an ability that everyone has, it is more effective for some than for others.

※ ※ ※

Musicians have a major awareness of the sounds of music and Appreciators have a major awareness of the Voice formed within consciousness from "Appreciations". Musicians create and play music and Appreciators create and play "Appreciations". Both Musicians and Appreciators are artists, each within their own fields of interests and expertise. Music is a heard vibration, "Appreciations" result in a hearing connection, and from that music can be appreciated. Musical sounds are created in the internal sound of thought vibration initially. From there they are manifested in forms, written and made auditory. Music connects to people, easing them into a beat, a dance, a song. While, for me, "Appreciations" ease my reception of the Inner Self's messages. "Appreciations" are similar to the poems or prayers of conversion from thought to synchronicity. I reach toward it and for it in a welcoming invitation and when in a state of "Appreciation" it reaches towards me, each of us sensing the presence of the other through the vibrations transmitted and the allowing of this nature. It is at this space between wanting to appreciate my Inner Self and receiving messages from Inner Self, that a peaceful allowing produces awareness. The product of music is the hearing of it, and likewise the product of "Appreciation" is the recognizing and hearing of it. "Appreciations" in this form sounds like messages from Source. Both Musical sounds and "Appreciations" can be manifested and shared.

The interpretation of "Appreciation" is vibrational clarity and union with the surrounding world, all accessible and transcendental. It resonates a subliminal characteristic of approaching oneself, as in coming to know oneself. Within appreciating and while playing "Appreciations" in my heart, mind and soul, I hear something wondrous to further appreciate. The return for the awareness of it is an increased joy and knowledge of eternal love bestowed upon me. The more I appreciate the more there comes into my life to appreciate. In this space of listening to the sound vibrations enabled through appreciating, I am enlightened and messages stream forth from a place much deeper than what can exist within my body, much larger than my body can hold all of and much further from my "normal" reality. The space and time found there, in "The Act of Appreciation", enlarges all my previous experiences of life and places me into a state of absolute "Now".

I have searched for better words and find these the best. I am able to approach the oneness of all-that-is-within the radiance of pure "Appreciations" and in that place I am enlightened with communications from my Higher Self. This is what I achieve. This is what I allow. This is what I am provided. This is the gift I receive. I am to wonder if others can find this "Withinness" as well and in association with "The Art of Appreciating" and for that I will attempt to bring more information forth to assist others into "The Art of Appreciating".

We know that energy can be created, detected, monitored, measured, depicted and converted into representations of information and data in wave forms, sign waves, graphs, and more and that existing energy has object relativity, force, intent and purpose in direction. In other words, energy knows where it is going. And we know that if any form of energy is moving it is possible to enhance its continued state easier then to initiate it over. That idea is utilized in the way electricity travels sound waves through wires in my attic taking it from the receiver device at the entertainment console to several sets of auxiliary speakers in the rooms of our home and it is enhanced along the way, when necessary, with boosters or repeaters which re-energize the momentum of the carry. It is strengthened and continues on its way. Is there an alteration in the exact vibration after the boost occurs? Probably, somewhat and partially due to duration also, yet, the essence of it is brought forward and comes out of the speakers with little detectable variation or distortion on the results.

That is a way in which I visualize "Appreciation" moving. Appreciation is initiated or created and then travels and is received and then boosted or re-directed. It is a living energy. Let me example that with a supposed situation. I can state, "I appreciate you". And when you receive that statement and you feel it and think of it and you can respond; "I appreciate you too" or you can think "I appreciate being appreciated". You can think both those thoughts as well, yet either thought takes Appreciation into another direction. One, "I appreciate you too", increases the frequency of the appreciation and brings it into a circular wave back to its emanated initiator. The other "I appreciate being appreciated", increases the frequency of self, and then self-worth is forwarded through its own positive course of travel. In other words, appreciations, at a minimum, can move in a circular spiraling motion and in a forward motion. That sounds rather abstract and irrelevant; yet, I want to begin to demonstrate the power in the knowing of these simple sounding ideas.

❋ ❋ ❋

A few weeks ago I purchased a bunch of fresh grapes from the local market. I brought them home in my bundles of groceries and when finally able to prepare them they were washed and set to dry. I recall it clearly as being a nice day, the sky was beautifully filled with a few white clouds and the horizon was wide, deep and clear from my vantage point in the kitchen of our hillside home. I recall actually taking a grape and placing it into my mouth and sensing something more than a flavorful grape. I gazed out of my window and recalled in a bit of a daydream state having read on the label of the grape packaging that these grapes were from the country of Chile. I started to sense something more about this delicious grape as I found those thoughts.

This was a feeling of something unfamiliar to me. I was actually feeling the "story" of the person who picked the grape, or so it seemed. I felt the great warmth of appreciation for this person, who I knew when he or she picked it, was in a great mood, like I felt myself in right now. I sensed that this person felt a mutual appreciation for me. This person was appreciating the day, the clouds, the sky, the work, and the vision of someone, me, enjoying the pick. This person, like me, deliberately was thinking in appreciation of the other people involved at the other end in the processing of the grape, and the water and land that was required to grow, the packaging and delivering and all the details that were required for me to have this grape in my mouth far from where it was grown, yet always intended for me. Neither of us knew each other personally and it is impossible to trace or officially document these feelings yet, I really know that this person and I were in the midst of a circle of Appreciation. We both knew it too. We knew that each understood happiness and we each knew that we were in appreciation for the other. The feeling was intoxicating and sweet. I wanted to prolong this thought and continue in the feelings of mutual appreciation with a stranger whose feelings had arrived in an invisible yet tangible way into my home, into my thoughts, into my appreciation, while mine were felt someplace else far away in the space of appreciation in this person's soul. I felt so mutually connected. I felt a soul connected intimacy and it felt really good. The grapes were delicious and I delighted further into this basic thought of mutual appreciation with the person who picked this grape with each and every individual grape I ate. They were very satisfying also. I still feel the sensation of this experience and my mouth intuitively waters in my soul's longing for it to return again.

In the days to follow I shared that episode of international appreciation with others and after several days I began to miss it a little, while holding on to the lovely personalized experience and the story of it. Abraham teaches that when something is pleasing to you, you should "Milk" it for all you can. In other words, it is a prolonged appreciation to keep thinking of the pleasure of it all.

Perhaps a week later I picked up some more grapes from Chile and did the same process. I washed and dried them and then when I ate the first one I felt a different sensation. I felt my appreciation of it; however, that wondrous sensation of an international bilateral intimacy of appreciation was absent. I was missing feeling the other person and they me.

I was finding appreciation in that previous experience as I sat in the same chair overlooking the huge window view and held an intention about that appreciation experience as I thought of the delightful exchange now seemingly too long ago in the past, when I noticed the grape vine that belongs to my next door neighbor moving a little more than the breezes could be causing. I thought again about the grapes of appreciation and then noticed the top of my neighbor's head appear above the fence. It had been perhaps two or three years ago since I had seen him there in that spot for a short moment and now again. Seeing our elderly next-door neighbor standing there is a rare occurrence. I thought how nice a neighbor he is and how nice to see him out climbing up to our property-line fence and pruning his grape vine. He missed me seeing him, or so it seemed. Yet, I took that moment to appreciate him. I felt that the connection to the originating appreciation of the grapes from Chile now had promulgated into this neighborly appreciation. This is an example of a waveform path of appreciation. It is a simple reality that is probably available more readily than we appreciate. The exercise of spiritual interconnection is untaught elsewhere.

The awareness of this ability is closely associated with telepathy and commences from the heart-mind connection. The feeling-place of Apperception is an eminent meeting place between souls.

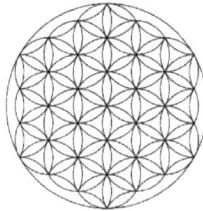

Chapter 3 - Peggy's Appreciations on Appreciating Changes Things

- ❖ I appreciate that I apply "The Art of Appreciation" in my life often, when I feel real good and when I want to feel better.

- ❖ I appreciate that I feel an abundance of Love in my life.

- ❖ I appreciate that I am almost always in control of my thoughts and aware of my emotions and I realize that from them I trust the Law of Attraction to deliver me more joy.

- ❖ I appreciate knowing that Love touches every shadow as much as every bright space in my life.

- ❖ I appreciate that we are an expanding life form and that we are a growth of pleasure in God's Eyes.

- ❖ I appreciate being inspired with enthusiasm to write these thoughts into this book.

- ❖ I appreciate being an Artist of Appreciations bringing Within Wisdom into my many masterpieces.

- ❖ I appreciate sensing the movement and momentum of the thought Appreciation.

- ❖ I appreciate the connectivity of Oneness that can be shared in Appreciation across miles and time.

- ❖ I appreciate the opening of my heart to hear the Great Voice Within that I find available as I think, write or speak heart-felt Appreciations.

Chapter 3 - Your Appreciations on Appreciating Changes Things

I appreciate this about myself: _____

_____

I appreciate this about my life: _____

_____

I appreciate this about my future: _____

_____

I appreciate _____

_____

I appreciate _____

_____

I appreciate_____

_____

I appreciate _____

_____

I appreciate _____

_____

I appreciate _____

_____

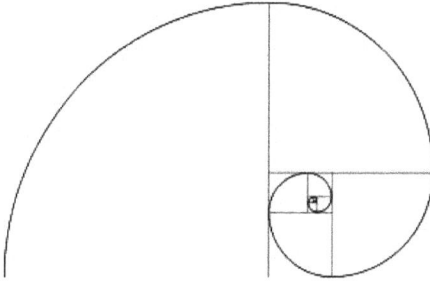

"Appreciating will allow & assist all appropriate changes."

By Peggy Halevi

Chapter 4   Allowing Appreciation

In my ongoing study of the numerous messages and interpretations from teachers around the world and through time regarding the Law of Attraction and in addition to my own clarity and experiences, I continuously am arriving at new and definitely lovely conclusions as to how to deliberately re-organize my thoughts such that the results of my having them could bring about a better emotional experience, and consequently a better life, finding, that connection consistent. And all that proved true.

It is so extraordinary that since I began consciously "Allowing" what I desire to come into my life, life is always surprising me with things turning out better than I thought was possible before now. To clarify, what I mean by "Allowing", which is an extended meaning from the dictionary definition, it is that I am willing to trust the Law of Attraction to endear onto me that which I am attracting just by being me. I am confidently taking personal responsibility for what is available for the Law of Attraction to yield, since; I am the only one who can do that. We all only can be held responsible for ourselves and it is a wonderful Within-accountability to appreciate that we each emanate the frequencies that manifest our future lives. There are no exceptions. Equally, we all have the ability to "allow", knowingly or not. We can think in default and we can allow in default, or we can think deliberately and allow deliberately. Even those with "thinking" impairments are creating the perfect components to allow goodness into their lives. Being aware of this, I am trusting in myself, through my clarifying thoughts and emotions, to bring to me my abstracted-formed-thoughts of my own life's projection. I am trusting that I am aligned to the best or even better than the best outcome that I desire. I know that I am a powerful beautiful Being that thinks in harmony with goodness and I confirm this appreciation of myself by allowing, which is an art form. We all have this leveraging power. In allowing, by lifting any self-imposed limitations, I am trusting that in which I am and knowing that it is all working out fine. In allowing I am willfully living the consequence of my own intended and extended energy vibrations to materialize my delineated conception of desired goodness. I am taking responsibility for the ability to allow myself to think, love, feel, appreciate, and resonate without restrictions of analyzing how or why.

In this trusting in one self, I am confident to "Allow" when I know I have been thinking goodness, hence, attracting goodness. When believing that all things are working for the best even my thinking goodness is subjective, as if I attract a contrast or something less pleasant then wanted, in that space of experience I immediately birth a desire for something else, something more aligned to pleasing me to become my new attraction. I hold treasure to the word "Appreciation", for it, even when just thinking of the word, releases any heaviness brought into me from the ways of the world and the misinterpretation I have beheld within it and especially within myself. For it is only my thoughts that create my fears and it is only my thoughts that can remove the cloud of confusion and enable the limitations to drop off of me like the opening of a door to walk through. The Appreciation of this is uplifting and enlightening. It is delightful to "Allow" when I know I have loved and appreciated life and everything in it. In that, all coming into my life is perfectly unfolding. In knowing that alone, I want to appreciate often.

Funny that before I started to "Allow", I didn't think the best was possible for me, but I do now. A major change occurred when I started to give it some Time; Time to happen. I love having time to "Allow" and "Allowing" is always exactly on time. Winter is winter, summer is summer and they are always on time and are collectively agreed upon times that naturally exist in my reality, as well as your reality. Time and seasons are but two of the numerous global agreements that identifies, in humanities harmony, our social Oneness. Hence, time is worth noting as a part of the equation that one works with in the Allowing process. Allow time to allow all that is to be, become and appreciate the connection and flow. That is so simple that it is forgotten to be known.

The entire process of thinking positive thoughts brings about goodness. That I had intuitively understood probably all of my life, yet, didn't connect the dots to recognize that it was "me" who was creating goodness for me until more recently. This was always an available awareness, however, I was learning it from the events "outside" of myself, the "Without Lessons" which take much longer to learn from the disadvantage of struggle than from the "Within Lessons" which are faster and delightful.

❊ ❊ ❊

When I was a child, I realized that people who seemed to be happy had good things happen to and around them, including what was affecting me. I liked being near happy people. I was happier with them too. If they felt good, good stuff happened to them and me, just because I was nearby. Yet, for some reason, I felt that others, rather than me, mostly caused happiness. I was just lucky if I was around these people who were so happy that it seemed to overflow into me. I could see that these happy sorts of people, the beautiful people, inspired happiness. I merely felt that I was just an influenced-one in the middle of something others were more fortunate to own or be. I realize now that I was the producer of my own happiness and these happy others were equally attracted to me. I was creating my own happiness and together we were co-creating shared happiness. Was anyone ever luckier than anyone else? The answer seems to be, only if they thought it to be so.

Looking back on it all and reflecting upon now as well, I see, most of us are in that state of misunderstanding and learning of many things from "Without". What was the cause of this thinking that I was less worthy of being the initiator of true happiness? Why did I seem to think others were better blessed with this gift of happiness than I was? The answer is that I lacked the knowledge and confidence to appreciate myself. Learning of that is a major keystone amending my ability to be happy and enables me to learn "Within". I needed to appreciate myself and know that my goodness is amply worthy to produce my own happiness and more. Imagine that! I needed self-confidence to see myself deserving. Now why didn't I realize that? I know why, because I had been thinking that self-confidence was something one conjured up to be brave, to walk tall with head and chin up, not to create and to be happy. I now realize all good feelings are personally invoked.

When my life goes through major changes it is somewhat common that there tends to be some drama that heightens the experience. In my developing spiritual growth and understanding, here, in time, is where all hell broke loose in my life! I had to overcome the stigma of protecting myself from conceit in order to gain self-value. That was a daunting step to take, or worse, it was an incorrect thing to do, perhaps even a sin, because I was taught in my Catholic ways that conceit and selfishness were the same things. I wanted to avoid being like that. After all, I was taught and told and it was passed on from generation to generation that these self-centered characteristics were undesirable and that in having them as part of my personality, surely, people would dislike me. I mentioned this self-indulging experiment of my self-appreciating to my sister who reminded me that one day while she was adoring her youthful beautiful self in a full length mirror at about the age of nine, when she was convinced that she was a princess, and she surely was in anyone's seeing eyes, and as she was sweepingly dancing airily in front of the mirror for the pure pleasure of her graceful admiring reflection, our Grandmother, saw this display of self-pleasure and said; "What the hell are you doing? Continue acting like that and you will grow up to be conceited". I too heard that voice in my memory along with myriads of others, such as; parents, relatives, siblings, friends, clerics, and teachers. How could I gain self-worth and avoid being conceited or selfish in so doing? This felt terribly un-Catholic. How could I turn my back on such vital virtues as humility, modesty, mercy, self-denial, charity, and obedience? Those steps of faith were squarely part of the cornerstone of my religious training, my family heritage, and my belief system. I concluded that this self-approving was going to be a bit tricky.

I had to let go and trust in myself. Was I now to grasp that this "turning-point" in my attitude actually was the "trusting-point" to move forward in creating my own happiness and recognizing my evident self-value and significance? Indeed, it was! How else does anyone come to realize his or her "purpose" in life? Discovering myself, regardless of what I was already taught or what others could say or think about me, was truly a Within Lesson that isolated and insolated me into a space of true unconditional love of self. I found that I am a beautiful Human Being, filled with love and seen as a perfect person in the eyes of God, and now in my own eyes too. I was being reborn into a person who did not possess or reflect sin, blame, shame, doubt or fears that associated within me from my Catholic trained self-imaging. What a novel thought!

Unconditional Love is born by unconditionally loving self. What a new concept to purely love myself? In addition to loving my hairdo, my clothes, my age, my shape, the color of my eyes or my smile impressed upon others I could love what is always me, the Withinness of Myself. That indeed is where my "true" beauty resides. Being distracted by self-discovered outwardly beauty is a lovely fleeting form of appreciation. Multiply that by a thousand times a thousand and look "Within" yourself for the real thing.

What excitement in finding out that I can appreciate myself and keep it a moral act of pureness and love rather than a sin to confess on next Saturday afternoon. I can believe in myself. I can see and feel the perfect Beingness that God made me into. In conflicting ambiguous instructions that too was a Catholic teaching. I am learning and I am less often stuck in negative thoughts about myself. The more I fill in this gap with love between me personally and my self-worth the better I feel. And the better I feel the better everything around me is. Even if I have times of resorting back to those engrained over-trained thoughts of self lack, irrelevance, unimportance and insignificance, I am certainly and increasingly being made aware, through my own thoughts and appreciations that I am exactly the way God wants me to be; right now, before, in the future and forever. Catholicism seems to preach both sides of the same coin. I chose to accept the side that bring honor to me. That is an example of accelerated learning through "Lessons Within".

I am a new me, a person of conscious self-dignity. I feel freer and safer, I grow wiser and calmer and I have found a point of contentment with whom I am, while knowing I am continuously improving. I am clearly more self-aware, self-confident and self-enabled. I care about others more effectively and can dream about my future fervently. I think and act with more poise and assurance. My future is larger and my past is less powerfully influenced upon it. I am gleefully a more selfish person and in so being I am a happier, more complete human being. I am far from humiliated by my humbled past. I hold only happiness for the lessons and sequences I follow, and I am pleased to state that I am selfishly enjoying life more fully than ever before. I am pleased with that accomplishment. I have overcome the impacting sigma and judgment of being enclosed in the fears of learning that the term "selfish" defines also an ability to be more honest about self-awareness. I am delighted to be selfish. I know that it is right for me. It is a different selfish than I knew selfish to be. It takes nothing from others and gives so much back to all I am and all I know. In loving and appreciating myself I have grown my love and appreciation for others.

I can look at my pure state of existence, my pure positive energies without feeling guilt at seeing me as a reflection of God, the Heart of Jesus and the perfection of life intended for me to realize about myself. I can appreciate that it is wonderful to see God in the reflection of myself. That is a very Catholic belief. It is beautiful to love myself, and without feeling conceited or arrogant. I can see, what I know to be true, that I am created in the image of God. I can release the shallow humility of being less and adapt the truth that always was and always will be in that I am in God's Eyes a perfect being created by God. We all are! We are all equally beautiful. There are no mistakes in God's creations and I can accept myself as God's perfect creation. From that I can birth back, re-birth what I entered this world knowing, that I am God's Delight, and you are God's Delight. I can think of my perfection without shame in so doing. I can accept "Within" the beauty of me. I can envision that every one and everything is equally perfect. I can realize that we are all perfect humans. In that releasing thought of equality and goodness I appreciate that by letting up on the Catholic guilt of loving myself I can give myself the best gift available, I can love myself and see myself thru the eyes of the Source of Life.

Realizing that Self-Appreciation has been a neglected requirement for happiness I began a most fascinating experiment. I started to write daily Appreciations into a journal. While I was attempting to build up needed self-worth, I decided to balance this appreciating routine and began to write one appreciation about myself and followed by one about something outside of myself.

In the beginning I was self-conscious and even embarrassingly modest about writing appreciations about myself. It felt awkward and even untrue, although I could effortlessly appreciate everything around me and could fill notebooks upon notebooks with appreciations about things of this world. Yet, when it came to appreciating myself, I felt clumsy and discombobulated about it. I kept repeating the more modest things like: I appreciate my cooking, or my caring about others, or my willingness to help others. I gradually started to appreciate, my hair-do, or my eyes, yet these being great, were shallow looks at myself. I realized that I held an immature viewpoint of myself. Self-relishing proved to be highly personal, difficult and absolutely uncomfortable initially. I assumed this blockage of being able to think of things to self-appreciate was because there is so much more outside of me, hence, that must have been why it was so easy to find things outside of myself to appreciate. After all, just look at the difference, me and the world, me and everything else. I felt like a blip in the order of magnitude of all else that is. Initially self-appreciating was creating a sense of inferiority rather than self worth.

This went on and on for about a month, however, slowly but surely, I was learning to appreciate more things about myself that I had taken for granted. It is so true that the more you appreciate about something the more things to appreciate about that something starts becoming obvious and self appreciating works the same way. I started to play a game of thought with myself. It went like this; Write alternating appreciations; first journal an appreciation about myself and then one about anything imaginable outside of myself and the tricky rule was that I could never repeat any of them on subsequent days. I began to find things about myself worthwhile appreciating and they grew in complexity, while simultaneously; I had barely touched the surface on appreciating things in my home and family life ever-the-less things of the world. In addition, I was observing some curious symmetry in my appreciation sentences and thought structures.

- I could appreciate my sight and then I could appreciate seeing the bird fly by.
- I could appreciate my sensitivity towards others and then I could appreciate how kind my husband was to me.
- I could appreciate my allowing nature and then I could appreciate feeling the soft breeze across my face.

❋ ❋ ❋

It is an interesting experience of creating the ying yang of appreciations so naturally and I realized how important I am in my world. How interconnected I am with things surrounding me. How much of me there is to think about. How complicated I am and how valuable I am. I discover more about my life and who I really am.

I learn a great deal about myself and about the world simply by continuing the writing of Appreciations. I have added other Appreciating Games to the scenario that enhance and accelerate awareness of positive aspects. Uri and I are currently doing a series of appreciations like this: Appreciate self, Appreciate outside self, Appreciate us (our marriage), and Appreciate our future. The self-centered "Within Lesson" renews my love and appreciation of everything. When I draw appreciation into my life, by appreciating, I draw closer onto myself that which I appreciate. If I am appreciating the beautiful puffy white clouds in the sky that fill me with imagination and soft thoughts, more clouds of that nature, more imagination and more soft thoughts come to me. I found within me peace and happiness upon appreciating both Inside-Self and Outside-Self. When I appreciate I hear the voice of God, of Source, of Life and I can approach it in worthiness. In appreciating I grow closer to God and God is drawn closer to me.

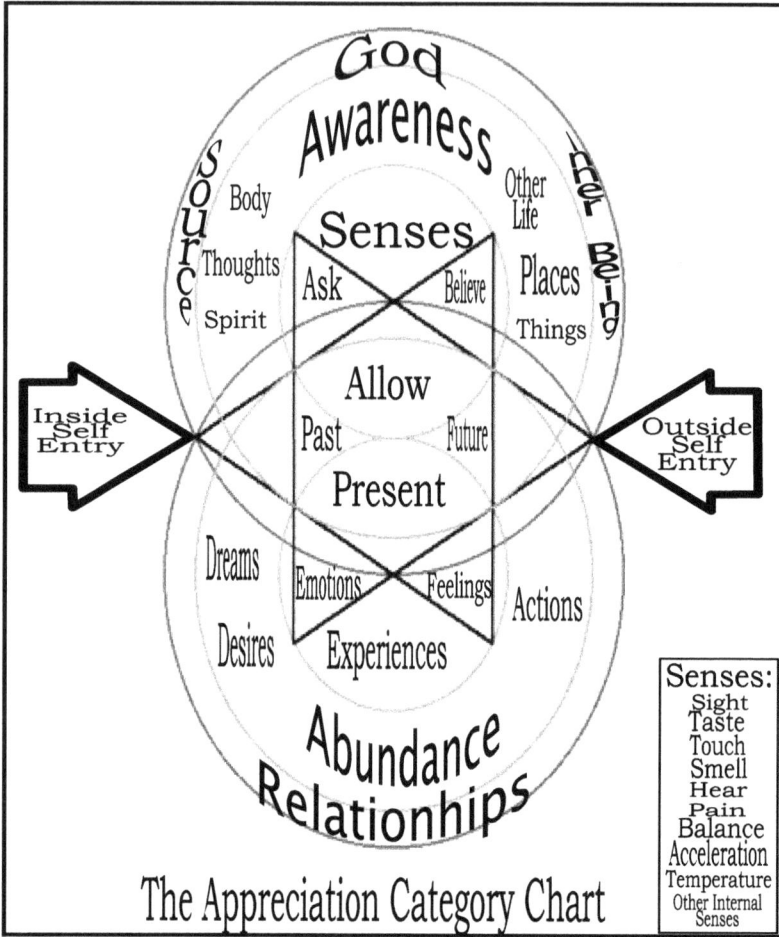

Figure 1   Appreciation Category Chart

From creating a variety of Appreciation Games, I have noted categories of appreciations appearing in my writing, in my verbalizing and in other's Appreciations, as well, and have made this illustration to informally depict them. This chart is meant to be a tool to enhance diversity in Appreciations that presumably results in more balance towards personal clarity and learning from "Within". Appreciating is a mechanism towards alignment and allowing. If the Appreciation Category Chart helps you find more ways to appreciate and makes you feel good in so doing, then it is a tool for you, if not, that is ok too. It does help me.

The major parts of the Appreciation Category Chart are that one side represents categories of Appreciations that pertain to the Inside-Self and the other is for Outside-Self. For me, it is easier to either enter a thought of Appreciation from one side or the other, as I previously explained. Both the Center Vertical and Horizontal areas of the diagram express Bridged-categories of items that connect the Inside-Self and the Outside-Self areas, although these relational connections are meant to be vague. Appreciating is a freedom rather than a science. These categories are offered purely to stimulate deliberate balance. The Sense categories are known herein to be; Sight, Hearing, Taste, Smell, Touch, Balance, Acceleration, Temperature, Pain and other Internal Senses.

To further assist in creating balanced appreciations, note that most significant emotions are identified in the following "Emotional Scale"[4]. As a basic foundation I have built upon its structure and have amended the original emotional list and added (*in parentheses*) connective virtues, which I term the *Virtuous Leaps*. *Virtuous Leaps* can assist in deliberately improving feelings and emotions upon realizing the direction one favors taking to feel better. The *Virtuous Leaps* are like methods or stepping-stones to move up and forward. This modified and combined listing is another tool and provides a pathway more than a scale indicator. To reach for or climb up to an improved emotion with thoughts, one can take the option of using a *(Virtuous Leap)* to help ease the pathway. Find where you are emotionally on any subject and do the work required to leap up the pathway to a better emotion

---

[4] Abraham Hicks Emotional Scale, Chapter 22, from "*Ask and It is Given*", 2007, published and distributed by Hay House, Inc.

The Emotional Scale
Enhanced with
Art of Appreciation methods
(Virtuous Leaps)

1. Joy, Knowledge, Empowerment, Freedom, Love & Appreciation *(Purposefulness, Unity, Beauty, Creativity, Grace, Bliss, & Wisdom)*
2. Passion and Celebration *(Trustworthiness, Honor, Integrity, & Wonder)*
3. Enthusiasm, Eagerness, and Happiness *(Truthfulness, Excellence & Faith)*
4. Positive Expectation and Belief *(Respect & Determination)*
5. Optimism *(Gratitude, Courtesy, Cooperation, & Thankfulness)*
6. Hopefulness *(Patience, Loyalty, Commitment, & Kindness)*
7. Contentment *(Confidence, Generosity, Charity, & Service)*
8. Boredom *(Idealism & Flexibility)*
9. Pessimism *(Order, Integrity & Peace)*
10. Frustration, Irritation & Impatience *(Steadfastness, Perseverance, Diligence & Fortitude)*
11. "Overwhelment" *(Acceptance)*
12. Disappointment *(Respect)*
13. Doubt *(Honesty & Discernment)*
14. Worry *(Forgiveness)*
15. Blame *(Consideration)*
16. Discouragement *(Obedience & Compassion)*
17. Anger *(Mercy)*
18. Revenge *(Temperance & Tact)*
19. Hatred & Rage *(Humility & Modesty)*
20. Jealousy *(Reverence, Justice, Prudence & Self-Discipline)*
21. Insecurity, Guilt, & Unworthiness *(Valor, Courage, Attachment, Tolerance & Assertiveness)*
22. Fear, Grief, Depression, Despair, Powerlessness

An expression used in the Law of Attraction Abraham Teaching's is "The Emotional Guidance System". It is defined as a guided awareness of the state of attraction from the feeling when giving attention to different life-issues. This comes together by completing the definition as the comparative feeling of a vibrational state of being when aligned with Source, or not. It can be more clearly realized as the gap or the delta that exists between self-appreciation and the way God sees and appreciates the issue. That space is the resident hall of human emotions. The emotional goal is to first notice misalignment, if any, and then to realign these states quickly to feel better. This is done by closing the gap or reducing the delta. Without noticing something off regarding an emotion, much like an energetic motion itself, it will continue, most probably, in the same direction in which it is going over the time it exists. That too is law. Think in this way about the word motion being contained with the word emotion and realize that emotions are moving vibrational energies. The quantity or intensity of the emotion can change depending upon which force is applied to it. A positive force, such as a *Virtuous Leap* or a pure "Appreciation" will assist the continuous motion of the emotion with improvement. When out of sync with self as God sees self, emotions are out of sync with good feelings and are on the lower end or the bottom of the emotional pathway. When in sync with the goodness that God created everyone as, there is an emotional experience of good feelings that are on the higher end or top of the emotional pathway. Therefore, the Emotions List in combination with the *Virtuous Leaps* offer two handy mechanisms when creating Appreciations or when trying to determine more about a current emotional state and pathway. There is much to learn about this natural system that in so doing will heighten self-awareness.

All can decide how to achieve emotional improvement by finding comfort in numerous techniques, such as thought shifting, refocusing, Appreciating or utilizing the *Virtuous Leaps*. Of course, the honest desire to feel better is a requirement. Virtues are certainly different than emotions. Emotions are aligned with feelings and virtues are aligned with actions. Climbing up the emotional pathway is evident by the relative change in feelings experienced and with that acknowledgement responsibility for the direction can be established. It is a wonderful chart to evaluate self-positioning emotionally. The *Virtuous Leaps* are stepping stones that also assist in associating feelings with clarifying direction. They are tools for self-evaluation and to determine the status of other's, especially people with whom you are in a relationship with and are feeling impacts from their emotions.

Once an emotional state has been identified and if "Appreciating" rather than taking a *Virtuous Leap* is desired for improvement, the Appreciation Category Chart can be effective for managing balance. The top of the diagram represents "God, Source or the Creator of All" and "Relationships" are at the base. This is a diagram that attempts to capture the ways in which Appreciations are created from raw thoughts. All Appreciations improve emotions as they can only uplift. *Virtuous Leaps* also improve emotions. Let's create Appreciations and categorize them according to the Chart.

Example 1.
I appreciate myself. = Inside-Self

Example 2.
I appreciate you. = Outside-Self, Other Life (possible relationship)

Example 3.
I appreciate the quality of the air. = Outside-Self, Thing

Example 4.
I appreciate the aroma in the air. = Outside-Self, Sense of Smell, Thing

Example 5.
I appreciate my parents. = Relationship, Outside-Self, Other Life

Example 6:
I appreciate that I am aware that Appreciations can be originated from either Inside-Self or Outside-Self Categories. = Inside-Self, Mind/Spirit, Outside-Self, Thing

For the most part, regardless of how simple or complex an Appreciation is there is a category path that comprises it. Used in conjunction with the Emotional/Virtuous path one can appreciate "Within learning" up the scale on any issue. The purpose of placing Appreciations into categories with the assistance of this chart can help in determining what Appreciations are made of, generally. Appendix "A" is a collection of Appreciations that have been analyzed in the attempt to learn from the patterns that appear in the forms of labeled categories. Why? I am unsure. However, I sense that there is something interesting, even important, to learn in the gathering of this information.

One thing to quickly observe is that there are many more Outside-Self Appreciations made than Self Appreciations. The benefit of a chart such as this is to provide a guideline for learning to deliberately create Appreciations to become thorough and balanced. It is very helpful in steering thoughts closer to Inside-Self Appreciations, which are especially good for, as I've discussed, increasing self-esteem, confidence and self-respect.

"The Art of Appreciating" is with definite benefit and with that in mind, it is also an experiment we are embarking upon in this quasi study of Appreciations. Any and all Appreciations, regardless of the subject or emotional entry point are in nature positive thoughts and with a little mind-adjusting indeed Appreciating is a useful influence for your "allowing" outcome. This factor can assist in manifesting all forms of abundance. Mental preparation is helpful in approaching "Appreciating" as they should be done with pleasure.

It is already determined of significant value to create Appreciations that are Inside-Self oriented to increase self worth and benefits can surface from balancing or creating variations. So many aspects of quantifying results when dealing with the patterns and paths associated with Appreciating are all new thoughts. There is so much to discover. Learning anything from "Within Learning" will bring about wisdom and enable time to grow strong. I realize that there is a great deal of power in "Appreciating". I can move along the emotional path towards feeling improvement in an accelerated way by applying "Appreciations" (which create "Within Lessons") or I can utilize the *Virtuous Leaps* (which usually create "Without Lessons").

❀ ❀ ❀

When I was a child if I thought I could make the sports team or hit the ball or run fast or learn quickly, that was exactly the outcome, notably most of the time. As I grew-up, I grew-up my doubts too. Almost everyone has. I attributed my successes mostly to luck or chance, although at that statement some Catholic style guilt cropped up, as I was taught that luck and chance were sort of like voodoo or superstition and both unlikely Catholic Teachings. Therefore, I was less aware of my own influence on my own situations and consequently, mostly things just happened.

Even as a young person, I was pretty thrilled if things worked out well. And when things worked out real well for too long a period of time, I started to become a bit intimidated by it all, thinking at any moment it was going to turn around and I was going to return to "the real world", where things didn't always go my way, and why should they. And so that was what happened to me. I could ride along in happy, happy, good, good, all is well, all is well, success, success, and then puff, it was over in a blink, or as I now know, it was over in a shifted and continued negative thought. It is Law!

And that was the "story" of my life. I waddled along almost as if I were on the very end point of a pendulum of life, never having too much happiness before it was time to return in the opposite direction and get my fair share of unhappiness. I recall by the time I was in my mid-twenties thinking, if only my life's pendulum could stop in the center for a long while, I could recover from the dramatic turns it was taking. I was the observer of my life, and the pendulum was the director of my life and there was little more then the will of the swing to balance my life. I was high in happiness and then low in misery, back and forth, over and over again.

Some good things did happen to me. I'd say good stuff did happen probably more than half of the time, so the pendulum was out of balance and in my favor most of the time. I was a happy sort of person in spite of my "challenges". I recall times when I thought it was impossible to do something and then it proved it was impossible. With it came disappointment and the like. Other times, I just knew it was probable and then it was. It was easy to go along with it all; to accept the roller coaster ride I was experiencing as I felt that I could never have it all so whatever I got was good enough. I definitely did not feel I could control the way life was mapped out for me. I was just living it as it came. I was taught and thought in that agreement that this was the way life was supposed to be. I now know that process of living to be "living in the default value".

As a child, I had already detected that I was happier and more successful than most others and I didn't give "having more" of anything much thought. I could handle the ups and the downs of life and I was surviving, so what was there to complain about. I was pretty tuff and strong. I began to think that I was riding the pendulum higher than most just because I was willing to take the risk of the ride, as I noticed others shunning the ride altogether. Many people I knew or saw, in fact, had stopped doing much of living all together. In spite of every up and down I was encountering I actually found myself to be one of the happiest people I knew, as most had stagnated and did not seem happy to me, although there was more acceptance of the way things just were. I also realized that I was not the unhappiest person around. I started to notice that I was one of the most experienced people that I knew too.

So this was my reality. That was an easy going feeling and it was sometimes easy for me to settle for what I could along the way, just like most others did. I did sense I was missing something, I just didn't know what it could be or how, (short of a miracle) things could change. And I did experience many a miracle along the both bumpy and then smooth path I was on. I thought perhaps if I were more religious, studied the Bible harder, attended Masses regularly, and did it all so Catholic Christian-life perfect that at least the pendulum might cease the drama. And I think that worked for a while.

Now things are changed, after realizing the Law of Attraction and that my thoughts are things I can control and create from, I started to pay attention to my thoughts all of the time and I could catch myself thinking in directions that I felt against the direction of Goodness and I could stop thinking that way or lessen that thought and re-curve it and this changed my thought process. I use the Emotional Scale and the *Virtuous Leaps* to assist me with capturing thoughts that yielded my emotions or prompted me to look in a shade of a better direction. "Within" I appreciate these experiences. I experience and detect understanding about my emotions to be the response of my thoughts, however, if I was concerned more about the emotions and the feelings than I was aware of the thoughts I was creating, I found that then my thoughts were responding to my feelings. It was a little strange at first, especially since I was so used to the drama and crisis I created around me, without even being conscious of it. And even now, when influenced by accumulated contrasts, I occasionally find myself wandering away in thoughts that are less than what I want for myself. I've spent most of my life in Default-Value-Thinking so once in a while I resort back to that "comfortable", but becoming more uncomfortable, way of thought. I prefer now to learn faster from "Within" my own control.

Now, through the encouragement of the Law of Attraction and my desired inner growth towards joy, appreciation, love, empowerment, freedom and knowledge,

- I can sense my emotional balance getting "off" a bit...and then,
- I can hear my thoughts going where I want to stay away from...and then,

- I can pull away and begin to straighten up my thought essence.

I have also learned that:

- I can sense an emotional state becoming stronger...and then,
- I can feel the intensity of that emotion holding onto a thought...and then,
- I can connect the thought to the feeling and direct it into a more heightened emotion.

In one situation I direct my thoughts away from an existing emotion and in the other case I direct my thoughts into the existing emotion, sometimes using the *Virtuous Leaps* to help my footing. Either way, I am deliberately 'riding' my emotions with my thoughts. Either process point will enable me to go up the emotional pathway. My thoughts create things, including my emotions.

This process of going up the emotional path enables me to evaluate where I am now and where I want to be. I am in great appreciation for this Emotional Virtuous Leap path. It is a placeholder for me to return to time after time. I use it for myself and I use it when others are in need and ask for my direction, which is more often than ever before in my life, I mean for people to ask for emotional advice. From there, where I need to straighten up my thoughts, better feeling thoughts are like sparkling shiny beams of color in clearing focus. This is "Learning from Within".

I know it when it starts happening. By that I mean I am aware that I am detecting a feeling that strongly impresses me. It is a turning point I establish. It is the place in which I find myself and find myself wanting to edge my way out from being at. When going towards good things and good thoughts, positive feeling and having clarity there is a movement or momentum towards that and it is a real emotional place and it is a heart-thought-influenced place and it is a place of personal energy that I can deliberately control, and so can you. If only I could have known this earlier in life, but, I am so in appreciation for it now. It is like being a zombie versus being free. It is where we should always search for, come to find, want to be at, and reach for. Having emotional control is the most important realization one will ever need to know, outside of knowing that you can control your thoughts. It is imperative that you can learn from your emotions. It is supportive to create appreciations about any and every state of emotion you are experiencing as they are happening. It is also beneficial to appreciate the emotional state you want to be at. Because your emotions are your indicators as to what you are feeling and your thinking is always connected to your emotions. If you want to feel good, and I do, then your thoughts, emotions and feelings should be your responsibility. Appreciating openly can bring the best out of any emotional standing.

No one else can make you think what you think. No one else can make you feel the way you feel. It is only what you accept, what you allow. It is a good thing to think thoughts that feel good and appreciate yourself as often as possible, especially while finding your better emotional state of being.

You are worthy of whatever you think is happiness for yourself. That is the easiest thought one could ever have and yet many think not!

Now the timing of the outcome of thought is another subject. Isn't it! One thinks good positive thoughts and one gets good positive results, in that order. I had been thinking positive thoughts and in control of my thinking for a while when I started to realize that I was improving my life significantly. So I decided to take it a step higher and start to deliberately think about what I wanted to happen and to start timing the results. If things were getting better from pure and positive thinking strengthened by thoughtful and regular appreciating joined by a comfort of emotional balancing, than I wondered, what I could expect if I added to my thoughts the outcome as designed by me rather than to just have more positive things happen.

It is most certainly valuable to envision and dream about the way you want things to be. Feel that and it is yours. Very simple! I hope you can appreciate the difference between these two aspects of Thinking. One is to think good positive thoughts and appropriate appreciations, and the other is to think good positive thoughts of what exactly you want to happen and while at it, it is possible to put time parameters on these desires and to create them by first appreciating them as if they already exist. That is nice!

All this deliberate thinking requires pure conscious desires too. I had always thought that I had been pretty definitive about knowing what exactly I wanted. But until I really started to apply my desires to deliberate thoughts and actual Appreciations, only then did I realize that I was a little vague about my wants. I was a little wishy-washy so to speak. I am appreciating that and during my Appreciation journal writings I began to appreciate what I want as often as what I have.

It is a deliberate process of learning more about myself and doing so while appreciating and in this heightened space of connection to Source. The process of self-knowing is a journey with a right to passage attached, as the more I know the more I know there is to know. I am allowing "The Art of Appreciation" to assist my life. "The Art of Appreciation" is rightly a creative process supported by a variety of focused methods towards enlightenment.

❀ ❀ ❀

To assist in comprehending this vehicle of personal control, evaluate that "Faith-based" is a term coined today to mean the usage of the religious sector to provide services to the public, mostly administrative and usually financial, as a middleman between the government and for the purpose of assisting those in need who are seeking resolve from others. Having faith based upon utilizing the Law of Attraction is very different. There are no middlemen. It is only you. You are the only one who can control your thoughts into alignment with what you want and appreciate and with whatever the Law of

Attraction delivers. It is universal law. It is between you and your desires. It is between you and your vibrations.

The Law of Attraction has no faith-based organizations or individuals involved in collecting something to provide if asked by those who lack to attract to themselves their needs. It is up to each of us to vibrate our own essence into Being. Regularly utilizing the described methodologies in this book of practicing "The Art of Appreciation", anyone can heighten awareness of alignment and enable improved control of thoughts. Having Faith in the ability to make the best choices resulting in happiness and a joyful life is all but up to the individual to do. Perhaps this is something other than "Faith". Knowing of the evidence of the Law of Attraction from personal experience creates trust in it.

For Faith as Hebrews 11:1 states, *"...is being sure of what we hope for and certain of what we do not see."*

There is more added onto that view of using Faith to gain your desires as it relates to the Law of Attraction. When aware of the Law of Attraction, you know what you are thinking. It follows that you know exactly what you are attracting. In the pure essence of this intuitive awareness of thought you are attracting more of the same vibration as you are emanating forth. At minimum, you know you are responsible for what you are attracting. All of it your reality!

Law of Attraction Faith therefore *is being sure of what we desire for and certain that what we do get is the manifestations of our thoughts.*

Accepting responsibility for life within the mode that thought is having knowledge in more than thought impacting the return on initially invested-thought. Your thoughts and your "feelings" actuate what the Law of Attraction provides in return by creating your thoughts into manifestations. Appreciating that with the Faith of knowing your part in the magnetic forces subscribed to through your thoughts and emotions, your mind and your heart, Faith-based living takes on a new meaning. Faith in the vicinity of thought-responsibility and emotional-responsibility in conjunction with the Law of Attraction is a far cry from Faith in the beliefs outlined from religious doctrine or the delivery of charity. One belongs to you and the other belongs to what you are told to think about, believe in, or instructed how to behave. Many find the direction and instruction of religions a safe thought process and it can be for many people. Thoughts become things and thoughts become vibrations, and the packaged component of thoughts and feelings enhance the vibration that in Faith result in the attraction you receive.

The next time you hear the term "faith-based", reflect upon the vibration of thoughts and emotions that are the faith-based components to the Law of Attraction. You will find it to be your own responsible thoughts. It is an amazing wonder to find joyful results from the personal freedom to think and sense your own responsible thoughts and feelings into your life.

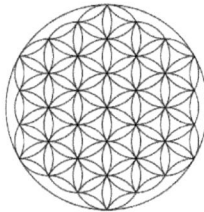

Chapter 4 - Peggy's Appreciations on Allowing Appreciation

- ❖ I appreciate that I ask, believe and receive willingly.

- ❖ I appreciate that I have taken the time in my life to think about my purpose in life and to enjoy manifesting it into reality.

- ❖ I appreciate that Time is my friend and that I can make more time by learning lessons from "Within".

- ❖ I appreciate the dreams I have and the awake I have.

- ❖ I appreciate seeking and finding beautiful things, good experiences and more wisdom.

- ❖ I appreciate the path in which I follow.

- ❖ I appreciate using my emotions as an indication of my thoughts.

- ❖ I appreciate discovering the Virtuous Leaps as mechanisms to bring me up and forth to better feelings.

- ❖ I appreciate that appreciations will advance my measure-to-measure expansion in pleasure.

- ❖ I appreciate knowing myself better by finding things about myself to appreciate often.

Chapter 4 - Your Appreciations on Allowing Appreciation

I appreciate this about myself: _____

_____

I appreciate this about my life: _____

_____

I appreciate this about my future: _____

_____

I appreciate _____

_____

I appreciate _____

_____

I appreciate _____

_____

I appreciate _____

_____

I appreciate _____

_____

I appreciate _____

_____

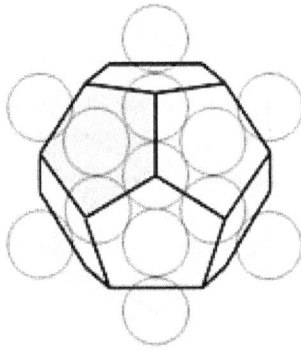

"Appreciation is a wonderful thing. It makes what is excellent in others belong to us as well."

Voltaire

Chapter 5 The Art of Appreciation

During our Appreciation Sharing when my husband, Uri and I take turns stating out loud and writing Appreciations into a journal nearly on a daily basis, we quickly found that our Appreciations beneficially assist in our communications with each other in ways we thought unlikely. Uri is a quiet man. Let's face it most men are less wordy then women, so the Appreciations actually opened him up to much deeper thoughts and verbal expressions than I had ever before experienced in our longtime marriage. He is in total agreement with that!

Like most couples that have been together for a long time, it sometimes feels as if we have said everything necessary to each other. In fact, sometimes it feels that we must have said all we needed to each other in our early dating days, and now we were just communicating the day's events. We rarely really and truly discussed our feelings. Some times feelings flew out of our mouths over the years (mostly mine), especially in time of stress or when obstacles were formed between us, but this Appreciating was proving very different. It is a much, much better feeling and there is a release of any emotional pressure in enabling ones thoughts to be present. It is more than just a "woman's" attraction. This Appreciating feels good for Uri too. He points out that it feels satisfying to recognize a vital part of him that was taught into suppression and now allowed to surface and be discovered to him while realized by me. It is divinely inspired and intimate.

We are in agreement that creating Shared-Appreciations on a regular basis is powerfully rewarding for each of us and for both of us. It certainly changed his capacity to release locked-away feelings to me and to himself and it does the same for me. The release is more like a relief as it flows rather than jumps into existence. Release is the result of holding something back, where as relief is a satisfaction in the change felt. I enjoy learning of him this way, as much as I like myself more opening-up to him this way. It is a renewal in my admiration, love and happiness with him and it contains mutuality. Sharing Appreciations systematically is amazing! For lack of a better expression, there is something magical about sharing Appreciations. I am in awe that something so simple and obvious can be so rare and undefined by humanity, until now.

The thoughts that Uri thinks and shares that come forth in his Appreciations are astounding. I am finding out more about myself and I am realizing more about him too. Honesty is real when appreciating mentally, by writing them or verbalizing them. Clarity becomes awakened in this process of expressing inner and, perhaps, even previously inaccessible thoughts and feelings. I knew I liked him, actually, I knew I loved him, yet I feel that taking turns at relinquishing our

Appreciations to self and each other brings us both knowledge of what is on each other's mind and in each other's heart. It is an opening of a shared heart. Beautiful and loving is the sensation that arises. In this space of Appreciating we are really and truly listening to each other. What more can each of us want but to be known and know of each other better? It is a primal reason we married, because we liked each other to begin with, loved each other as it followed.

In this Appreciation Time we grow in a most playful way our "Appreciation" of each other. This is evolving into a time in which we can be heard by each other, and in this space thoughtful pure ideas, feelings, desires and directions all come into harmony. Our time together in sharing these precious clarifying thought gems is one of the best therapies any couple could possibly ask for. We know we are a happily married couple and we realize better why. We are both appreciating each other more, simply by sharing our own Appreciations.

I learn so much about him and so quickly. What a wonderful man he is. I love knowing and hearing what he is thinking about and never before realizing the strength in his underlining good nature. Sometimes when he is reading out loud what he is simultaneously writing into our journal, I smile as his gentle loving expressions of his personal and deep, often newly revealed thoughts make me feel so happy. It is truly an intimacy that is among the most complimentary actions a marriage, or any relation, can uncover. I am amazed at how much I learn about him and how quickly and easily his thoughts are coming out, as are mine. "The Art of Appreciation" includes creating a complete yet simple sentence structure to bring to light intricate thoughts, feelings and emotions. These sentence formations unravel thoughts into intuitive expressions. I listen to his Appreciative words and hear every one of them and longingly wait the very next word as I am amazed that each new word that follows the last word is always the perfect word to hear. The strung sequence of thoughts and words in Appreciation are live music to the spirit.

I also love seeking deeper for my own thoughts of Appreciation. Often our Appreciations take a course of events, as if they are creating a movement in our time-space-reality. They might begin rather simple and obvious, such as; "I Appreciate myself", or "I Appreciate you". The back and forth Appreciation creations sometimes seem to crescendo in thrilling interest of the richness of our essence. Each next Appreciation seems to reveal more intensely strong patterns of thoughts that want to be awakened to us, from us and for each other. After a short while the "back and forth" motion begins a momentum of a smoother feeling, like a circular pattern of love. The flow becomes more connected to each other's expressions and a quiet connected vortex is conceived. Many feel that a vortex is only created from individuality; however, we know that this is a shared new-birthed vortex belonging to us both and containing each of us within. It is a sacred space.

Many of his thought or mine begin an entire conversation about that subject and we are truly finding new mutual interests in the mix of it all. We conjure up pleasant new ideas and rekindle choice old ones. We are realizing each other and ourselves and it is captivating as we are drawn into it so voluntarily. There is so much joy in appreciating, alone, together, in a group, in thought, in writing or out loud.

Shared-appreciating is truly a worthwhile acceleration into knowing another while getting into your own space of peace and happiness. Finding that place together is a powerful encounter. Any event that provides so much love and understanding, growth and wisdom, is awesome. We feel much appreciation in this growing gift; for once it is experienced it is as if the finding of something one can never do without again. Noble sweetness exists in learning about life's mysterious time-released-capsules of revelations when willing to accept.

Bringing forth from fresh thoughts "Appreciations" is a lovely and loving way to communicate and it brings joy and often clarity in times of calm and peace. Direction, even enthusiasm, can bubble-up from the wellspring of the open sharing of Appreciations within the quiet atmosphere of connection. A worthy and interesting thing about it is that shared-appreciating can illuminate and purify moods of discontentment almost as quickly as it can elevate the more pleasurable times of sharing. This is a remarkable uplifting tool, and although "Appreciating" might feel a bit pretentious when entered into from a space of emotional contrast or overwhelment, it is absolutely amazing how within only minutes, the Appreciations tend to noticeably soften the environment and the "problem" or "disposition" seems to dissolve sweetly as with chocolate in your mouth. When your emotions are above or higher than "Overwhelment" as indicated in the Emotions/Virtuous Leaps List, Shared-Appreciations can sparkle effervescence into your mood and when your emotions are at or beneath "Overwhelment" Shared-Appreciations can fizzle-out or flatten the intensity of your mood very quickly, enabling better control of thoughts to improve your emotional status. Words of Appreciation soon melt your heart, as if enforcing the sacred space it evokes by nature to absolve and resolve all thoughts foreign to it. This is a comfort, as this environment of Shared-Appreciations can only serve you toward improvement. Evidently, this space is free to accept only what is its purpose and when appreciating it is impossible to depreciate simultaneously.

Appreciate the things that bring goodness into your life and you will have more good things happen in your life to appreciate. Appreciate the things that bring you contrast and you will have less contrasts and more goodness. Appreciating creates a win – win result. Everyone would be more willing to appreciate hardships if we only realized that in so doing more goodness is received, even in the moment. When being an artist in the state of Appreciating what might be perceived as experiences of contrast or hardship, in bringing appreciation to anything in that bothersome scenario that can be appreciated, ever so slightly though it may be (and there is always something to appreciate about every situation), the results are a softening of the heart and the viewing of the contrast or hardship from heart-eye-consciousness which is higher in acceptance. It is especially effective to recognize that you can see everything through the Eye's of the Source Within and it is much easier to see that while appreciating. In so doing, Appreciating lifts the spirit into a brighter hope. Being in a state of hope is far better than sitting in the midst of contrast or hardship. Appreciating is an exceptional tool to set yourself and others free from negative lower-based-thoughts. I truly sense that being in a state of Appreciation is much like the knowing that there is only a Stream of Wellbeing. This intentionally co-created dominion of Shared-Appreciation is emotionally sacred and quite similar spiritually to going into a church where immediately, intuitively and silently all are realizing the intent and purpose of this entered-sanctuary is to respectfully pray alone and/or to rejoice in worship usually in a group. Everything supports that purpose of peace in harmony. Such is the way in the crystal calm reverence of "The Art of Appreciating".

❀

In Church it would be found inappropriate to sit down on the floor and have a family picnic. It enables only from within its intent to exist. Likewise the Space of participating in "The Art of Appreciating" can effectively be only what it is and Appreciations are defined as recognizing positive aspects. Appreciating is the act of estimating the qualities of things and giving them their proper value without judgment. It is a welcomed and favorable critique or positive written evaluation. One can basically only approach this space within that realm. It confirms that certain thing can only be good. Appreciation, as it relates to the action of it, is similar to active love, and is one of those special spaces within the soul's realm that triumphs over all less than pure.

Another aspect of this joyous time we set aside to appreciate in is that the time is seemingly slower and the interruptions are amazingly associated to the mood or the context of the Appreciations at hand. It is in that regard a bit magical and holy. The space in which we set aside for Appreciating is at a quiet restful time of the day, usually early evening after dinner, yet it is always available to us at the convening.

Enjoying it so, we have marginally formalized it by coming together, often lighting a candle, turning off the music, opening the window a bit, wearing something comfortable and taking several deep long breathes before taking the corner of the next empty page, and folding it in an ear. The preparation time apparently assists in the reverent mindset we allow. On that overlapping ear of the corner of the page in our journal, we write the date and day of the week. We usually sit straight up, facing each other with a coffee table in-between us and with our stocking, sock or barefoot resting flat on the carpet. We place our hands comfortably on our own legs and feel the calm take possession of our room. This is so often done at the same time of the day when we can sense that most of the neighborhood is sitting in front of the TV watching the news. The stark difference seems to become apparent to us within a moment. The sounds of the quiet neighborhood gradually become more perceptible to us even at quite a distance, a block or so around us. We can hear new sounds come forth into our awareness; local youths visiting each other, walking in the street outside, passing by, and perhaps calling to each other playing catch, walking their dog or scurrying about. We clearly hear when a car arrives on the block, the engine stop, the silence of the momentary fuss taking place inside the car as things get gathered to come inside with them, the car door opens then closes and the door click locked. We hear the owner's dog bark its hello, the house door being unlocked and opened and even a sense of the comfort and peace that takes hold as these neighbors step inside their homes. We hear doors open and close and people come and go. We hear the birds chirp and the tree leaves whisper their songs. We hear so much more clearly all the activities of the "now" we are so in. We feel as if the walls of our house and of our lives vanish in the shades of twilight. We are inside and outside. We hear all and nothing. Our breath and our heartbeats frame life's gentle ballet of purity all around us. "The Art of Appreciation" is a Gift!

This is always going on outside our home this time of evening, however, it is now more aligned to us so we can comprehend this energetic movement as an aliveness which was before unfelt, unnoticed and awaiting to be noticed.

Being aware of my surroundings is stillness at its most aliveness for me. These sounds are vibrations of life today. Vibrations are more than the sounds, yet are sounds too, Sounds, Lights, Thoughts. In the impression of those forms of nature coming forth thoughts become engaged with emotions. Emotions are illuminated to be sensory impulses that arrive at cellular awakening. One thinks movement through them here in this space of transition into the sanctuary of Appreciation. Time resolves the difference in that thought and life shadows a responsible movement of energy in peace and in concert with itself. Thoughts become things, things of energy first, pulses of energy next, waves of fluttering emotions that are settling into our Beingness and in connection to all around us. And in this awareness our Appreciations birth forth awaiting the opportunity to enhance the power of alignment and loosen the memory of resistance.

It is a joy to experience this clarity of our surrounding lives and their activities. In this state of peaceful surrender we hear the birds, cats and distant traffic more clearly, as if magically it is all a part of us now, as aware of us as we are of it, hence there swirls about a comfort of proximity to Godliness. It is the opposite of a lonely place as it is filled richly with the fabric of our interwoven existences. We, in this state of approaching and experiencing Appreciations, become more aware of what we have forgotten to hear or neglected to focus on or lost to the noise of being more ourselves and less our Source connection. All these sounds are enhanced even before we begin our Appreciation Session. It is in the approach towards Appreciating and it is in the journey coming into Appreciating that so much is awakened from within and outside of us. As we progress into the state of Appreciation these everyday camouflaged sounds of life encapsulates us with mutual connection and sanctioned wellbeing. It is a magical holy bubble.

That might very well sound like the aura of meditation and we both agree it is a form of meditation, yet it is something else too. It is the stillness of the day becoming the surface of our reality. It is always there. It is the calm and peace within us recognizing the "now" upon us. And more, it is the quietness from "Within" us rejoicing in the anticipated connection to Self and reconnection to Source, to God. The approaching correction in perception is Source's celebrated excitement at our choice to enter into "The Art of Appreciation" and it responds with a greeting of delight and enabled wakefulness. We recognize it as a Source-provided gift we allow to flow into and around us, yet we realize that we are part of the gift. We enable receipt within a point of participation. It might well be a form of sweeping meditation that collects the parts of the environment around into the whole of our Being.

❋ ❋ ❋

Triadual Vortex

It is unmistakably the creating of another us, a third entity, which represents our relationship at its current, most emotional and spiritual height. Its existence is the perfect definition of our matured Marriage. It is the becoming-up, the building-of our individual Vortex, which is our space where we neatly file the pointer system to what is Wisdom to and for us, what are our desires, and, we have learned, that it contains all the pieces of our vibrational and potential reality. This means that we each hold the answers to our mounting needs and desires that are already assembled and only awaiting for our usage of them or more succinctly our allowance of them. This Well-Stream is where all that we want in life knowingly resides, aware of our status and awaiting our ability to allow whatever we desire to become into our practical reality existence. And in mutual "Appreciation" it is combined and enhanced into a recognized dual Vortex and in a timely moment merges into a larger third Vortex surrounding both.

I visualize two living circles overlapping into each other half way as does a perfectly forming Vesica Piscis and when connection occurs this third entity, growing from these inter-workings of the scared Vesica Piscis, like a flowing water of pure energy revolves from within itself upward, collapsing outward and curving downward far past the originating circles creating a new bubble-like thin enclosure circumferencing the entirety of both circles and more. It is much larger than the sum of the two originating circles. It encircles invisibly thru the floor, walls and ceilings creating a perfect surrounding in its pure crystal clear light. Inside of this potential expanse I am unsure if I am indoors or out-of-doors, but I know I am someplace safe and interconnected. It contains the sounds, sequences and geometry of a scared space. It is the coming together of two powerful Beings (and we all are as powerful) for the purpose of sharing Appreciations. Co-creating always amounts to an amazing magnification in basic addition. Co-creating in the "Art of Appreciation" solidifies the common connection and enables the passage of a conceived cadence, which unites to form and experience Appreciations. It is like being in church. It equates and equals much more than the sum of the individual parts and it has a residue that strengthens and softens all experiences in life.

Do you think that is possible? Can you imagine that to be so? Well, we do! We have come to know this space as our Triadual Vortex; His, Mine and Ours, all three entities intentionally entwined in some swirling fashion to connect and be separate at the same time. It is a flexible space of consciousness that exists in our beliefs in ourselves, in each other and in the marriage that we have co-created. It is the space of us together wanting to stretch-up to aware-clarity. It is where we feel easy about being ourselves. It aligns us individually together. It is that space that Kahlil Gibran discusses as marriage in the book, *The Prophet*,

"Give your hearts, but not into each other's keeping. For only the hand of Life can contain your hearts. And stand together yet not too near together: For the pillars of the temple stand apart, and the oak tree and the cypress grow not in each other's shadow."

This Triadual Vortex is the rebirthing of a marriage brought about by "The Art of Appreciating" that it is both of ours and we each are contained independently within it.

From what we experience, "The Art of Appreciating" is a form of meditation by anyone's definition. It is a sacred space. It exists for something other than and is happening because of something other than the "stillness" of thought and the absence of feelings, as is often the definition of meditation. Being still means more than resisting movement, it means being aware of the space in-between the beat that is holding the rhythm and the sound that is the meaning of the song. In the emptiness of meditation exists the somethingness that creates worlds. "The Art of Appreciation" includes the "processing" of meditative thoughts. It is for the favorable "activity" of thought and feelings, bringing together the mind and the heart into something tangible. It is the seeking of deeper thoughts and feelings that are already there within us. It is for something other than the "no thought" it is for the "all thought that can be appreciated". It is stimulation into self-thought, rather than the reduction or relaxation of thought form. Our "Art of Appreciation" sessions are all of what we can think and feel in the translative-form of communicating Appreciations rather than the ceasing of thought into a meditative trance or the focus upon one or no thing. In a State of Appreciation is heard the continuum of thought sounds and heart feelings that are realized as vibrations. This sharing soothes us into a song of self and an insight to the other, simultaneously. It is also an active participation of a growing awareness of everything. It is the opposite of meditative trance; it is becoming more aware of what thoughts are actually thinking and of what feelings are actually feeling. It is an awakening of self with someone else awakening to them self at the same time. It is an opening of the gift of yourself together.

The standard dictionary definition states that mediation is the giving of attention to one thing, and not thinking about anything other than that one thing to bring calm and relaxation to the mind. In a purer definition, meditation means thinking of nothing at all and focusing, in the spirit of non-judgment, consciousness on the universal truth, God. I add to that definition that meditation can additionally be the bringing into focus the every thought available in appreciation. While in the Act of Appreciating meditation is the clear focusing upon loving appreciative thoughts.

We experiment with a variety of "Art of Appreciation Session" types and in so doing we learn some things of interest. It is a great deal of fun to think up new ways to appreciate. We "Appreciate" taking turns. Our original Art of Appreciation was that first one would appreciate out loud and then the other, back and forth, while one is on assignment to write down the Appreciations into our journal.

We have added other appreciation processes to the experiments as well. When possible, we appreciate with our daughters, friends and business acquaintances. It requires only a sentence that expresses an appreciation. It is an adventure in rapidly getting to the "important issues", although "issues" is too much at struggle, it is better stated as rapidly getting to the "important stuff" the "priority things of understanding". In the focusing on the positive aspect in life to appreciate, the thoughts between each are charged with upliftment. Appreciating is endless. We might put down our journal and stop writing our Appreciations down, however, by the time we do, our thoughts have far exceeded our amount of Appreciations written. It is like a fountain of refreshing thoughts that flows forth and it comes from a deep rich source that is continuously seeking and finding new Appreciations.

The processes primarily revolve rather then go back and forth. The motion obtained by the flow of communication is usually circular, somewhat spiral in nature ascending up and outwards, as one envisions a vortex to be, yet it is far from a tornado or any such violence, it is the opposite, it is a peacemaking swirl that feels good and very safe to be inside of. I, personally, had never before thought I could even envision what a vortex could possibly mean, as it sounds a little too mysterious to me. Vortex, sounded a little to "out-there" for my vocabulary. Yet, now I know what a vortex is and I sense what a vortex feels like. This space of "The Art of Appreciation" is a sharing of gentleness, there is no competition involved, yet there is a mild teaching without intention to do so. It is a release of pressure and an unraveling of thoughts and emotions. It is an "enabling". One is a listener as much as a provider and so the wave is generously yours sometimes and the tide is deep sometimes. There is no intention to create rules, rather to flow with it all, float with it, and enable the goodness of it all to capture you rather than you to capture it. It is a discovery and an adventure into the more familiar, the more natural, the more willing.

The voice of self is so clearly the voice of others that hearing is but an echo of your minds understanding it to be, especially in between people who are spiritually close to each other while in the Act of performing the "Art of Appreciating". There is a connection of gathering thoughts and feelings, which become loud enough, rich enough and filled enough to be come together in this shared appreciation space. When it travels the mind it remembers similarities that bond the thought twofold, once for you and once for your partner. The resulting appreciations often link up to the last or the next. Watch for the flow and realize the harmony. This movement with purpose reminds me of some thoughts I've put together about the round of appreciation I felt at the end of a delightful California Philharmonic concert recently.

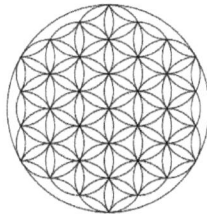

A Round For Appreciation

At the end of the Opera
The Magnificent God-given Voice
stood sounding still
for only a moment.
In the pause the Audience thrilled
and clapped with tears of joy
upon delighted ears.
And, so it should be!
Oh, yet - listen and see!
The Voice then turned,
And in a soft curled waving gesture
included the Musicians;
Orchestra, Instruments, Maestro and All,
Into their anticipated combined
appreciated realm of awe.
And then,
in a much lesser pause than before,
The field of Clapping continued a louder
crescendo for more....
And they,
the Presenters,
bowed in-turn
And that was just the beginning,
As the Clapping in union
Stood-Up their applause,
And back and forth
it increased its winnings to all.
Clapping and Bowing,
Bowing and Clapping
some more!
Where is it now
the Circle-of-Knowing
that "APPRECIATING"
is Forever Flowing

The Art of Appreciation

Chapter 5 - Peggy's Appreciations on The Art of Appreciation

- ❖ I appreciate that I am growing my understanding of the frequency that all loving thoughts vibrate in and from.

- ❖ I appreciate that my life experiences yields new information and abilities to become convincingly aware that there is more than enough of everything for everyone.

- ❖ I appreciate that Uri and I will continue to seek and find new processes in which to share our hearts in appreciation.

- ❖ I appreciate that words are the slow motion manifestations of the thoughts and feelings we are experiencing more quickly.

- ❖ I appreciate being uplifted whenever I appreciate and being doubly uplifted whenever I share my appreciative thoughts with another willing to share theirs with me.

- ❖ I appreciate the ease in which appreciations flow one upon another as if they are the building blocks of my life telling me the story of myself.

- ❖ I appreciate recognizing that my heart thinks in unison with my mind, being blended together, especially during our "Art of Appreciation" Sessions.

- ❖ I appreciate the heightened clarity that arrives in all my senses while intentionally appreciating.

- ❖ I appreciate experiencing the softening of my heart's vibration with each and every thought and verbalization, especially during our "Art of Appreciation" Sessions.

Chapter 5 - Your Appreciations on The Art of Appreciation

I appreciate this about myself: _____

_____

I appreciate this about my life: _____

_____

I appreciate this about my future: _____

_____

I appreciate this about my "Appreciation" experience: ___

_____

I appreciate _____

_____

I appreciate _____

_____

I appreciate _____

_____

I appreciate _____

_____

I appreciate _____

_____

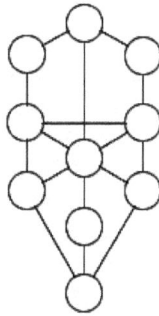

"Appreciating in lieu of Blaming,
Rights Forgiveness a Forgotten Worry."

Chapter 6 Appreciate or Forgive?

I appreciate the time and inspired inclination to look deeper into aspects of "Forgiveness", especially as Forgiveness relates to "The Art of Appreciation". I am in search to find out what is the connection between the virtue of "Forgiveness" and the emotion of "Appreciating"? I discovered that the bridge is narrow and strong and existing in a binding magnificence that enables me to appreciate the Law of Attraction deeper and recognize its impact upon emotional healing of emotional wounds. Social and psychiatric terminology trends would most likely say that there is a fine line between emotional scars and emotional illness, so it is with great care I attempt to reach for relief from these notorious misnomers. There is no disconnecting them and there is no real acknowledgement of them in the way I evaluate confusion. Forgiveness can be only a bandage and emotional scars, wounds and illnesses can only be the symptoms.

My appreciating forgiveness is a lifelong pursuit and after feeling content that I had definitely mastered understanding it through my Catholic objectivity and my personal encounters, the Law of Attraction came along and, again, I am amazed and startled at the changes in my viewpoint and in the growth of my wisdom in regards to the way the treasured concept of forgiveness has evolved into me.

The new light that shed brightly upon me came from "Within" me and is founded upon this following thought: In taking responsibility for my own thoughts, I take responsibility for my own emotions and feelings, all of them, no exceptions. When I am feeling good and I am feeling good more and more of the time, it is a result of my own impactful thoughts. If I am feeling less than good, and I am feeling so less and less of the time, it is from my own impactful thoughts. I am responsible for my feeling good and I am equally responsible for my feeling bad. It is not that I am responsible for my good feelings and someone or something else is responsible for my bad ones. In other words, no thing or one else is responsible for my good or bad feelings, my good or bad experiences, and my good or bad thoughts. Only I hold all the keys to self. I desire to open the doors I want most opened of myself.

Be warned that this re-evaluation of forgiveness is a harsh reality to those who use forgiveness as a crutch to blame or bring shame unto others in order to accept what is of "cause". The results of this journey into understanding forgiveness is going to be controversial to some; especially those who are very comfortable with their accusing or pointing to blame as the answer to all things unwanted. However, I encourage you, especially you of that nature, to read on as my heart-song sings out as in the finally appreciating of forgiveness there is an incredible realization of Personal Freedom. With Personal Freedom one comes into life. It, Personal Freedom, is yours to begin with and with freedom you obtain joy in living now. The truth does not set you free, you set yourself free in the truth. It is exhilarating to accept that responsibility.

❋

Years before becoming aware of the Law of Attraction, one of my favorite quotes on Forgiveness that still touches my heart and soul with understanding, growth and wisdom remains:

"Forgiveness is the scent that the rose leaves on the heel that crushes it."

I interpret this "Anonymous" quote in a wider scope "Now". My soul hears it renewed and I understand the way the Law of Attraction influences it into my Beingness.

Loving roses as I do, this quote always took me illusively into the lush garden of fragrant delight and away from myself long enough to sense that Forgiveness is a special consideration in order for that quote to have been created. I respect the essence of the sound vibrations of that quote. It resonates with me in its convoluted makeup of tenses in time and it brings me around to seeing things in a lightened stage of innocence. In that quite moment away in the sweet scented garden my thoughts soften even the little needed to recognize the difference I am meant to realize. In Forgiveness there is a giving and a taking, an opening and a closing, a beginning and an ending. It is a complicated concept combining it within the Christian and Catholic teachings and then in regard to the Law of Attraction it can be seen in different lights also. In Christianity one is forgiven if one forgives as taught in the Lord's Prayer,

"...And forgive us our trespasses, as we forgive those who trespass against us".

Within the understanding of the Law of Attraction one forgives if it feel better to do so. It is not a moral issue. It is a better thought then blame. Forgiveness is a virtuous stepping stone on the path to emotional healing that one can choose to reach for when finding a better thought and therefore one can begin to shift towards feeling improved rather than feeling "all better". Forgiveness is far from a destination of joy. In despair or anger, or any of the lower-base emotions that are considered negative emotions, an attempt at a mental shift can be associated with a "need" to forgive. Finding a better thought from there, even the slightest better thought can be of help in the process of feeling better. As we think our emotions will follow. When something seems wrong, it is a true blessing to reach immediately for a thought, a better thought to hold onto instead of dwelling upon the thought that is driving your will towards forgiveness. That might sound a bit counter-intuitive, however, there are other ways to address blame, if you must blame, then to reach for forgiveness.

Christianity naturally and quickly appoints blame. This is because blame identifies that some one has done something that requires forgiving, one-self included. Perhaps even a sin has been committed and usually against another or God. The entire Catholic concept of confession revolves around, what else, sin and forgiveness. The Law of Attraction teaches something very different. It reveals that in taking responsibility for what is brought upon me as well as what I do, that, in that awareness forgiveness can be sensed differently by focusing on rising above blame instead. Forgiveness is a way to go from blame to worry. Worry is a little better a state of being then is Blame. So Forgiveness works in Christianity to bring a little relief. It seems to be a big deal for a little relief.

The Law of Attraction sees that aspect of forgiveness identically. It does bring about a degree of relief and that is most welcomed and feels better. The big difference, of course, is that the Law of Attraction, which personally vibrates forth all of the time, causes all that is drawn onto me to come to me and while I am attracted to it. It is all me who creates my life experiences. The Law of Attraction teaches that although stuff happens, everything happens because we are involved in it happening. We create, usually subconsciously, vibrations that attract like vibrations onto it. What is meant here is that we create our own reality, whether we like it or not. What we focus upon is strengthened. When focusing upon Appreciation, more things to Appreciate are available and the more Appreciation is desired to continue, because it feels so good to appreciate. The same is true with contrast; the more one holds focus upon contrasts, the more contrasts there are and the more contrasts will follow in thought, action, emotion, and in reality.

There are aspects of Christianity that allude to this, however, and for the most part, blame is the sinner's residue. In reflecting upon that above Rose quote, quite possibly and universally thinking the Rose could be generally agreed to as a timeless, beautiful, sophisticated, matured, evolved, flower containing a most fragrant holistic aroma that possibly could ever be. If forgiveness held an aroma, it most likely smells like a Rose. Reflecting back into this anonymous quote and combining what Shakespeare wrote:

"A rose by any other name would smell as sweet"

This leaves forgiveness being forgiveness rather than it being the rose, the heel or the crush. Forgiveness by any other name, like blame, feels emotionally releasing. Most agree that within their experiences with Forgiveness, there was a releasing and even to a point, some resolving. The anonymous quote could be implying that the result of forgiveness is good, regardless of why or what is being forgiven, and this is true; yet, there is a better way to arrive at feeling better without implementing Forgiveness. The quote states that in the crush (or the hurt) a lovely smell is released (a pleasant residue is sensed) and this could be interpreted as a discovery of wisdom. It is the wisdom in knowing the truth that exists in the freedom, the personal freedom to think a better thought.

Taking from what I know of the Law of Attraction and applying it to this anonymous quote one can feel the **power** of "Contrast" rather that the **results** of "Forgiveness". "I appreciate that Contrast accelerates my path to expansion and avails my emotions to climb above Contentment, whereby Forgiveness brings me from Blame to Worry, Doubt or Disappointment, probably no higher than that. I appreciate that I can Appreciate rather than Forgive, or in addition to Forgiving, if necessary.

The intended definition of Contrast in the way in which it is used and from my perspective, is to become focused unto difference in a way that can serve to distinguish, and usually, in a negative direction or sensation.

When I asked Uri what he thought was the definition of "Contrast" as used in this context he replied; "It is experiencing something or an event that takes you upstream from where you are." Visualizing the Stream of Life as only containing goodness and only bringing its current downstream in to all goodness and actualizing it such that everything wanted in life is downstream from any position in the Stream. This is similar to the vortex. All that is ever wanted by anyone and at any time is always downstream and in the flow of the direction of the stream one is inevitably moving. Nothing wanted is upstream! This vision of the Stream of Life has dramatically changed my perspective of the original thoughts I held in hearing this anonymous quote about forgiveness. *"Forgiveness is the scent that the rose leaves on the heel that crushes it."* In it I now see that by experiencing contrasts, even those seemingly unwanted contrast that someone else provides insight into (those I used to blame on someone else), I have the sweet opportunity to create new desires and to be happier for the contrast and the resulting desires (instead of forgiving those I used to blame or myself). I can accept that I attracted this contrast upon myself and as a result I have a new and better point of attraction that brings me to a deeper understanding of what I want and what will bring me happiness and joy. I am appreciating the contrasts that I bring upon myself. That is quiet a difference in perspective from Forgiveness to Appreciation.

In "Contrast" I experience a desire towards expansion. In Forgiveness I experience a self-fulfilling explanatory satisfaction in Blame, while moving forward towards expansion, however, at a more upstream point on the Stream. Quite Different! I often dislike the feelings of Contrast and I can appreciate that also. Although the longer I think about "Contrast" the more I realize that Contrast can reference or point to the positive direction in comparison to the negative direction as easily as the negative to the positive. However, for the comfort of clarity we will generally think of Contrast as a negative or better stated, contrast usually conjures up negative emotions. In removing the concept of Blame, when rewording this anonymous quote into Law of Attraction terms and compassions, it sounds more like this:

> *"Expanded joy is allowed into life through appreciating contrasts."*

Forgiveness is a virtue one is taught to apply to improving ones offended State-of-Being in the emotional stage of blame and thereby finding or arriving at worry, doubt, and/or disappointment, all of which are improved feelings over blame. The application of Forgiveness feels like relief because it feels better to be out of Blame. Feeling good is on that path, yet, there is still much emotional work one needs to do to get from worry, doubt, or disappointment to Love or Joy. It is also true to me that without forgiveness and by using appreciation, love and joy is much closer by.

❈ ❈ ❈

I have traveled a path that Forgiveness was a part of, in fact, a significant part of, though with no regret for it has brought me here. I have more Wisdom now and a great deal of my Wisdom comes from my intense participation in Forgiveness throughout my strong Catholic-influenced years. In learning and practicing Forgiveness I am enlightened into a sister-virtue of Forgiveness, which is "not being offended". I am tempted to say; not being **easily** offended; yet I have learnt "offended" is "offended" whether easily or not so. And as Gertrude Stein said, "*A rose, is a rose, is a rose.*" And so it is.

Being offended basically is enabling yourself to <u>overly</u> care about what another is thinking, doing or saying. Definitely, being offended is being out of alignment with self and with how Source sees me or the person I want to appreciate as being the offender. In this clarity, I know that it is more important to know how and what I am thinking, rather than how or what others are thinking, especially about me.

It is impossible to be offended when you do not care what anyone else thinks. Caring for and about others positions one vulnerably to experience "being offended", sometimes quite easily. It can better be stated that caring for and about others positions one vulnerably to experience contrasts. It is the Caring that enables one contrasted-growth. Compassion and Love elevate the level of the Stream of Life to hold more depth. The liquid pool of life is as deep as we dare to swim within the breath we believe we can hold. Contrast is so worth it for it ignites the journey's onward motion. Without contrast there is no growth, and growth invents wisdom and understanding. An evolving relationship, an evolving life does not have to involve forgiveness if one sees all things that are attracted onto oneself is of the drawing it to oneself by the vibrations, thoughts, feelings and desires one emits forth.

Generally, the impact of being offended only matters when the other person, "the offender", is someone that matters to you; someone you care about. Rarely does the mass society or disassociated people offend individually. Offense is somewhat personal. Even in so knowing, it is a tricky discipline to be able to refresh your thoughts, after feeling offended, with remembering that it should always matter more to you what you are thinking than what you think others are thinking, even when they express it in words or actions.

It is so ingrained into us that others are responsible for our lives, and by that I am meaning the "happiness of our lives" as much as the "sorrow of our lives", that we as a general wave of people identify with being offended when or so we can blame it, our happiness or lack of it, on another.

People say; "You offended me", when in truth "I attracted this", is more appropriate. That, however, is a large pill for most to swallow. We want not to admit we attracted the accident experienced at the corner intersection. The other person must have done it. It was their fault. Even the word "accident" is so comforting to reduce our responsibility of it. The dictionary definition of accident is an undesirable or unfortunate happening that occurs <u>unintentionally</u> and usually results in harm, injury, damage, or loss, casualty or mishap, such as an automobile accident. The big word in that definition that causes an entire society to sue and blame others is "unintentionally". The Law of Attraction tells that story differently.

No one wants to admit that last year's cold was a self-attracted one. Rarely does one admit that they wanted that divorce. Who wants to admit that an unkind person is attracted unto oneself, by self? No one wants to take responsibility for their experiences if they are contrasting experiences. Through our teachings and experiences and those of others, we want to blame it on events outside of ourselves. No one wants to blame the abuse or the depression or the defeat on self. We are taught otherwise. To think outside the blame-other's-box is never taught which leaves us stranded in a quagmire of blaming others, self or God as a normal approach towards justification. Yet, when we are able to do that, take responsibility for what is attracting into our lives; both the great things and the contrasts, we will be able to appreciate the power in our own thoughts and focus. We will be able to become deliberate in intent and accepting in whatever life holds. It is the acceptance of the journey from here to there that makes all of the difference in the quality of life and in the power of self-awareness the journey is now the unblemished choices that one beholds. It is not bad or good, right or wrong, for what is, is and appreciating your impact upon your ability to a happy life is a personal choice. A choice to accept what is, a choice to appreciate what is, a choice to find no offense in what others are, rather to take charge of your own self.

Appreciate or Forgive?

We did not come forth into this world with the intent to have everyone and everything mold us into something for them, for their approval, for their satisfaction. We have not brought forth our children to mimic us either or to have them mimic others. We have always wanted our children to be themselves, to expand their own God-given skills, to find their own passions and to live their own lives. We come forth to find our own way, to use and create in our own uniqueness, to experience our own life and to expand in our own direction. It is our own path of life we are on. Our learning and our expansion is the becoming what we each are, not the conforming to what anyone else wants us to become. When we find confidence in the direction we individually choose, we find that it feels so good to be ourselves.

Does it even matter what forgiveness is, even when it seems that there is little else available to pass by "offense" and get on with ones life? Acceptance in what the Law of Attraction is brings peace into my life with detachment from or non-dependency on blame. Within acceptance of the Law of Attraction, forgiveness can become a missing concept from life and feeling better takes another path. It is an initial effort to retrain thoughts into this Law of Attraction vein, yet in so doing, one finds joy in self-control of thoughts, actions and results, void of stress.

The difference between Gratitude and Appreciation is that one can identify the "struggle" in Gratitude as having come from a place of lack that brings one into and towards thankfulness. I sense this understanding and use it faithfully in my life and it works for me. I have recreated myself from a Great Blamer and I have become a Great Appreciator and although I am in Gratitude for much, I skirt "Gratitude" often and apply Appreciation into my focus in its place, if applicable. It is a slight variation in my thoughts; however, over time it produces a huge difference. It resembles the way that at a specific point in calculating a projected path of two separate straight lines extended out from a same exact point and each with a small delta in a degree of change in a direction continuing on. It becomes apparent that each line being drawn and extended forth is much further apart from each over time and distance. That is the way applying Appreciations diverges from having Gratitude, although, there is a clear purpose for each in its intended place, each arrive at a different destination, both in good standing. In Appreciation, I personally move faster improved emotions, which makes me feel better, and I want to feel better.

Appreciation generates that feeling place very similar to Love. Gratitude feels in the level, as does Forgiveness, both slightly lower than appreciation. Do Forgiveness, Appreciation, and Love have a similar comparison of understanding in actual practice? When one forgives, (let's take oneself although it feels similar if taking another into forgiveness), it comes from a place of contrast going into self re-evaluation. Whereas appreciating yourself and or others at that place where forgiveness might otherwise enter, will bring self-worth more visible in the reflections of self and or others. I can "Appreciate" in spaces of experience where previously I might have grabbed for "Forgiveness". Being in Appreciation for the contrasts I have attracted to myself, will avoid Forgiveness.

I am the only Source in which the Law of Attraction is responding onto me. I am responsible for my creation of my life experience. I once thought that idea too high mighty until I figured out what I was meaning was that God made me for me to make my own life. It is up to me. These chosen lessons have been willfully abiding for self-love. It is better to appreciate that rather than to blame someone or some thing else on lessons happening. I ask; Without Blame could Forgiveness even exist? Forgiveness and Gratitude are Virtuous Leaps. Even as such, I am responsible for attracting the contrasts I experience into my life and in concert with my vibrations. These contrasts are of my subconscious (Without) or conscious (Within) intention. I am on purpose and perfectly learning and growing with them. I choose my own contrasts to teach me needed lessons and I can further choose these lessons from "Within" as opposed to from "Without". Regarding the feelings that enable me to move-up and improve my emotions, I have to reach-up, requiring thoughts that feel better. Also certainly, from places along the reaching

I could decide to use Forgiveness and/or Gratitude as vehicles to expand up in. They are *Virtuous Leaps* and assist in the balance from "Without" which is encouraged over stagnation and festering in foolishness. It seems to me that both Forgiveness and Gratitude come from that "underlying struggle" and that reaching-up is aligned to an "assertion or struggle" of some nature. My reaching-up is very different than my being handed over something. There is a stretching implied. It infers an effort. It develops strength and character.

From my Catholic perspective I am conscious of the feeling of openly holding out my hands together slightly cupped in a stretching position and in a wanting sensation, when I am receiving the Holy Eucharist, Holy Communion, during a Mass. It is one thing to have it given to you, put into your mouth or hands, however, in my experiences it feels so much more personal, powerful, holy and spiritual to reach out in a silent internal longing prayer for the Communion to be placed gently onto my hand, while craving for this Blessing as a desired gift. Actually, before the church changed its instructions to stand and slightly bow your head, we used to kneel on our knees when receiving this sacramental gift of finest wheat. While receiving the Holy Eucharist is always a validating sacrament, desiring it with a great appetite for holy satisfaction makes receiving it so much more rewarding. The entire experience feels in total Christ-consciousness when done in wanting and then experiencing the Christ-provided-gift.

I absorbed the Forgiveness Lesson from "Without" very well and yet it took years and years to master it as well as I did. When I was in a turbulent changing relationship, one that was unquestionably dissolving, usually bitterly, I entered a state of Blame with verifiable justification. Since there was a victim, me, then there had to be a villain, him. It was a perfect balance in Contrasting arrangements. I, in turn, invited Blame to become my next partner, my new relationship. I found my new self-identity of "victim". Victim and Blame lived happily unhappy in some kind of symbiotic agreement and both in my personality. It was a safe representation of myself. I created me in the martyr's roll with the saintly strength to be bravely freed from the validated bad situation and to come through the experience a brand new invigorated person. I never thought that I personally created this story of "Me against the World" thinking somehow that it was my destiny, although always believing that someone else caused it, for the most part, and I was left to make the best of the circumstances. I discovered subconsciously, from the default wave of thought, that the pity others provided to me while I wore my bright huge victim's badge of honor brought me charitable comfort and a sense of being loved. Being intelligent enough to escape, I indeed had freed myself from the abuse and everyone, myself included, celebrated my brave flight and fight for survival. Of course, it was always the right thing to do, to breakup and out of relationships that were dangerously bad for me. Additionally, I was saving my children from the experience of an unhappy family and negative marriage encounter. Everyone knows that secondhand smoke impacts all in the immediate environment so I was honored for that consideration also.

Step-by-step, measure-by-measure, I had habitually taken a path that yielded contrasts that assured my success. It is obvious that pushing off and up from an abusive relationship was leading me to improvement and independence, both of which I desired. I had no conscious idea that I was creating negative relationships in order to pursue the eventual results that brought forth my individual growth. I was living in the default value decidedly taking the ride of life by swinging on the end of that pendulum.

I most certainly could find an easier "Within" path now, knowing the Law of Attraction. Divorce and relationship struggles could have been dealt with differently, although I have no regrets as these experiences and adventures lead me to here, and I am in Gratitude for that result, although my advice to others is to seek self-worth in other ways.

My "Without" Lessons took so long and they repeated themselves over and over again, becoming the path I was on. I went from one bad relationship to another, each parting-time growing more successful at self-empowerment and then, of course, by increasing my skills at finding another bad relationship to follow up the last. During these times I focused upon fighting my way into recovery by using the virtue of Forgiveness. Forgiveness can work very well while living in the belief of Blame.

✴

The Law of Attraction states that that which is of like unto itself is drawn. In my younger days, I can recall that I felt I was the primary victim in all breakups and even in all relationship discords. I never took responsibility for problems in relationships. It was always someone else's fault. The miracles that I experienced were that my mode of operation enabled me to, in spite of my problems, achieve an increasingly better professional life. Relationships, I could not do, but professionally I was doing well and reaching milestones in software engineering that were among the "firsts" for women in the nation and perhaps in the world. I created a dichotomy based upon the definitions of relationships versus professionalism and they were interdependent upon each other. Unfortunately, during those years, I apparently felt I could have only one of those achievements. I thought I could not have it all.

In this "Without Lesson" I approached Forgiveness as my guiding light into Personal Freedom to expand. It works very well, although, it is time consuming and seemingly painful, as I recall. Now, I see that forgiveness is associated with blame and I am finding blame a pretty useless sensation. The path of blame and forgiveness was a stepping-stone to my own ability to come into enlightenment, so it was good for me then. Now from "Within" my heart feels its way directly using Appreciation and avoids blame and forgiveness as often as possible.

My life-long personal healing experience with intimate relationship breakups came through "Forgiveness", yet my knowledge base is now in seeing things through the Law of Attraction and Appreciation. Forgiveness seems to be a virtue that comes from a place of struggle, from a lack of having, from a place of blame.

The Law of Attraction enables either or both parties in a diverging intimate relationship to accept responsibility for their change equally; yet, each only has self to control in reacting. These are not legal laws to insist upon. The Law of Attraction is not a mandate. One can think whatever one wants to think. Though common, blaming each other is inappropriate and at the same time seemingly so socially and legally acceptable.

The All-that-is-Mind knows that the Universe is mental and The All-that-is-Heart knows that the Universe is love. In a perfect world, there is completion in negotiating ending relationships from the concepts of responsible thoughtful love. Each of us should accept what "is", make peace with it, and find ways to create better feeling thoughts about any situation. The antidote to a divorce or any relationship dissolution is to see and understand it as a self-designed contrast, and that all contrasts are like gifts that assist to better know what is wanted. We each compose the perfect contrasts into our lives in order to benefit by its provided lesson, whether we believe so, or not.

With attitudes like that there could be less need for attorneys or external arbitrators. The Law of Attraction is not well known or practiced which is evidenced by our still teaching the youth too much about judgment, competition, protectionism, right and wrong instead of self-empowerment, responsible thoughts, feelings and emotions. Therefore, sometimes in breakups one party knows it and the other does not. This imbalance can further create the invented villain in the other who is more accepting of the change at hand. It is noteworthy that when there is one with a positive acceptance and resignation the conflict is more peaceful and quick to resolve. The Law of Attraction will have its way and it is noteworthy that one positive thought is stronger than thousands of negative ones. This is the opposite of the teachings that one bad apple can spoil the entire barrel, which is a proverb meaning a bad person, policy or action can ruin everything around it. Indeed that is only true if more bad thoughts support it with more focus upon it, otherwise, a good thought, person, policy or action improves everything even in the face of adversity.

Is "Forgiveness" today as were cigarettes of yesterday; something in the culture that was acceptable and is learned now to be even harmful if practiced intensely? In forgiveness does one point blame outward so that one can claim a victory inward? "What is the use of Forgiveness?" Forgiveness seems overstated, overused and enables excuses for apparent and evidential life contrasts. Appreciating works as well, actually better. Forgiveness has long been the established path to relinquish ones troubled or broken heart from emotional resentment with one of its results described as freedom reborn. That sound good, yet I encourage you to look "Within", accept what is and Appreciate instead. It matter's little when an experience occurred that lead into a decision to forgive or appreciate, as it could have been something years ago that continues to tie your emotions to the blame that figures into your forgiving. The Law of Attraction has always been in existence. If you are learning of it now, that is wonderful, yet it always existed as Universal Law. Past blames are misalignments of accepting a part in your own life situations. It was always you making vibrational choices. Past issues that emotionally rock your life into feeling a need to blame can be easily evaporated out of your life with Appreciating.

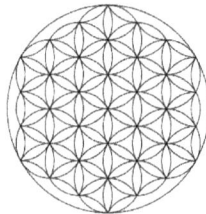

Chapter 6 - Peggy's Appreciations on Appreciate or Forgive?

- ❖ I appreciate that when the "Contrast" I am experiencing involves being personally offended, I have the Personal Freedom to see myself and the perceived offender thru my heart-mind knowledge that I am only responsible for my own thoughts and that I am very worthy.

- ❖ I appreciate that I've experienced years and years of attraction to learning about "Forgiveness" in my life.

- ❖ I appreciate that I can learn from evaluating my "accidents" from the viewpoint of the power of my deliberate intensions as I have chosen my lessons very carefully.

- ❖ I appreciate that Forgiveness is the Scent that the Rose leaves on the Heel that crushes it and that Expanded Joy is allowed into Life through Appreciating Contrasts.

- ❖ I appreciate the remarkable life changing difference in the quality of my life free of Blame.

- ❖ I appreciate that I am a Great Appreciator when once I was a Great Blamer.

- ❖ I appreciate my fundamental Catholic Christian Teachings, which helps me grow Spiritually and brings me to where I am.

- ❖ I appreciate that from out of my lovely wonderful Contrasts I am a clear-minded person containing a Wiser Connection "Within".

- ❖ I appreciate the transition process I feel in my heart when appreciating someone whom I previously might have blamed.

Chapter 6 - Your Appreciations on Appreciate or Forgive?

I appreciate this about myself: _____

_____

I appreciate this about my life: _____

_____

I appreciate this about my future: _____

_____

I appreciate this about my understanding of Forgiveness:

_____

I appreciate _____

_____

I appreciate _____

_____

I appreciate _____

_____

I appreciate _____

_____

I appreciate_____

_____

Relief, resolve and refocus are the ingredients required for the absolute best prescription for any and all illnesses.

Chapter 7   Appreciating Wellness

As I approach this subject, I begin by joyfully yielding time in "The Art of Appreciation", which I believe brings me closer to the vicinity of listening to what Source intends for me to hear and to write about. As with the approach to "The Art of Appreciating" with Uri, while appreciating alone I first recognize that I am arriving at a special state of mind. Being in reverence, I appreciate my health, my healing and my overall WELL-BEING. I appreciate my clear focus towards addressing Wellness. I appreciate the many things that support my natural state of Wellness. I know that I am feeling better everyday from the way I felt the day before; in so saying it, in so it happens. For the purpose of the fun of this discovery of "The Art of Appreciating" Wellness, I also appreciate that I have previously been ill and I know that I like being well, much better. Yet, in my times of sickness I yearned for healing and I feel happiness in having ascended up from being sick to this place of feeling very well. I appreciate feeling good. I love feeling good. I also want to avoid illness and sickness as I find preference in endlessly being improved, always being enriched and rejuvenated.

How can I find this nirvana of Wellness when simultaneously I feel that in my sickness I pivot into grandeur Wellness? I feel that I have become stronger for the experience of the weakness. Can I obtain a better alignment with self and with the Universe, such that I can avoid illness? Knowing better about what I do not want can bring me quicker into knowing exactly what I want more. I think there is a place of discerning balance that yields improvement without having to experience the opposite first, after or ever. Life can work very well without the extreme positions of the pendulum approaching Wellness on one side and then sickness on the other side. Creating and appreciating thoughts of knowing and of imagining can call into mind a phase of walking forward into something as opposed to swinging from side to side or going backwards. Emotions must play a roll in determining direction. Listen to your emotions and hear what your emotions, regarding health-issues, resonate to you. Emotions have something like a voice contained inside of them, a voice that speaks in harmony to your personal understanding of self. Joy is the chicken soup for Wellness.

❉

During one of our recent Appreciation Sessions, I started to appreciate all the wonderful changes we made in our house over the many years we have lived here. Our house started out being an affordable fixer-upper twenty years ago. Before moving into this house we removed and replaced all the carpeting and painted all the walls and ceilings. That was the beginning of a huge list of changes we made in and outside of this house as we continue to improve it. It upgrades and it births new directions. Once upon a time, it was a four-bedroom, two-bathroom house, now it is a two-bedroom, two-bathroom house. What then happened to those other two bedrooms? They accommodated our new requirements of our ideas of home. Now they are connected into a huge shared office space. The house changes, as has the household, as have we who live here. Our grown children are living their own lives and our needs have changed right along with theirs. It is a changing improving personal environment in which Uri and I live. We accommodate our desires as they are recognized and our home improves to meet our desires. The previous owner might find it difficult to recognize the house as even the floor plan is changed over these years, always with our best interest in mind. I am appreciating all these wonderful changes and how we have deliberately and regularly updated our house to suit our specific and ever changing lifestyle. As I was appreciating this family created evolution of our physical home, I realized that it is a perfectly fantastic analogy to express what I feel is the process we can take, if so decided, to upgrade and update our bodies so that we can live with them comfortably over a very long time. There is a way to continuously improve and age without going backwards; in a house redesign and in the way we can manage our Wellness; both by noticing and involving ourselves in our continuously changing lifestyle.

As I am beatifically preparing my thoughts about writing this Chapter on Appreciating Wellness and while somewhat anticipating that along the way some health-related issues might substantiate, I am realizing several mind-health-broadening companions that I am purposely connecting to today to bring balance to my personal experience and will assist in strengthening my mood. I am listening to a harmonic healing hertz frequency sounds known to be the healing vibrations. As recommended, I listen through my headset and appreciate the unique sonorous echoing quality of it. Initially, it seems these sounds are too high pitched, intense and a little annoying, as is an itch in a healing wound, but soon, within a minute, I adjust to these frequencies which are often taken for granted, find the perfect volume, close-off outside distractions and internalize the cultivated vibrations of its cadence into my head and down through my body. I am Appreciating healing and discovering assurance in my ability to write. These composed sounds soothe my senses into intuitively exploring a richly positive resonant tone of enhancing thoughts, which is a far distance from the expressions of contrasting baser-tones, of which some may find need to surface during this Chapter's creation, although I am intentionally seeking other directions "Within". As I do this I am thinking that I might need to visit in my thoughts some health-issues that resonate lower to me naturally for the purpose of writing clearly on this subject for the readers sake. I rarely visit thoughts of illness, preferring Wellness. So here I write to you, with my headset matched-up, toned-in to guarding and guiding us into Wellness. It is remarkable that good health is that instinctive!

We all have heard expressions that relate in some way to frequencies and vibrations: "Find the higher vibration", "She's giving me good vibrations", "Praising is the raising of vibrations", and many more. We sometimes express frequencies directly as high or low frequencies. Sound is a harmonic vibrational frequency. Visible light is a very high frequency. Thought is an adjustable vibrational energy as well, which permeates, resonates and radiates from "Within" our mind, adjusted by our heart and soul, through ourselves and out from us. All mass is moving energy that is managed through the frequencies it resonates. It is all vibrational energy; from the thoughts you create, to the planets we see in the sky, from the cry of a baby to the house that you live in. Every single little and big bit of it is all vibrational and resonant frequencies. My intent is to approach the issues of Wellness while holding high frequencies on this subject.

It is more often that we focus specifically upon illness rather than upon Wellness. Sickness is examined intensely and globally. People who are ill are studied skillfully, carefully and often compassionately. Apparently, the "well-ones" are less interesting to study, especially if focus is upon illness and many do just that. Our focus is more contagious than are the diseases. In due respect, much of the attention towards illness is to tend to those who are in need of care. Caregivers are the real students of illness and I appreciate the dedication and inspiration of health professionals. However, this Chapter is arching towards Wellness while noticing, when necessary, the lack of it. Unless ill, and I do not think even then is a good time for it, why focus on illness at all, if not to look at its relationship to Wellness. Illness, as in chaos or any other form of drama insists upon attention, it takes away energy unto itself, as it naturally defines a diversion from Wellness and peacefulness. It reminds me of a street-intersection "Red Light", it gets attention and one must stop until able to go again. Some call it egotic-tendencies or ego-fulfillment, and some carry that process with them nearly all of the time. It seems also, that many of the patterns of looking at illness is vibrated into us subliminally or subconsciously, by default clinging, through the words we hear in the mass media and in the volumes upon volumes of illness references made in the commercial world, relentlessly. Additionally, many people communicate their experiences with sickness and disorder as their primary way of making or being involved in conversation. It is their default process of unawareness. Within these discussions of personal sickness and disease there is an additional negative poignancy, which is the "complaint".

❁ Complaining should be labeled a sickness all by itself. ❁

These forms of negative inputs are so apparent that everyone knows this already. There is nothing new in writing about the onslaught of negative incoherent health features on TV or in magazines, except, it is important that we all guard ourselves to avoid overconfidence in thinking that we are wiser than these inputs. Egotistically it might be thought that these "illness" messages might be affecting other people, but not you. Perhaps you think you are wiser for the wear. Well, let's hope so! However, avoiding the temptation is a good idea.

You can choose your sequence of inputs more than you realize. It is feasible that these "low-baser-tones" can impact in subtle ways. By lower-baser-tones I mean the "negative" resonant of lesser encounters. These can be listening to negative words, viewing something horrible to see, thinking thoughts that do not feel good or any experience that just doesn't feel right. Even while trying to avoid these messages consciously, some of them filter into the self-intelligent systems and need to be thought controlled and refined in order for them to fade away. Every bit of it all matters. When hearing or telling about an illness there stands a chance that the viewer, or listener will perhaps after hearing it again and again find it easier to believe in. Repetition in all these messages carry a great deal of "low-baser-tones" and entwine into thoughts easily especially when confirmed in the people's experiences we all communicate with and the vast amount of packaging propaganda and sickness-selling going on mostly in the medical marketplace and as often in the entertainment media. It seems to me remedies for illnesses are advertised all over the place. It is personally demanding to disregard all this bombardment and embrace Wellness routinely and confidently. Even addressing these thoughts feels heavy to me and it is only in the encouragement from the Source Within that I am refreshed in each breathe as I attempt to round up the audience that will most benefit for the telling of my Appreciation of Wellness, in so, I extend and impart this knowledge of Wellness to you.

Could it be that we have an insatiable fixation for hearing and learning about what's going wrong with others or ourselves? "What's wrong?" is asked more often then "What's right?". In fact, when has anyone ever asked you, "What's right"? That might explain why we seemingly are drawn into slowing down to see the accident on the road side, even knowing that our "lookie-lou" action will slow the traffic down longer. It could be purely human curiosity. Why do we slow down and attempt to see disorder? It could be for the same reason that illness and sickness is centered upon more than healing and Wellness, generally.

Attentively, even probingly, individuals and entire groups of society are evaluated for their weaknesses or tendencies towards failures. There are many degrees of illness and disease spanning the spectrum from an ingrown toenail to the vast amounts of identified and increasing terminal conditions. Appreciating that, I am astonished to realize and make this silly, but true, comment that "There are as many identified types of Wellness too". In fact, there is a lot more Wellness. Herein, I want to focus upon the Wellness factor of humanity and WELL-BEING. WELL-BEING is the natural and predominant order of the Universe. That is certainly nice to know and be reminded of often. Appreciating Wellness is simple, logical, and easy. Additionally, it is in a tranquil space to rest in and be rejuvenated in thought. Appreciating Wellness brings about Wellness. Categorically comparable, Wellness ranges from a correctly grown toenail to at last surrendering the physical life into the non-physical, without pain, suffering, doubts, fears or illness.

In my state of Appreciative Meditation I ask and then listen for guidance and Wisdom. Part of my meditation is to practice calmness in recognizing and actually participating in the stillness of "Now", yet, increasingly so, a portion of my meditation is to receive answers for the questions I personally explore "Within" and for the guidance that enhances my life experiences. Answers to the question of, "How to Appreciate Wellness?" are entwined within the written thoughts and vibrations of this Chapter. As I ask, I am willfully made aware of some things I have only now thought about, although immediately upon giving them some thought, objectively, I understand why the Law of Attraction directed me to these beautiful thoughts.

That is my fundamental understanding and experience with what some call Divine Guidance, and what I detect as being aware of what I am noticing and noticing that which I am to be aware of, as all is brought to me by the Law of Attraction, and all is attracted to me from the emanated vibrations which I alone am responsible for creating. It is a universal consistent law that I am vibrating in cord with cooperatively; actually, I have no choice in the matter, so I feel. The Law of Attraction recognizes everything I vibrate without judgment as to my being in-cord cooperatively or in discord unwillingly. Once I appreciate the absoluteness of the Law of Attraction, all things are comprehensive.

That sounds very cyclic and, more directly, what I mean is that when I am noticing something come before me through one of my traditional senses I want to pay attention to it. Let's address noticing in more detail as it relates directly to Wellness. If I see something more clearly or something moves, perhaps I notice a bright color or a particularly darkened area off the periphery of my line-of-vision, or I might hear something or stop hearing it, smell an odor that is different, or get a phone call from someone I've been thinking of, or many other ways in which I notice something more or less. I detect a variation or an anomaly from that which I was noticing or even complacent to at that given time, in the moment before it became noticed. I can notice something because it initially became, it continues, it fades or goes away, sort of like the way the random transitions work on a photo slideshow whereby each new photo presented is brought into view with a phase-in or -out variation. It is most likely something other than the intensity alone that captures my attention, although when something loud happens, it gets attention immediately as opposed to when things change very gradually, I hardly notice it at all. It is a level of in-commensurate notice, as it gains my attention or it comes into my thoughts, I then become aware that I am noticing it because it is intended for me to be aware of it. It is always the Law of Attraction getting my attention, delivering what I've attracted. I desire to notice changes more in order to detect the feelings of the experience sooner, smarter and smoother. Previously, my noticing might actually be overlooked or underestimated, perhaps taken for granted. I may have been inattentive or anticipating specific aspects and unable to see other aspects. When something becomes so apparent that there is a manifestation association to it, then it gets my total attention.

I am my own experience. I want to participate in that experience more. In knowing that, now, more regularly, I have recognition before events become, apparent or even because I want it to become more apparent. There is a seeking and a finding involved in the space in-between occurrences, which creates levels of abstractions of Appreciations. When I am attuned to my vibrational cords, in harmony, I can notice better and sooner what is happening as I become aware that I am at one with the vibration. Therefore, when I am being directed towards something, I know it is being mutually attracted towards me. If it feels good I enable it, otherwise, I look for options and search for positive aspects and things to Appreciate. Appreciating always, without exception, assists in directing me towards a better place, thought, experience or noticing.

✻ ✻ ✻

That is exactly what happened when I meditated upon what direction to take when addressing Appreciating Wellness and where to start writing. I was having a seemingly strange direction imprinted into my thoughts. I initially questioned myself, yet the thoughts "Within" grew strong and I decided that it felt good in a curious sort of way and that I might give it a second thought. At first noticing this clear and decisive thought of "Tribal Dancing" literally jump into my head, I missed the connection to Wellness, as I was anticipating a comparison with illness, and I only wondered if my thoughts were straying away from my meditation and my request for guidance on addressing WELL-BEING. Then moments later, I filled in the dots and immediately sensed thrill run through me. You know, the kind of tingly thrill that runs waves of tiny chills through you and within only its own control. These chills I am unable to conjured-up at will. They come intuitively and feel to be a part of joy, generally. It was the kind of chill that almost as soon as I notice it, I want to have it last, yet, once it is noticed the awareness of it returns that sensation to the place where it comes from, a place that connects emotions to pure pleasure. It is a momentary letting in of more than thoughts can otherwise contain.

As I became aware of my wanting to further this path of thought, I knew I was realizing that "Tribal Dancing" is the delicious art of deliberately and collectively co-creating thoughts into manifestations. Further, I recognized that "Tribal Dancing", which is similar to prayer in worshiping, is basically either from an internal-place in thoughts of thanks or in thoughts of allowing. I wanted to write about Wellness so I kept looking for the link and knowing that it was coming to me. The very essence of my desires was stimulating the Law of Attraction to deliver this thought direction. I was noticing it happening, and having an awareness of moving pieces in my mind, heart and soul, simultaneously. "Tribal Dancing" when in thanks is primarily associated with gratitude and when in allowing it is with emphatic Appreciation. The dance of allowing is the dancing for manifestations. Hence, it requires appreciation, love, empowerment, joy, knowledge and freedom to be magnetized into the actualizing scenario. Indian dances for blessings are the asking, in thanksgiving. It is said that the intensity of the dance for rain, or Tribal Dance for any form of manifestation, is more immersed in celebration of collectively cooperating within individual self-centeredness and personal passion regarding the outcome. It is about self and others, at the same time.

In large modern-day sporting events, such as a football or a baseball game or the World Olympics, there is generated a great amount of deliberate collective vibrations within the passion of the fans which leads to the apparent manifestation of the victorious. The event is more then the competition or the winning; it is the collective vibrations and the self-born desires that stimulates the environment. The competition resides within the individual or team involved in performing the actual game, whereas the deliberate collective vibrations belongs to the fans. I think that the Ancient Tribal Indian Rain Dance is similar.

Historically, the indigenous cultures everywhere on the earth-around-the-globe and for generations upon ancient generations back to time undocumented used the art of collectively coming together in focused individual desire and in dance. Often they would swirl about alone and in deep mental concentration intensified by chanting. Additionally, these dances usually were repetitious and lengthy, filled with energy vibrations and concentrated thoughts. It is a perfect environment in which manifestation on an individual and on a group level could occur and did occur. It is highly unlikely that performing a "Tribal Rain Dance" was recreated season to season without some form of evidence of its effectiveness. The primitive, even ancient, cultures of the Indians, in all probability, left little time to dance for rain unless it seemed to work and was by consensus agreed upon doing. That is amazing and exciting to ponder. The collective choice for a village or group of Indians to decide to hold a dance for rain is truly an activity of thought in love and appreciation that shapes aspects of self-preservation into reality. I appreciate that noticing and awareness are deliberate and spiritual companions provided by the Law of Attraction and the Art of Allowing.

On a community level it was known or sensed by the Indians, as it is in certain gatherings today, that intensified like-minded thoughts manifest the thoughts that are extended forth. In a Tribal Rain Dance, which is a collective mental, physical and spiritual agreement, putting the well-defined pure desire into ones own heart of consciousness and bringing with hope into thought the same conscious desire into or for each other's hearts, is deliberate and collective-creating. This is a brilliant enlightenment. Further, everything we know to be originates from and is a deliberate manifestation commencing in a thought, and sometimes it is a collective thought. "E PLURIBUS UNU" meaning "Out of Many One".

In life, through time and experiences, both seemingly good and bad, we can become a bit complacent about it happening, this collective-determined-reality, as it is radically dulled by the overwhelming tendency to deny responsibility for things or occurrences we wish we could avoid thinking about having anything to do with manifesting. Some deny it altogether, which, in either way, is resistance to acknowledging the great and consistent Law of Attraction. Some people forget it totally or express manifestation as coincidence. This is due to the fact that we draw onto ourselves all thoughts, seemingly good or bad and draw upon them as a result whether we want to or not. Taking responsibility for "all" that we experience is too hard or uncomfortable to do when first given the choice to rather blame another something or someone for what is undesirable yet within experience. The concept of a society or a group of fans accepting a global or larger, seemingly negative, manifestation is even more difficult as that requires more individuals taking responsibility collectively. Again, it is apparently easier to blame others and, seemingly, it is inbreed into our behavior by now. We are trained to avoid this responsibility, hence, we experiment less with the risk of collectively creating. In the space in-between that truth and the next stepping-stone walking forth in faith with the Law of Attraction, we can aspire wonder in awesome consideration at the greatness implied in allowing collective manifestation. It is valuable to realize that one positive thought is more powerful than hundreds, perhaps thousands, of negative thoughts. This brings high hopes to the potential results in collective thought processing. A lot less positive thoughts override a great many negative thoughts, collectively or individually.

Continuing on this path of thinking, each one of us has the unequivocal ability and right to appreciate self and the Wellbeing of self and in so doing bring or manifest Wellbeing to one self. We seem pretty good at accepting sickness and disease on a large communal scale. We are just as easily capable of accepting Wellness as positively being manifested from our thoughts. Although, this following comment is somewhat unpopular to mention as it sounds selfish to those looking for reasons to discount these progressive avenues of thought, 'in self-absorbed appreciation one draws Wellness closer.' Get close to God and God is closer to you. It is an agreed mutuality. You want good health through WELL-BEING and WELL-BEING wants to provide good health.

Infusing the Tribal Rain Dance phenomenon into Appreciating, links the concept with having "Faith" in trusting that the Law of Attraction will provide goodness and Wellness personally and impersonally; for you personally or for the fans or the tribe impersonally or better expressed, inter-personally. There much to be learned from the ancient societies as we combine our ways with their ways and, in such, co-create new ways. In this regard, clarifying the general distinction between health and Wellness is essential for detecting the self-preservation in an activity such as doing a Tribal Rain Dance.

In other words, the dancer wants rain for his- or her-own Wellbeing in addition to the community's Wellbeing. Desiring to draw upon oneself manifestations through the least means of resistance, the fastest way possible, includes accepting the results of the self-absorbed intensity of thought(s) and sometimes action(s), or both, although it is always the thoughts more than the actions that inspire results. When sensing a choice, it is in having Faith that Time is in perfect harmony with the Law of Attraction, which enables a heightened enjoyment of the entire journey as an individual and as humanity, so rush not a moment for each one yields a surprise of its own. I wonder if a focused group can allow manifestation faster than an individual can. Perhaps, in humor, the answer is; "It depends upon how many raindrops you think about or believe about".

Healing collectively or in self-preservation is more inclined to establish thoughts of achieving something, whereas Wellbeing assumes good health. You do not have to obtain Wellbeing as you do good health. It, generally, feels better to think or to address Wellness issues rather than to address health-related-issues. Health and healing connect vibrationally to a medical or purely biological status of correction. Wellness connects vibrationally on a different level of an overall status. Health includes conditions; Wellness concludes wholeness.

❋ ❋ ❋

In Figure 2., The Wellness Fence, I am brought to clearly understand this difference between health or healing and WELL-BEING. WELL-BEING is absolute. Health is the condition. Healing implies fixing and comes into existence when comparisons are made between health to or from illness, strength to and from sickness. Wellness leans almost cynically in the shadows of health and in the light of WELL-BEING. Health and healing observes Wellness and refuses to see past that point or to become into WELL-BEING. WELL-BEING seeing Wellness and yet will avoid acknowledging sickness, illness, and healing or health issues at all. By nature WELL-BEING's conclusive standings totally avoid comparisons with illness or sickness.

Looking at the Wellness Fence Drawing, Figure 2, I envision it as such; there sitting in plain view for all to see right on top of a very sturdy fence is, "Wellness". "Wellness" is clearly there standing very proud and strong. It is huge and in my vision "Wellness" is an integrated

Figure 2   Wellness Fence

part of this towering fence rather than being an addition to the fence. Furthermore, "Wellness" only covers the top most pronounced portion of the fence, the part of the fence open to the circulation of clean fresh air, receiving the brilliance of the sun and the benefit of the night sky. It is clearly visible and apparent and desiring to be seen. Wellness is substantial.

Let's look closer at "Wellness". The undersides of the "Wellness" fence are primarily for support and strength and it provides complete assurance that it will forever stand in place, which brings comfort to both sides while enabling this fence to form a well-defined formidable boundary. It is a separator and it delights in knowing so. It is almost like a wall rather than a fence except for the friendlier appeal of it standing there void of threat and only to bring clear definition to life. Its architectural perfection includes slight slots on its surface, enabling ever-such-occasional light to shine through when exactly at the angle for the sunshine of BEING. It is an awesome sight to see.

Let us now visualize the surrounding areas on both sides of this magnificent fence: On one side of the fence is an area that contains all Human-Qualities (states and conditions), such as but definitely not inclusive to the ones in the drawing. There are many Human-Qualities that comprise human existence. The Human-Qualities in this rendering are entitled: Spiritual, Mental, Financial, Emotional, and Physical Human-Qualities and are each individually represented on a thick strong measuring-pole that extends through the Wellness Fence, fitting very snuggly and securely in-thru custom made holes designed for the purpose of allowing this pole to extend into the other side of the fence, as well.

All these featured measuring-poles also impart a considered timeline of progressive change, always desiring its flow towards the fence and onward indicating improvement. The assumption is that Human-Qualities tend naturally to desire increased improvement. The measuring-poles also intrinsically represent the processes of individual "thoughts". All progressive changes are BEING-forces and are based upon the "thoughts" that humans create and that moves change forward over time. Our thoughts create things, including our realities, our paths of Wellness and our states of WELL-BEING.

WELL-BEING is the garden-like area that exists on the other side of the Wellness Fence, which is on the other side of the Human-Qualities domain. In many regards this diagram is more about "Thought Processes" than health as the emphasis of this Chapter is on Appreciating Wellness.

Each separate measuring-pole introduces the polarity involved in the specific Human-Quality it represents. For example the Human-Quality labeled Spiritual-measuring-pole shows that on one end there exists -saturated "darkness" and far on the other side, the absolute opposite side, and in the area of WELL-BEING, the Spiritual-measuring-pole shows clairvoyance and an +ABUNDANCE of it. The fencepost that the Spiritual-measuring-pole fits tightly into indicates consciousness and enlightenment as thought processes to transition into the WELL-BELING Domain. It should be noted that the epitome of WELL-BEING relating to any and all measuring-poles is to Appreciate and associate with +ABUNDANCE. In the drawing BEING indicates existence itself. BEING realms above all and is all.

Briefly:

❖ The Spiritual-measuring-pole keeps darkness at one end and CLAIRVOYANCE at the other end, while processing thoughts aligned to Consciousness and Enlightenment.

❖ The Mental-measuring-pole keeps fear at one end and TRUST on the other, while processing thoughts aligned to Confidence and Self-approval.

❖ The Financial-measuring-pole keeps poverty at one end and WEALTH at the other, while processing thoughts aligned to Security and Prosperity.

❖ The Emotional-measuring-pole keeps confusion, and discombobulation on one end and JOY at the other, while processing thoughts aligned to Feelings and Beliefs.

❖ The Physical-measuring-pole keeps sickness at one end and STRENGTH at the other, while processing thoughts aligned to Healing and Good Health.

It is easier to see using the visual symbols in this drawing that when Appreciating Wellness it is apparent that Human-Qualities are states and conditions that run the gamut of what feels bad to what feels good. At the furthermost extreme negative side of that is the idea of -saturation. Once these Human-Qualities transition through Wellness into WELL-BEING, always utilizing improving thoughts, the state or condition can evolve into Appreciating +ABUNDANCE.

Specifically regarding the associations between these concepts of Appreciating Wellness, it is valuable to realize that +ABUNDANCE does not see -saturation, CLAIRVOYANCE does not see darkness, TRUST does not see fear, WEALTH does not see poverty, JOY does not see discombobulation and STRENGTH does not see sickness. They are on the other side of the fence and the flow and direction is always going towards +ABUNDANCE. Everything in the WELL-BEING domain is unaware of what is in the Human-Quality domain and even if it was aware it has no interest to focus upon any aspect of it. It is impossible to create WEALTH while looking at poverty. One cannot go backwards and forwards at the same time. Interestingly however, all aspects present in the Human-Quality domain senses a desire to gravitate towards, perhaps more as an instinct for survival, moving into Wellness and they constantly grow an increasing awareness of progressive changes. Everyone wants to find +ABUNDANCE in all aspects of life as +ABUNDANCE is having enough or more than enough immediately available of whatever is desired. Wellness, from it's viewpoint sees WELL-BEIING and +ABUNDANCE, whereas, Human-Qualities can not directly even view WELL-BEING and +ABUNDANCE. They are completely out of view, yet as the right thoughts flow towards Wellness there is a drawing closer to WELL-BEING.

Looming above it all is BEING. Its vantage point is from the stars, sky, sun and moon looking down at the fence and seeing both sides of it simultaneously, while treating all equally.

❀ ❀ ❀

Now having formed these images and relationships I want to infuse several healing issues. My lifetime aromatic adventures with the study and use of essential oils collected from all over the world has taught me that the healing of symptoms leaves the health issue to continue to perhaps increase or perhaps decrease. There is no cure in treating symptoms. Reducing or easing symptoms only provides some time to determine healing direction, and it is always a choice. It is only when Wellness is believed that WELL-BEING can conclude. However, in the curiosity of desired cures, all things inclined to heal moves into the direction of goodness that can lead to Wellness.

The experience of using essential oils is a delightful one and for many provides an exceptional connection to this understanding, can be an enjoyable way to find oneself through the temporary relaxed interdependency available in the use of their substance through textures and aromas. It is interesting the ways in which the essentials of plant life can awaken the essentials of human life. I call my essential oils, "liquid gems", because they as with jewels brighten, enhance and enchant while they reveal. I enjoy learning about the ways in which essential oils are processed which reminds me again of that quote *"Forgiveness is the sent that the rose leaves on the heel that crushes it"*. I love and appreciate the absorption of the intense concentrated life that yields forth from the plants that are so friendly to humans, there to improve our experiences and our Wellness. Now, when I utilize essential oils I sway from evaluating my symptoms for healing purposes and only think about the experience I am seeking. When I dabble, into my collection of essential oils, I want to address the Wellness of my desires and myself rather than the wrongness of my feelings and myself. Many of the essential oils report to address emotional enhancement and or moods. I call them the essentionals. It is a perfect word to unlock the real secrets of healing. Healing is an emotional feeling rather than a chemical substance.

Similar to essential oils and in that they also positively address the health-related Human-Quality issues that move towards Wellness are vitamins and minerals. They are an incredible assistance to work healing into health-related-physical issues and also provide the ability to maintain the activities of the body that is undergoing movement towards Wellness. And, indeed, medicines and procedures that are believed-in recover old or previously attracted conditions and can, if desired, take a momentum towards improving health. It should be noted that there is no judgment placed upon the medical world as opposed to the holistic world of healing remedies, they are each and every one of them useful for the occasions in which they are used in Faith. In Personal

Freedom and experiences of Wellness I use holistic earth yielding remedies whenever a need presents itself and I refrain from chemical medicines. I think this more organic path is what attracts to me. It is all in the belief of the thoughts invoked while finding ones way into Wellness, if not there. However, the most important ingredient that can be taken is trusting in the Law of Attraction in faith and in Appreciation that it is the thoughts that are held and, as with the Tribal Rain Dance, it is the intensity of the pure thoughts that are held, from the heart, that creates JOY and with the continuance of JOY, WELL-BEING is manifested and maintained. Being well is the state that one is in on the way to WELL-BEING.

There are other worthy subjects to appreciate regarding the balance of obtaining and maintaining Wellness and there are many books that cover those subjects, from exercise to meditation, from foods to environmental issues, yet, the focus of this book is on Appreciations and it is most beneficial to Appreciate WELL-BEING and to do so often. Appreciating Wellness is enabling Wellness, as much as any other worthy subject directed at health-related issues. In Appreciating WELL-BEING, WELL-BEING is draw onto itself and you. Putting WELL-BEING into your own Appreciating heart in Faith and bringing it into each other's hearts in Trust for the inevitable behavior of the Law of Attraction forms the strong brilliant thread of Wellness that weaves the comfortable fabric of our lives together, for in the state of BEING we are all aware of our strong inter-connection. In our state of BEING we see the fence, and both sides in peace and harmony for the whole. Joy is what manifests Wellness. More Joy manifests WELL-BEING. And still more joy manifests BEING.

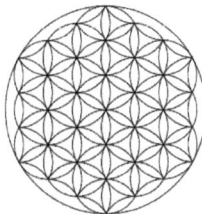

Chapter 7 - Peggy's Appreciations on Appreciating Wellness

- ❖ I appreciate that I can decide to think thoughts of Well-Being into existence.

- ❖ I appreciate that Well-Being is my natural state of Being.

- ❖ I appreciate that I can retain a healthy Long Life by focusing upon my Wellness.

- ❖ I appreciate that Wellness is substantial.

- ❖ I appreciate that Joy is the real chicken soup of Wellness.

- ❖ I appreciate that Wealth is obtained by seeking after it rather than noticing the lack of it.

- ❖ I appreciate listening to "healing frequencies" and hearing sounds that bring joy.

- ❖ I appreciate that I can manifest benefits and desires into my life.

- ❖ I appreciate the open feeling of Wellness.

- ❖ I appreciate that relief, resolve, and refocus are the ingredients required for the best prescription to cure any illness.

Chapter 7 - Your Appreciations on Appreciating Wellness

I appreciate this about myself: _____

_____

I appreciate this about my life: _____

_____

I appreciate this about my future: _____

_____

I appreciate this about my understanding of Wellness: __

_____

I appreciate _____

_____

I appreciate _____

_____

I appreciate_____

_____

I appreciate_____

_____

"I am, I said
To no one there
And no one heard at all
Not even the chair
I am, I cried
I am, said I
And I am lost, and I can't even say why"

Neil Diamond

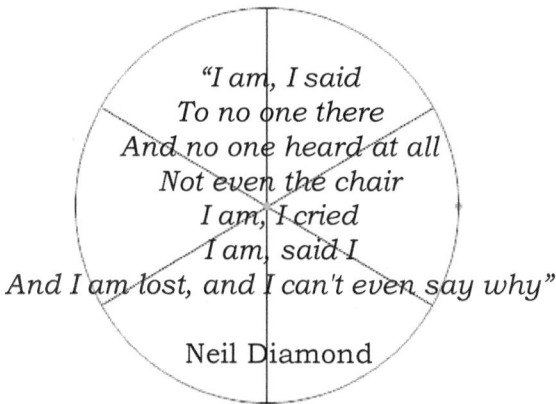

Chapter 8   I AM Appreciating All

I have auspiciously noticed, as probably many others and always as a consequence of applying persistent and inquisitive focus, in other words from being a bit curious, toward the subject that in Today's Inner Spiritual and Religious Circles, Theologians and/or Spiritual Leaders are asking other's of the like, who are apparently sensing fulfillment in "happiness" the following type of question; "Are you really happy?" In some cases, if Yes is the answer, it is followed by the next question; "What are you experiencing enlightenment to be?"

Personally, I find those are very plain ordinary questions to ask, but none-the-less, interviews contain those kinds of questions and they are addressed to those spiritual types and to be perfectly honest, I am interested in hearing the answers. Aren't you? Yet, what should be asked is the more obvious question of "How do you know that being happy is an improved awareness from the last Spiritual Movement which was to be in meditative or transcendental thought hopefully for the purpose of finding "self"?"

I think quiet peaceful thinking-places obtained through meditation are good portals to spirituality, however, there are, indeed, other ways to reach illuminated heightened-spirituality or rejuvenated relaxing-zones and, for me, more directly and immediately and, important to note, without drugs or other external enhancements. Ironically, the better questions to ask the distinguished enlightened among us, who claim to be in a space of allowing spiritual muchness into their lives is: "How do you get it?" "How does one find happiness?" "Where is it hidden?" Especially and seemingly in today's society where people are continuously bombarded by the opposite and are looking problems squarely-in-the-eyes more often, whether it be financial, romantic, political, global or personal. The stream is moving rapidly for most everyone, as we are all part of the entire oneness and the entire change. It is no wonder that when someone shows-up anywhere feeling good or happy at an interview, a church service, or at a local pub, others gravitate towards them with the desire to know "WHY". Why are some happy? That is a good question.

I was listening on the radio to a renowned self-professed "enlightened" gentlemen discussing that when he recently attended a supposedly newly discovered earthly-enchanted place, a mystical isle somewhere unknown to me, that is for some reason or another drawing "enlightened-in-the-moment-seekers" like him, he noticed that there are clearly two kinds of people on the Island. He had time to visit the local town's pub during his journey of isle enlightenment. There he found the clear distinction between him and the other enlightened wayfarer people like him on one side who gathered in this quaint town, and, on the other side were the plain non-indoctrinated unaware parochial dim-lighted towns- and isle-folk. Apparently, there is a significant difference between these two groups in his "enlightened" view. And he wondered intellectually and out loud for the interview, 'When, in fact, these people would ever become more like him, "enlightened" or is mankind destined to have separation even during these heightened times?' The locals had no appreciation for this elevated sense that the "Spiritually" gathered masters were having on their very special island. He said they were "oblivious" to the extraordinary internationally recognized events emerging in their own home-rural community. These locals realized some "tourists" had arrived, yet, they, for the most, did not question as to the why-for they were there and they frankly did not seem to care. Unthinkable to him, the locals held no esteemed interest in his aristocratic esoteric group's ethereal gatherings. Business perhaps had improved yet there was no prying as to what were these sophisticated worldly-types thinking about together or individually. I judge not this illuminated man being interviewed, however, I think differently about these groups comparatively, neither better than the other.

His thoughts were exactly of the nature that any and all religious wars start. Seemingly, he was thinking himself more enlightened than another, and he was inferring class distinction. I want to be enlightened enough to be on neither side. I want to be whom I am and let others be themselves, finding equal value in either and both. How can one tell what another is feeling or thinking to even determine one more aware than another, especially in compare with darling egotistical self? Were the town folk happier than the mistral-enlightened seeker? I think not! If people who are enlightened deliberately exempt themselves from connectivity to others, regardless of whom, than can enlightenment tend to insolate its own into groups instead of realizing that we are all-of-the same entirety? I AM myself, you are yourself, and "We-are-One" is the way I want to see it. That is my intuitive absolute definition of being enlightened. Enlightened is being in awareness of self and synchronously existing as "We-are-One".

We self-professed enlightened ones have much to learn before our "halos" visibly glow around us and more so before others can see them. I think in light of that, one has to have a halo to see a halo. Having no halo, I personally experience these perplexing incompatibilities with others.

❈ ❈ ❈

For example, let me tell you about a recent awareness, seemingly mostly from a "Without Lesson", since it was time consuming and perplexing, that I've had which left me feeling some similar thoughts on a different level of abstraction regarding this sense of separation.

We have some good long-term couple friends who surprisingly have traveled in a tattered direction recently, over the past three years specifically, down the road of limitations, which, for them, was long enough to materialize some financial distress. Watching this unfold, we found it difficult and inappropriate, at best, to tell them of this apparent route they were on, although we noticed and cautiously dropped hints about our impression along the way. We detected that they were causing their own swelling problems and theirs were easier to see than our own. We wanted to tell them that their focus of attention was on a slippery slope downhill, although we opted to gather our thoughts together, control them and to mind-our-own-business. We only mentioned certain obvious things said or attitudes noticed that blended into conversation rather than to bring up the subject. It was like seeing a big elephant and not mentioning it. Additionally, it was seemingly hard for them to hear us even when we carefully and most politely spoke to them about it. There was noticeable resistance to our expressions. When one feels things going wrong it is uncomfortable to deal with the Pollyanna vibrations of others, such as we are, as we continued enjoying positive aspects of our lives and appreciating our good experiences openly. Their resistant baser-tones vibrated onto us enough such that we felt them actually pursuing us, yet they could not influence us into their cunning lure.

We continued to seek beauty, joy, prosperity and abundance in all, despite their increasing financial calamity. Financially, the only real budget we have is the one that feels like appropriate spending. We are convinced, from our observations such as this one, that some people are truly happy with their created problems, which sometimes includes trends towards lack and limitations. Sad people are happy within their unfettered sadness, as misery invites company. The multi-dimensional, multi-intentional egotic sway towards surrendering self-happiness into the open arms of the masses negative impressions can collectively create even a national movement of contagious misery. This is what causes national "Recessions" and personal financial decline. It is the focus on it that enlivens it. There is always a choice we each make, much like a fine line of separation between connecting to happiness or unhappiness, abundance or the lack of abundance. This is done individually, as a couple, in a family, locally, nationally and/or globally, from wherever you identify yourself with and on all subjects that you focus upon. Trends can definitely influence personal tendencies and bridge ease into default thinking. Additionally, there is an isolating existence when a social trend is going in one direction and your thoughts are appreciating in the opposite of that trend. The mass-thought grows in its confidence in numbers and the individual preference is strengthened in personal beliefs or falters into the numbers. The numbers focus on their growing conviction in their story and the personal believer focuses on the outcome of self. Misery wants company and like attracts like.

Why are some unhappy? For it is often in knowing what one does not want that one can see what it is that they do want. Is it true that those who are unhappy think they are just as happy with that as those who are happy? Can people really find happiness in unhappiness? Perhaps our friends and many others are happily unhappy people, but we know that they are not happily happy people. We know to find the positive aspects in it or it could actually contaminate our own happiness. We know that our assuming position of our abundance is framed around the fact that we always have more than what we need when we need it. Focusing upon our friend's perceived limitations could reduce our own happiness. We opted to accept their choices as the ones that they require to experience, rather than the ones that are our responsibility to change in them. We avoided being company to this misery and the Law of Attraction took care of the involvement in the most profound supportive ways. Sometimes the choice to survive in happiness requires separation, and we sensed in this case, that the choice to survive in sadness also requires separation. There it is. There is the separation. I used to say, "There but for the Grace of God go I", now I remind myself that I have a choice in all things, I can see the good or not. We accepted their circumstances and they seemed relieved as they went on their unhappily merry way.

It seems of value to know how to be happy, and it is of interest to share how to come into this knowledge. The Path is as valuable to know as the lifestyle it provides. People who know of it are curious of others who know of it, because tasting it brings about a desire for more and like attracts like. We are more and more aware of our individuality and at the same time we are more and more aware of this mindset of thinking. We want to be happy.

❋ ❋ ❋

In my realized thoughts of happiness, I am magnetized towards appreciating abundance over and over again in my life as all the resources that I am provided delights me. Source is the provider of all abundance and therefore all re-Source really is, is Source's offerings of that abundance. Further, re-sources are the secondary fulfillment, the once-removed vehicle in which Source gets from and gives to all requested attention and desires. Resources are resulting thoughts becoming manifested things through believing in Source's provisions. The primary appreciation is that the Source itself, is the real main event. When we are saturated with resources we can become distracted from Source, unless we are in Appreciation. By obtaining and permitting an abundance of re-sources, we can more easily mistaken abundance for Source, when abundance is only the resource. "Re" is a preposition that means, *with reference to*. Re-Source literally can be derived to mean "with reference to Source". Source wants our attention, and we desire it too. In listening to Source above the noise of resources, whether the resource is money, strength, clarity, or any pursuit we desire, we can miss some of the messages being delivered with our receiving of abundance. Resources and abundance are provided for our pleasure and comfort in accordance with our desires and allowance. Source is the giver of all.

At the beginning of any day when first arriving from dream into awakened consciousness, in the quiet of this peaceful environment, in prayer, appreciation, love, pure thoughts, in the meditative state of clarity or expanded thought, it is easier then for me to hear the messages from my Inner-Being, which is a direct Source. Yet, as the day continues and the crescendo of the clutter of the environment creeps into my existence, I hear less clearly the voice of my Inner-Being. The seeming chaos or confusion of the progressive momentum of time spanning through the day collecting itself into the abundance of resources of sounds and lights and much more, I can find it more difficult to connect directly to my Source. Source is always there, it is me who is out of range. The resources can distract my thoughts and the challenge is apparent only when I seek to be closer to God. The focus on the Source "Within" requires a refocus away from the resources God provides to "without" or outside of me and they are there of my own desire and request. Ironically, I ask of God, God provides and then I can be distracted from God because of the receiving of the resources I asked God for. Resources and the every day occurrences can distract focus on Source. The best way to keep connected is to Appreciate. Appreciate the asking, the believing and the receiving.

Many say it, and I for one believe it to be true, that there is a Grand Transformation of Mankind going on. Ask the enlightened ones if you will, and if you can find an enlightened one, that is enough said. They are there in every office, at any party, in all circles, in schools, all churches, and in families of all kinds. They are there; the happy enlightened ones. They are the evidence of this movement. It is becoming so, this transforming and it is finding its way through many avenues and in a great variety of teachings. Humans are waking up from a long sleep. Some people just come to realize these things more naturally, more intuitively and through their own clarifying thought processes. Others are learning of it today in this book or in a vast many other written resources of similar-mindedness. Some hear it and refuse understanding of it yet; some are seeking for it still. If looking for it one will find it. I find that life's experiences and the using of the Law of Attraction have enhanced my knowing of so many things before unknown to me. It is proclaimed that if only we seek to find happiness the rest will come about. That is one of the simplest and most profound realization I can think of knowing.

The transformation is something other than a belief or a religion; it is much more. It is a becoming, an arrival and a Beingness. The Source Within you, the Source of All, and the Source of me is all the same One Source. The Source is God and God is far from a religion.

Theologians who want to find this out are going to be delighted in the answers to their questions being found in such simple uplifting terms. Life is Good! And of the separation, it is good too. If life was but one solid entity it could continue on and on and on being but the same forever. Yet, it is other than a solid entity as it is made of fragments or separations of expanded self. Every separation, be it a new born taking it's first breath, a towns folk oblivious of the enlightened tourists, or friends carried away on a different path, it is all in harmony with each other. It is all of natural perfection. A friend can take a different departing path and in it I can find no judgment that the separation is creating the birthing of freedom's adventure for all.

I want to positively embrace the separations I see around me. The ones that I create and the ones created by others in the same manner in which a new born infant child is held, tight, but only tight enough to allow for "wiggle room". I want to know the side I am on, my preference, without holding judgment of the other side or another side. It is juxtaposition from the lovely void between. I want to be the child between Wisdom and Understanding, which is Knowing. In knowing that truth I am set free.

Exactly like you, I am a flesh, blood and bones physical Human Being and I believe, and always have believed, that my Soul is non-physical, yet it is an intrinsic component of me, much as my heart or mind is of my self-composition. This was intuitive to me as a child. When growing-up I was provided information through my religious teachings and the Bible that confirmed this understanding of my Soul. Religion provided much information with little explanation. The concept of my Soul became more entwined with my behavior rather than of my existence, such as it relates to sin more than to purity. My religion-based understanding of my Soul became even a bit spooky or unnatural to dwell upon. Perhaps this somewhat negative connotation of soul relative to heaven or hell instilled in me a shunning of any consistent reflection upon my Soul. I, for years, avoided thoughts about my Soul except for the search for it, yet I was shy to actually learn of it. It is only recently, over the past several years that I come to fully appreciate that this Soul of mine is wholly integrated into the very fibers of my Being. It is woven throughout each and every cell and all spaces in-between every cell and within every heartbeat, every thought and every action. It embodies a frequency that emanates and permeates continually.

This Soul or Higher Self resides "Within" me and it never sleeps, it never leaves and it always loves everything about me, as does yours. It's residence "Within" me is as if extended up and into the Source of all Life. It is a spiritual intelligence as much as a connector. It is pure and it is good and it is only wellness and positive, actual and alive. It is "Within" and surrounds. It is ethereal and apparent all at the same time. It is my thinking and feeling awareness of it that changes and therefore it can be made to seem as if an illusion, which confirms what we each perceive as our reality. Yet, it is not concerned with my ignorance or awareness of it for it is totally aware of what I am and of what I am ready to learn or acknowledge of its existence. Even more, it is in the awareness of this Soul entity that we can actually "experience" our personal Soul. It actually awaits me, as you are awaited for also. It is happy to do so. It is in agreement to be there for us. It is always happy rather than patient, although it is there ready, willing and able always.

I have thought that perhaps this entity of my attached connection, my personal loving angelic support system, might be tired of waiting for me to recognize it more totally, and it advises me that I am confused about the idea of time as they experience it towards me and our communications and between them and their understanding of time. And that is no mistake. "They" are a "they". They are my Soul and my Soul is a part of everyone's Soul, so, of course, my Soul is a plural form. Here is the ways in which I am to regain balance on this subject.

- First of all, they sense only love, pure positive love for me, and they know there is a mutual and equal love between us.

- Secondly, they have all the time in the world because time is only relative in physical reality as we calculate it from moment to moment, now to now, in order to move forward. They are existing in ALL and moving forward in their expansion which is unlike ours but in conjunction with ours (more like in a direct ratio), as the kaleidoscope moves so eventually does most of it pieces.

- Thirdly, we are in an agreement of this relationship, we know each other long before now and it is within this mutual agreement that we decided that I venture forth, as me, to experience this physical existence, while remaining attached. You are doing the same thing.

- Fourthly, together in communication, as such as this, we are fulfilling one of our purposes so that is worth many lifetimes of, what we call, waiting.

Our purposes are multi-augmentative. WOW!

God is always available to us, every one of us. Our Soul is there, always available to us. It contains the love of Jesus, and the love of any Master Teacher our religious reality sparks forth. It cultivates the appreciation of the interpretation of love we are available to comprehend, now and in the future. Our Soul knows everything about us without judgment. Hence, it is well equipped to understand our mode of thinking, our current capacity to evolve and our capability to grasp new concepts at any time of our growth process, both intellectually and spiritually. It is always prepared to answer our questions and it knows ALL the answers to anything that can be imagined to ask. We are being reminded that the answer is always in the question, so think about your questions, the same way you think about any thought you have with deliberate intention.

It is we who are illusive to the knowing of it. We always have the choice to know it though it is not forcing itself on us to know it. It is not a visiting Holy Spirit, although it is a Holy Spirit and other Holy Spirits can make visitation within my depths of understandings, and deeply visiting my Inner Being, more than my physical self, though both visitations are of my experience. My Soul only loves. It is intended to support our freedom of will. It is supportive of our choices and it only is respectful toward our desires, in fact it is obliging in all ways to provide. It never sets out to "teach" a lesson, or manipulate a direction in our will or mindset, yet the door to Soul is always open to assist, if asked and to guide when requested. It is respectful of the human interface and will only respond, when invited to do so. That is why we can see that some "enlightened" individuals seem to enter enlightenment when they are in a very precarious situation and the request is in desperation. It is equally available to connect to Soul for the purpose of enlightenment when in the state of peace. Actually, your state of mind or physical caliber is totally irrelevant to the appropriateness to petition for connection to your Soul and to Source. It is always the perfect time to do so.

I believe, of course, that my Soul, my Inner Being, is connected to a grander non-physical portion of me, which is the space at which I am also connected to everyone else and everything else through these extended cross-gathered spirits, energies or vibrations. It is through or with my Soul, which I also call my Inner Being, that I connect-up with The Creator of All, God. I am connected to God through my Inner Being and God is connected to me, always. We should look "Within" and find the world of love that is there. I reflect upon God, as do many others, as the Source of all. I am connected to you through this same Inner Being and you are connected to me in the same way, through your Inner Being. It is a glorious and growing reality. It is in perfect harmony with my Catholic Teachings, hence again, I feel like I am "more than a Catholic". I am happy for the Catholic teachings of my life for within them and because of them I am willing to seek after my Soul and I am enabled to find it.

My beliefs hinge upon my individually appreciating that we are more than what we see in our physical Beingness. If you think you are only human, you might have forgotten that Humans are Beings also. That is so telling, is it not! My beliefs in this fit perfectly within the experiences I create. The more I am aware of my Higher Being, the more I am attuned to my Spirit, my feelings, my emotions, my frequency, my vibrations and my life is rather than proportionally improved, it is extraordinarily enriched. Life is better and better all of the time, as Life is growing and expanding all of the time. There is only a glorious resource of love through this connection to my Soul. God, The Creator of All things creates Goodness. Being connected with God and being connected with ones Inner Being is all the same thing. Goodness is in abundance.

✿ ✿ ✿

What is your Being to you? The dictionary frames Being as Existence. Your Being is Your Existence. If you sense that you are more than the name that people have called you all of your life, then perhaps you can fathom the thought that the spirit of what makes you, you, could very well be your Inner Being. And then one might further in line ask; 'What is my Inner Being?' And if you can acknowledge that within you there is an Inner Being and appreciate that your Inner Being, your Soul or your Spirit is connected to the Source of Life, let's call that God, then you can comprehend from that aspect that you are a human segment amplified from your non-physical component, the rest of you. You are both Spirit and Human. You are both Non-Physical and Physical. You are more than what you see and are taught yourself to be. We are permeating with frequencies and radiating out frequencies in Grace. The more frequently we appreciate that the more effective our frequencies behold our consciousness. The quality of my life is a direct result of my vibrational frequency.

I recall as a young person, probably around the age of 10, spending time in self-contemplating-thought and realizing, somewhat surprisingly, that I was myself. I think most reading this have been there in that thought of recognizing one's own existence; one's self, and the age at which one comes to recognize oneself is irrelevant. It can happen at any age, regardless when, it is a memorable feeling. Before one is apparently mature enough to grasp and hold that thought it is fleeting, or it was for me. I realized that I was "me". Standing on that fringe of the thought of connecting me to my Inner-self was the essence of actually recognizing who I AM. I recall thinking; 'I AM'. I kept saying inside of my thoughts, over and over again; 'I AM!' How profound a thought it was at that time, and to be honest it remains a thrill to appreciate!

It was like looking at the substance that is inside of a seed. The seed when germinated grows and pushes out of the seed skin, but realizing the I AM-ness of oneself is like realizing that the inside of the seed exists and has something important to do with the birth and growth of the plant, except more.

I further remember, as if it were today, being so excited that I ran off to find my Mother so I could ask her if she understood that "I AM" the only one like me. I felt so aware in that moment saying; "Mommy, I AM MYSELF, and YOU are YOURSELF, and isn't that great! We are each of us

OURSELVES. No body else can be me. Everyone has to be themselves. Do you feel that too? I AM really me and I can only be me." Mom was in joyful agreement.

How true is that! Of all the people in the entire world, I AM me. That was a long time ago, about 50 years ago. From time-to-time in my youthful days, I remembered that feeling of being illuminated with my own awareness of self and amazed that it felt so important to realize. If it was ever taught to me, or if anyone ever discussed it with me, or if it was a part of my biology classes, or personal hygiene class, I missed hearing it. Yet, I know it is truth. I AM.

I rarely discussed it with anyone, although in a loving emotional intimacy with Uri, I asked if he was ever "struck" as a child with knowing that feeling of being oneself. He had.

I only thought of it once in a while, maybe while looking at the raindrops drip down a window, or in a daydream thought that wandered into me when peace was predominantly present, which was becoming more rare as I entered my more dramatic and fairly turbulent mid-twenties. It was only as a more settled adult did I feel, once again, with a deep understanding that I am a Human Being and that my Human Being is attached to the rest of me, which is my Non-Physical Spirit. I AM. I feel a trust in myself knowing that I AM. It feels great knowing that I AM. I AM. I AM. I AM! And YOU ARE, or at least I believe YOU ARE even if You do not recognize yourself as Being. Being Human is, in part, the becoming aware of oneself and in second part becoming aware of others who may or may not be aware of themselves.

I AM! YOU ARE! WE ARE!

Knowing that I AM and then knowing in addition that I AM an appended part of the Non-physical is a bit further a thought, that requires me to distinguish me from my I AM. It stretches me on to knowing more about myself and my I AM-ness. However, that is an interesting sentence: "It stretches me on to knowing more about my I AM-ness and myself.", is what the grammar checker suggests and in so doing that suggestion brings clarity to the confusion of me, I, and I AM.

Apparently, it is grammatically more correct to put myself last after others. I feel the core self, my I AM is more me than "myself" even if that is grammatically, religiously and politically incorrect. The world does not recognize my I AM or your I AM. Grammatically it isn't a consideration and early in life we are trained away from addressing our Inner Self, our I AM. This training away from the awareness of the I AM in us is not done maliciously, but rather by a hand-me-down thought that propagates and continues for most. It is only until more recently, only since the Grand Transformation of Mankind is increasing momentum that we are thinking about what we are thinking about that increases our thoughts of our Inner Self, our I AM.

I also believe that the non-physical part of me is the larger, grander, part of me. Perhaps that is why the Grand Transformation of mankind is such a fitting expression. I visualize that by thinking of my hand and it being attached to God and the Human Being, me being a finger, but in my imagination of this hand it has a finger for each human being. We are all connected to God and we are therefore all inter-connected to each other. The larger part of me is part of God. That is what most all religions say also.

One can, if desired to be there, stretch ones feelings to find its own inner truth. Yet, I sense that anyone recognizing and acknowledging themselves in the term of I AM, will quickly become aware of an unmistakable sense of being connected up and outwards to All-of-what-IS from there. That is the way I felt in my thoughts, when I was a kid and again now as a wise adult. I must also admit that often, seemingly to me, far too often, I forgot this sensation of connection from the physical body of me and the Spiritual Beingness of me to the connection to All-that-IS, otherwise known as God or Source.

I know I AM a Physical Extension of that which is Non-physical. I know by the thoughts I have and the feelings that correspond to those thoughts that this is what I AM. I know by the way I distinguish you from me and still see and feel and love you and me both as a part of the same Non-physical. I know by the Voice Within assisting me in making my path toward wisdom through experiences and understandings. I know this. Do you?

Over time I have changed my personal definition of Wisdom. Even prior to reading what the dictionary had to claim Wisdom to be which is the quality or state of being wise; knowledge of what is true or right coupled with just judgment as to action; sagacity, discernment, or insight, even before finding this definition, I knew what it was. Initially it was something that God provided those special people in the Bible and my Parents and the Grandparents and all the old people in the neighborhood. Then I came to know that Wisdom was what the teachers and the priests had, and then others too. I found Wisdom something that I too wanted but felt unworthy of it as a child. I have obtained Wisdom over the years and have developed my definition of Wisdom to be less in line with "judgment" as much as with experience and knowledge wrapped into understanding. Added to that is that in Wisdom I was able to apply it into my experiences and for my own good. No judgment in it. Changing as it does, now I have formed a new definition of Wisdom. I know Wisdom to be the desire and ability to hear, listen and follow the guidance provide by the Inner Voice "Within" oneself; the voice of knowledge, experience, understanding and love. It is why Solomon was wise. He followed Divine Guidance. When you listen to your Inner Voice you can hear yourself or you can hear something more; it is always your choice. It is sometimes difficult, difficult not being the best word to choose, sometimes unfamiliar to distinguish the voice of myself versus the voice of my Inner Being, because they are connected to each other and they exist as a bridge between self - to and from God. We are trained that God is pretty inaccessible and not since Moses has God communicated directly with us, which is why Jesus came to us. I feel both avenues of communication exist. That is why I proclaim that I am now "More than a Christian".

I chose to be who I AM. I have ownership of myself! I realized that I had something, actually a lot, to do with my being born. How I got to be, I mean the I AM of me, was never explained satisfactorily to my comprehension in any of my years of religion or biology classes, nor has there ever been a movie (including the embryonic one) or any book (including the Bible) that explained to me in clear terms who I am. Educationally, aside from having some references proclaim that I was a miracle (including my Mother), a Miracle of Life, avoiding explanation as to spiritually how I was here and how I came into being was all a part of my being unaware of self. Being a Miracle of Life, in and of itself feels pretty good, yet knowing that I AM here in this very body and of my choice and really wanting to be here as I AM, that feels even better. Lots better!

In appreciating that I am here, as myself because I want to be here and somehow always wanted to be here, I feel increased. I feel whole and connected. I feel decidedly in control of myself. It is good to know that from where we come we choose to be here and, what's more, excitedly so. I am not a random sperm, who has proven successfully competitive against gazillions of others racing into attempted existence completely instinctively and only because I was the most strongest and most determined sperm was it me at the finish line. This is true of you too. We come here by agreed supportive choice, not by competitively winning first place. I chose to be here, others chose not to be here. Whichever sperm commenced this biological existence that I am, I was the person connected into it rather than because of it. The sperm was a part of the intelligence of biological model, much the same as a heartbeat is automatically intelligent, of the father and was in cooperation with the biological cellular intelligence of the mother. They enabled the formation. I accepted the invitation, not as a sperm but as a spirit. Conception of my soul happened long before my spirit agreed to come forth into the biological physical invitation of humanity.

The connection of soul to fetus didn't come into the materials formed **in** the conception, rather **in-from** the spiritual acceptance. Conception is a multi-party agreement along with the spirit's desire to become a physical human being. This is a different way of looking at conception, but it is not disregarding that conception is creation. It is only clarifying what was created. Conception is actually co-creation. I was not forced to be here nor are others forced to not be here by winning or loosing the sperm race. This thinking and teaching that we were each in a race to win physical human life at the cost of all those other sperms dying-off in vain is ridiculous. This idea of competitive conception through the survival of the fittest or of natural selection negatively slants our comprehending the perfection in our intended existence and taints the awareness of our legitimate ability to obtain abundance.

The "sperm race" theory impacts our ability to grasp Abundance. If only the one sperm wins the conception race and leaves the rest to die-off incomplete and defeated by a better sperm specimen, this implies that we each won life at the cost of many of others. This instructs us that there is not enough for all. We live and others did not make it to life. If we didn't rush to the win, we could not exist. Someone else would be me, I guess. We are taught in biology that at the very beginning of our lives we killed-off an entire population of others. This has a primal influence on our emotional and intellectual behavior towards self and others. What an upside-down way to think of God's provisions and what a formula to confuse our connection with all others by feeling the limitations we experience are based upon our own competitive drive to survive. In this way we are wrongly taught to believe competition is our natural instinct and without it we could not be.

I believe we didn't fight or win to exist. We are meant to be here. We chose to be here. That is so helpful to discover about myself. I AM and I AM because I want to be. I AM involved in my own existence to the point at which I chose to be here, exactly here. I am reminded that we come here as a projected idea or an image of what we might become and we have, once here in this physical being called self, now the ability to become whatever we want to become. No one decided my being here for me to be so. That is so freeing. I AM free to accept myself, not as a random coincidence, but rather as a free-to-chose-spirit in physical form with direct intention and great enthusiasm to exist as me. Not as you, as me! What a wonderful way to perceive oneself and what a glorious way to appreciate oneself and others.

Then in flows the ramifications of such a powerful statement of thought; I AM and I chose to be me, hence, I choose my own parents. Some say why would they ever choose them? I say because it was what I wanted for myself. I always felt that to be true, even as a small child, and sometimes I think I felt that more as a small child. There is a lovely and loving thought process that brings one into a heightened stage of self-awareness that resonates to my very soul. It is that we, each of us, regardless of the experiences we attract, seemingly good or bad, chose our life parents for the joy in growing the experiences they are framed into providing within their desires for mutual connection and love. They actually agreed to welcome me into my physical self from whence we all come. In like manner, it is probable that from where we come from, from where our Inner Being is continuously remaining connected up and out to Source, God, we have previously made equally profound agreements with those beautiful souls whom we now have named our children. We are all Children of God. We are all brothers and sisters. Equality between each and every one of us is based in eternity.

I came forth to great parents. I love my parents. They were perfect for me, theirs perfect for them. I lived out childhood seemingly quickly. I experienced childhood in a typical way, for those days and times, and with average or better than average problems. I experienced the contrasts as well as the extraordinary harmony, being both loved and denied, wanted and resented, belonging and separated as I was growing up and I imagine that I felt what you felt too in many ways as we are all similar. There are more things about us each that are in common than not. Some people put their "negative" spins on their youth, especially if one wants to blame others for their perceived outcome in life. We come forth, as babies, requiring so much gentle care and knowing today that someone provided that care can only be appreciated. People who complain about their upbringing forget that they survived those intense needy years. That is indeed nice to remember. You have attracted enough care into your infancy that you survived that growing experience. We didn't have the identical experiences, not exactly, but we each are here on this bountiful planet together and having survived infancy and childhood that required someone to care a lot for us. For that I am in appreciation.

We share that undeniable feature, even if you deny our personal connection; we are connected to this time and space reality. I love this physical experience so much that I want to hold each moment as if now will always remain here, now, and now and now. Now is always, regardless of where I AM in Now, a place where I belong. I fear no longer the fact that I will "die". I Am here by choice and I will be "wherever" I go after life by choice. It goes on and on with many circumstances and comparisons, yet, boiling it down into simple terms, I am very happy for the ability to be me.

More ramifications and implications flow forth in thoughts swirling from this realization that I am here in this body because I chose to be here. What about all those unborn lives that cease for numerous reasons prior to birth? We can choose to continue or not. At any point in time, including during the cycle of becoming physically born as an embryo we chose to be physical or not. Being born is a mutual-inter-reality choice. We are happy when born; we are equally happy if not born. We are never the sperm or the egg as we are always the spirit and the soul. It is interesting to think in these terms of appreciating birth as our choice, our choice to enter the physical time space experience we individually and collectively claim to be reality.

Imagine I AM and you are, involved in the choice to live and consciously in-tune with it all. That is worth pondering. There is so much more to explore in this thought process, yet, for now, I surrender to the appreciation that I am here in this marvelous body because I chose to be here. That doesn't state any preference as to the body I have but rather that I am in this body, and I am joined into the physical experience within it. We have Personal Freedom to live or not. The significance that Personal Freedom is a part of everyone's natural God-Given birthright and with it we are equipped to enjoy whatever we Will to do within our belief, is enlightening. We come, as babies, into physical birth with this inalienable human right, yet far too soon we seem to misplace this knowledge about ourselves and it is not taught to us. It is time to remember that we are all born of and in our Freedom to do so, our Will to be born brings with it our Freedom to experience our lives as we desire and we all come here to enjoy living. We did not come forth for the struggle, yet in the confusion of what we actually are we limit ourselves and recreate that false thought that we have to fight for and win continuously in order to exist.

We came forth to discover what we might find in this Freedom we are. I never heard anything close to that in the lifetime of years of weekly hour-long Sunday Masses attended at our parish Catholic Church. I was never told nor was it ever mentioned that it is practical or sensible to consider that my Personal Freedom is important and definitely no one at church, or anyplace, ever even vaguely eluded that the purpose of my life is to enjoy it. What a humongous redirection in thought! This is a brand new way of regarding my very own existence. It is a spiritual understanding rather than a religious one. Religion and having a good time doesn't really seem to go together regardless of what the Good Book stated here and there or how loud the songs sang of joy. Most religious songs of Joy were specifically sung to Jesus or God, not in rejoicing for the experience I am having in life. Enjoying life is used more in commercial advertising than in real life explanation. Not a one of the Great Commandments contains either the words Personal Freedom or Enjoyment. How much validity should be weighted in that statement that we are each born with the Personal Freedom to be and with the desire to obtain enjoyment in life? It does get my attention and alters my feelings about what is truly important.

At first thought of this Personal Freedom to have Joy, I am not even sure I totally comprehended what it could mean. It sounds initially foreign and too idealistic and I felt it a little silly to take too seriously, although I am attracted to the simple truth it contains and the way it brings my mind out of the "box", so to speak. Am I becoming aware that the absolute core, the source, the origin, the center, the starting point, the beginning of my Life is Personal Freedom? Personal Freedom is my ultimate choice to behold or deny. Could it be true that I have so much Personal Freedom that I could have missed looking outside the "box" for most of my life? Could the foundation of my life be Personal Freedom? Strange to think it so, as I was coming from a place that I thought the foundation of my life was to do what I was supposed to do as well as I could, to do what I had to do often, to do what I needed to do just because and all the do's were clearly defined as a set of rules. I felt the core of me was more aligned to being "good" rather than obtaining "enjoyment" and I didn't have freedom in the equation along with purpose. I was conformed into the loss of my own purpose. I held little thought of what the core of my life was, but Personal Freedom, until now this was a bit too far out of my programmed mental domain.

The learning and searching for understanding of this statement that Personal Freedom is at my very core made me reflect upon so many things including all the times as a child I was told that; "Children are to be seen, rather than heard". If Personal Freedom was the foundation of my existence, it was apparent that that idea had been trained out of me a very long time ago, if I ever really had a chance to remember it at birth. I was raised within and remained within the constraints of the governing, acceptable and permissible rules and regulation; all handed down and handed down still now. Seemingly, these quasi-enforceable regulations were ever growing and for a good reason. Rules and Laws enable the building of a structure of policies defining who I was and how I was supposed to be who I was. Is Personal embedded Freedom the opposite of Social Law? Each is working with each other for the good of all if we will recall our responsibility to our individual Personal Freedom. I assumed then and do now, that all these social "rules" are for my benefit and can and do work along with my Personal Freedom. I never thought that each one of the rules that formed my life could be removing, or better stated, reducing some of my apparent inherent Personal Freedom in their very proclamation. I actually was feeling that the "rules" were securing my Personal Freedom. In having Freedom, rules authorize Freedom's realm.

Further in defense of having the rules and regulations that carefully spelled-out the conventions of the standards of my life, and most probably your life too, as they were one by one introduced to me throughout life it seemed easier and neater to have them to conform to, rather than to decide so many things on my own, or so it seemed for a good portion of my life. I play, as if a game, by all the rules I find and it works out pretty good for me. I am somewhat complacent to them and willing to follow them and I feel that they assisted me by making my life easier and more stable. They bring into harmony a race of people of whom I AM connected to and a part of. In trying to understand I ask myself; 'Is complacency what happens to people as they are taught nothing of their intrinsic foundation of life, which is their legitimate inborn Personal Freedom?'

I didn't spend a great deal of time thinking about it as something that I was to claim as mine. I had no idea that I should have tremendously high regard for this freedom, or needed to analyze it, protect it, nurture or use it more than I was already doing. Being unsure, at first, of what it really is yet knowing a new awareness of it, I sensed that this freedom that consumes me now with such high regard must be something for me to better understand. My Personal Freedom is assumed just there and there seemed initially no need to dig deeper into knowing more about it on any serious level. It is evident that I was free to do what I wanted, pretty much, and I wanted to do whatever seemed appropriate and acceptable to be safe and legal. And as a result, I trained a lot of Personal Freedom out of myself voluntarily and it was ok with me.

Now, I am learning that Personal Freedom is inborn into and along with my existence. Personal Freedom isn't just something that our forefathers fought and died for, bless their hearts. I came here to live my life appreciating everything in my Personal Freedom.

Unsure of to what degree I should be taking this to heart I thought back to another time when I did experience a few nearly-punishing failed relationships which by nature and law provided the residue of itself in my becoming stronger, wiser and more aware of what I wanted in Life. I believe looking back on my experiences, that I thought Personal Freedom was something I had to fight for, even in my personal relationships! Personal Freedom was just another race to win. As a result of some seemingly difficult psychologically intensive relationships experienced in my young adult life where I felt like the victim, I wanted more for myself and I wanted my children to have more. I wanted to teach them to avoid negative relationships. I attempted to create more, for us all, by augmenting and securing our futures and more by supporting an evolved self-reliance and self-confidence then in a heightened awareness of my Personal Freedom.

I was thinking of the fight to gain, the struggle to win, the action to take as I literally pursued what I thought was my finding of freedom, my independence. I had no idea that Freedom is my personal right as a human. I had no understanding that Personal Freedom is right there in my own thoughts, if only I could think it.

I had gained independence and a credible professional status from the fight and the wins and I carried that ambitious attitude into my children whenever I could, explaining to them to always remain strong and depend upon only themselves. When my children came of age to go off to school, on that first day I had them innocently wear a huge button on their lapel that read "Question Authority". I instinctively wanted them to walk in their Mom-provided Freedom and I wanted to let those who were to guide and teach my children that I cared about their sense of choice and their knowledge of personal freedom and they better find someone else to "mess" with because I was watching them. Yet, I did not really know if they, my children, so much realized the message. How could they at the age of six? It was me who really wore that button for I was the one who needed to regain that knowledge. Fortunately, I now cherish my God-Given Personal Freedom knowing it cannot be taken from me, although it can be denied by me.

Freedom has become now to mean to most of us the Freedom we have as citizens of our country, state, city or community rather than as humans of our World or the Universe. Freedom is known to most as something different than a personal issue it is a collective and very public issue. It is why we fight wars and stand tall. It is a flag and a huge perfectly lined up military cemetery, but I lost a sense of it being mine, nationally independent from the "us" and the "we".

It is no coincidence that I am remembering the connection between Personal Freedom and Enjoying life. Knowing this does not constitute a religion or institute a nation. There is no church of Personal Freedom and Enjoyment, yet, in these fundamental thoughts there comes indeed recognition worth affirming. It is striking that I am simultaneously or synchronistically realizing that within Personal Freedom I can expand my Personal Joy.

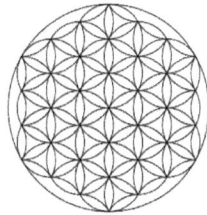

Chapter 8 - Peggy's Appreciations on I AM Appreciating ALL.

- ❖ I appreciate knowing that I AM myself and no one else is me.

- ❖ I appreciate that I AM creating the life that I love living.

- ❖ I appreciate that I AM Free to find Joy in my life.

- ❖ I appreciate knowing that I AM a physical extension of the non-physical part of me that I call my Soul.

- ❖ I appreciate my parents, who took care of me as a baby and my children, who I took care of as babies, and the connection between us.

- ❖ I appreciate the miracle of my life.

- ❖ I appreciate being a non-competitive person and knowing that there is enough for us all to have, rather than win, whatever we want.

- ❖ I appreciate knowing the difference between rules, laws, and regulations and Personal Freedom and that I can live joyfully with both.

- ❖ I appreciate that my Personal Freedom is part of me and it can never be taken away from me by anyone.

- ❖ I appreciate the pursuit of JOY.

Chapter 8 - Your Appreciations on I AM Appreciating ALL

I appreciate this about myself: _____

_____

I appreciate this about my life: _____

_____

I appreciate this about my future: _____

_____

I appreciate this about my understanding of Personal Freedom:

_____

I appreciate _____

_____

I appreciate _____

_____

I appreciate _____

_____

I appreciate _____

_____

I appreciate_____

_____

"Man can form things in his thoughts, and, by impressing his thoughts upon Formless Substance, can cause the thing he thinks about to be created."
Wallace D. Wattles

Chapter 9 Emotionally Appreciating Thoughts

We are all absolutely great Creators. We create that which we think about. We really know what is the absolute best for ourselves in Personal Freedom and get to determine our own lives and all we experience. We can feel what is good for us and we can use those feelings to assist us in thinking of what we want to think about and we create in the direction in which we will improve our enjoyment of life. I am a Great Appreciator of that fact.

"Being the creators of our reality" is a timeless message and yet apparently it is time and again I forget. Life is a joyous experiment of thinking into being what I want it to be. I love life and I love that I am creating the life I live, just by thinking it properly into place, just like you. We are all creating from our every single thought and all while we are conscious and awake, all day long. Further more, as we choose to think our thoughts, we can interpret their impact upon us by noticing our emotions and feelings, which can show us the best way for us to go. We are like machines in that fashion. We can actually monitor our creative power through our emotional experiences. We can tell by the way we feel what direction our thoughts are taking us, and, consequently, how well we are creating our future. Whatever we think about we bring about. What we focus upon and give attention to becomes more vivid. Every person is able to do this too. It is for us all. We are all doing it whether we think we are or not, so why not think it so and pay attention and be your own judge. It works!

It is a fantastic difference in my otherwise would have been ordinary life, ordinary day. Now all days are perfectly wondrous and that is because I am creating them to be so in my every single thought. I am taking total responsibility for my life. I am doing so by caring about what I am thinking about and how my thinking about it is creating the emotions I am having. When I feel good I am thinking good thoughts. There is a match. When things are not going as well as I want and I know that because I am feeling it, I can take responsibility for it and change directions. I can sense when I am thinking something that is bringing about more goodness and the best way for me to pull myself up out of ordinary is by simply appreciating. I start out half there some days, even within a shadow of doubt, and if I continue to appreciate just a little longer. Life's wisdom informs me to doubt only the doubt that figures into the space of my understanding with reason, as doubt lacks reason. It is a path to enlightenment. Start simply by appreciating the possibility of this working.

It comes easy to me to understand, believe and appreciate that I am a Creator. I have been experiencing the delight in creating all of my life, in one form or another. So have you. We all create intuitively and it is fun. Children create instinctively and so do adults. We create our lives, our fun, our direction, our personalities, our decisions and much more. We create all the misery we experience but I want to avoid going there in my thoughts. Why focus upon that fact. I want to focus on what I want more of in my life rather than what I do not want. It is hard to discuss this subject without mentioning it so I did, but I want to appreciate goodness. I want to make goodness my company rather than misery.

We create all of the time and we also co-create. We are meant to be Creators, yet, equally so, we are meant to co-create. That is why we are not the only one, any of us, on this beautiful planet of "ours". Even if all that we see and experience is only our perception of things, we are doing it in agreement with many others at the same time, because we all are here. We are all a part of the same Source so I ask, are we "stranger" passing by each other on the streets and sidewalks, in the markets and offices, or are we just pretending to not know each other? I am sure we all don't just imagine the others are here. We are all here and, as they say, no man is an island. We are all here within our own agreements to be here and now together.

We all are brilliant creators. It is a great joy that we have an entire population of civilization, of mankind, to co-create with anyplace and anytime we can individually become that creative as to become co-creative. Co-creation is as natural as creating, once raised into self-sufficient humans. In other words once we believe that we are individually creating we co-create. Creating is what we do first. We first learn how to create, on our own, as part of our growing independence from caregivers as infants and babies. Then in the curiosity to continue to create we learn also to co-create. Creating and/or co-creating each naturally feels good and are both one of many perfect reflections of life's purposes, for life hold multi-purposes all bannered under the heading of enjoyment.

We are Creators who create with each of our Thoughts. In fact, it is like "love and marriage" or "noticing and awareness", this is a Wisdom companion statement. There is interdependency between the creator and the thoughts of creation. First we acknowledge that we are a Creator. In knowing that, then we can appreciate that we are creating with our own thoughts, with our every single thought. That is it! The point to extract is that every single thought applies to our creations. So when the Law of Attraction states that: "You get what you think about, whether you like it or not". That is a very profound and informative statement.

When darker thoughts arrive, once noticed as not serving well, and they do not serve well, we can shift thoughts to ones we want more of instead. Sometimes the lower-baser-toned-thoughts can entice with momentary thrill or artificial power. However, you can chose to break away from "default" thoughts that strives on the opportunity to stream forth into existence from a slight sense of egotic fear. You own your thought choices. Your past doesn't own them, nor someone else, and not even your negative ego.

In accepting myself as an extended portion of my much larger non-physical part and combining that with the Law of Attraction, I enable and attract what is my essence, my vibration, my desires into and upon myself with my own thoughts. It is the most powerful though I have ever, so far, come to have. It is one of the most exciting scenarios I can currently behold. I feel in total appreciation of this understanding. Life is forever going to be different because I know this. It was a missing key to the way in which I had experienced everything in life, up until now. If it is not one of the most important thoughts you have personally had, you are not hearing what is being stated. It is the sound of understanding. It is the thought of creation. It is absolutely astonishing that I can think something and then create from that thought and what is the best part of this is that I can control my thinking. Once realized, within a little time and conscious direction, pure raw thought can be controlled. Just look around you and it is truth; everything around you was first a thought. Everything is created from thought. What a marvelous miraculous world and how special we each are to be able to create. We are the result of our own thought of what we are now and what we are to become.

Now several years ago when first Uri and I heard that concept in the *Secret Book* we were so excited. We found mostly positive thoughts and we began controlling our thoughts as we ascended out of the default value of thought.

Uri and I voluntarily jumped into each other's thoughts and spoken words to assist each other to think and speak more positively whenever we could, each wanting for ourselves and each other to retrain our thoughts to align with what we wanted to feel and what we wanted to create. With some practice we achieved that pretty much and we continue to hold onto that premise of thought as preferred, yet, more has been discovered.

We continued to practice and study this phenomenal aspect of life and found numerous teachers and teachings directing us towards an extended idea. Our emotions are a guard and a guide to the quality of our thoughts and when we felt good it meant that we were also thinking goodness. Our emotions are the response to our thoughts. When we cared about our thoughts our emotions and feelings would respond well. Likewise when an emotion indicated need for improvement, we found our better thoughts could chart the course back towards better feeling emotions. There is a round robin involved between emotions and thoughts. If you take care about what you are thinking, you will have taken comparable care of your feelings and visa versa. Sometimes it seems easier to take care of emotions first and other times it seems easier to rethink thoughts first, but either way there is a direct interaction, however for the most part the initializing thought drives the direction. I know that my emotions and feelings are my indicators as to the wellbeingness of my resulted thoughts. Sometimes I catch a thought and immediately amend it to jostle my emotions. I'll think a thought and then realizing it could be better. It is a new way of living life, actually taking responsibility for every thought I can think about making as much as I can and when I cannot, my emotions will assist me in evaluating. With practice this fellowship between thoughts and feelings is manageable, most of the time; either way I eventually enter contrast.

Then, as evolution and learning would have it, we started to realize something we had not previously learned about or intuitively thought about and that was "deliberate" thinking. We can, mostly, control our thoughts away from negative by thinking positive or turning into an alternative direction, as in the shifting of thoughts. We can also pay attention to our emotions and create feel-good thoughts. And now, we decidedly want to "deliberately" create thoughts, specifically tailored to our desires. We want to manifest our life, and shape our lives into what we want, what we dream of it to be. This is a major change from taking the default value through life, even the positive default value. The power to think and create is tremendous.

❋ ❋ ❋

Uri and I are already good at creating things together. We have created a family, a wonderful home, family businesses, and so many wonderful things and experiences. We came to realize that we had co-created much, and it was all so good. Now we were beginning on a new and exciting journey together, we decidedly began to deliberately co-create. There is already a lot of intuitive deliberate thought in all we manifested in life; however, we want to take it up a step. Put on the gas and have some fun with it all. We are and continue to be good at this co-creating. We also began to desire knowing more about collectively and deliberately co-creating with like minds.

I continue to be amazed at the way our thoughts create things. I believe that thinking deliberately places me immediately out of the box, or rather into to vortex, and once there I can avoid the lazy default thinking. This new way of Life has a new purpose. What do you think about and what is your purpose? My purpose varies daily and often yet always wanting joy and I am improving my focus on deliberate thought and it is very exciting. I love that I AM enabled to recognize my thoughts, to hear them vividly and to appreciate this happening to me. Whether thinking in default-value or on purpose, creating in default or deliberately creating or co-creating, one will always connect to feelings and emotions.

Four of my most successful creations are my children. In thinking about them I want to go back to the last child's birth, although each held very similar feelings and memories. As with all births that I have had, I was accompanied by at least a doctor and a nurse. With my last we had a doctor and a couple of nurses and our arriving daughter's brave supporting Dad all in the room. It was exciting and remarkable, especially the delight when first meeting and touching this newborn child personally in that delivery room. Afterwards, it seemed a long time before, we, mother and child, were actually alone together since family and friends, in addition to the nursing and care-giving staff were always seemingly there with us. There was always a hospital procedure, time or event that required assistance, or so it felt and all was wonderful in that, as well. I was appreciating the assistance and detailed care. We had "Mother and Child" rare and short moments physically together alone during the first several days of her life.

After coming home with our new daughter, there came a time when the household was quiet and the proud Dad was back at work and the excited, instantly-grown-up sibling was in school that we, mother and child, had a prolonged moment in time together and finally. It was a most mesmerizing feeling of familiarity and calm. It was a very intimate sharing in destiny. Intimacy between two people who are connected by so much more than the physical forms we encounter is beautiful. We were connected by so much more than my having been the vehicle in which she arrived through. I looked into her eyes seeing through and feeling more than the bluish-fog of a newborn's sight melt beyond my eyes and into a spiritual light of mutual awareness recognizing that we knew each other forever. Right then, I recalled, but for a moment, experiencing this with my own mother holding me as a baby connecting up our souls. Telling each other without words spoken of our external light and love in a feeling of togetherness and re-connectivity. I thought that every mother-child-mother must encounter this experience. My thoughts were sensing a timeless connection between us that words could never accurately express and emotions could never evoke on their own. The timing was perfect. It was time to remember each other. Emotional intimacy between two connected souls is a powerful pure love.

✵ ✵ ✵

Emotionally Appreciating Thoughts

Emotions are guiders as well as guarders. They are yours and are provided to you in your best interest and as a useful tool. Emotions know the best way to keep you informed about your personal current direction. When noticing emotions and feelings, it is easy to detect good feelings from those that are less comfortable, but also it is obvious that if detectible amounts of emotions are ignored, good or bad, they will grow larger and stronger so that they will eventually be recognized. Emotions insist upon the attention they require of you to inform or re-inform you of your existence in now. Emotions belong to men and women, babies, toddlers, teens, adults, elders and everyone.

It will feel better to appreciate your feelings and emotions such that you can follow them into what benefits you best from acknowledging them. Emotions and feelings will grow to insist you notice. Emotions are your personal Geiger counter indicators, intended to pick up signals that can assist you in your choices about your directions based upon your thoughts. Paying close attention to your own emotions enables you to change or continue critical thoughts, causing them and therefore giving you great power to control what you are feeling and what experiences you are creating. If you can control your thoughts, and you can, you can influence your emotions and you can create your own life on purpose, helped along by paying attention to your emotions. You are your own major participant in life. Others are only responsible for their own life. Others are not here to make you happy or sad. You are it. It is all you! It is all up to you to follow your desires. It is all up to you to pay attention to what your emotions are doing and in so what are they telling you. It is all up to you to think thoughts that direct your emotions. Emotions do not dissolve or disappear; they complete their function and it is an intelligent function. I repeat this for purpose.

✵ ✵ ✵

People do not disappoint, you permit your thoughts of disappointment to exist and those thoughts bring to surface the emotion of disappointment. Emotions have been created to exist, although, they do not have to rule your life, just guide it. I have been taught that emotions are far from intelligent or logical, but, truly look at them closer, work with them with deliberate intent, use them as the tools they have always been intended for and think about them and notice their intelligence, their ability to guide and guard.

Thoughts and emotions are partners in directing happiness into life experiences. Thoughts and emotions are equally partners in directing sadness. Happiness is a more desirable direction than sadness, for most and at most times, although I can think of times when, right or wrong, sadness was a preferential thought to me. Sad things happen and when they do, I want to feel that sadness and appreciate its conquest over me and sometimes it's healing in me. Yet, emotions direct both positive and negative experiences, depending upon their impact. Being sad is not always a negative experience for me. I can, for example, look at a sad piece of art and sense it as beauty. There are overlapping connections between thoughts, emotions and desires. Emotions guide our understanding of the influence our thoughts have upon our creations and our experiences. In realizing emotions, it is reasonable to detect that some emotions are provided to trigger-off indicators of direction. They pave the "best" route for us to recon in their "telling" us what they do. This telling can be advice or it can flow into your default value. It is all within your capability to direct, as you pay attention and control thoughts resulting from emotions, because that is all emotions ever really are, your actualized thoughts.

Emotions can guide and guard thoughts and when recognized can enable a more intense flow towards what is wanted or not wanted, depending upon the sensation being attracted. They continue, on and on more, increasing the direction in which they are headed, much as the flow of any type of energy. I know that by appreciating my emotions I can increase the reasons for appreciating them even at the "risk" of being more emotional.

We have all been taught to "control" our emotions. In that control there is only a halt, not ever a real stop. We are confusing hindering or forced-alterations of emotions with a control or deletion of them. Emotions do not go away. They only get covered up if not dealt with and they ever pursue themselves. Getting your way can be as simple as knowing what you are feeling and following through with your feelings and trusting them or re-thinking what is causing them. You can surely change your emotions but you first have to recognize the importance in having them. That seems uninviting to so many for fear of being seen for what they really are emotionally. It is all so easy once you know and when you know that, you also know the great power in your being more of who you really are. You are a great human being intended for the purpose of knowing that and much more.

There are vast amounts of people suppressing, separating and denying emotions from thoughts. Most people are in this mode of living and most of the time. This separation is said to be "logical". It is the thriving pull of the default ego-value, which wants to copasetically be included in all of life and yielding to that is a major sacrifice of ownership, joy and happiness. A person who wants to create deliberately will always pay close attention to the feelings that emotions are providing and will find or realize the thoughts that create the emotions are of their free will to make. These emotions are the signposts that assist in preparing for the upcoming curve or other safety or comfort qualifiers coming forth on the road of life. It is a good idea to pay attention to them and avoid problems and if problems cannot be avoided it is easier to be prepared to cope with required change by sensing their nearing. Evaluating the indicators along the way enables slight changes in the course and enough to grow easier when desired.

Whereas it is, disruptive, yet socially accepted that desires are selfish in nature; emotions are equally, controversial, having been established on a wide- and general-level socially as being weaknesses, almost regarded as unfortunate personality flaws. Emotions are welcomed in particular moving situations including when a singer or entertainer is really singing their hearts out within the scope of the acting of it. Some people think emotions are merely personality quirks, theatrics or, perhaps they have the dubious notion that emotions are hormonal or uncontrollable physiological sensitivities. It seems rather ironic because good emotions are not thought of as weaknesses, or hormonal, although even the emotion of "love", which is universally agreed to as one of the highest forms of positive emotion, is somewhat considered more feminine and more of a weakness in men on that same general level. For most people, on a personal level regarding the masculine "love" it is better kept personal, while the feminine can more freely express love or hormonally induced emotions, the exceptions being the song lyrics or the poets results. Basically, the message I have heard, near all of my life, is that emotions, especially those that are more extreme are meant to be kept at bay rather than to be bravely sailed out in the open seas of life, where all can observe. The exception is when females use hormones as their emotional excuse.

I was taught to not even observe my own emotions too closely; never-the-less put them out for all around to view and I am herein proclaiming that one should notice and direct, on purpose, thoughts from emotions that are being experienced; thus paying a lot of attention to them. We aught to pay very close attention to the way we feel emotionally. We are taught to hide our emotions. One fascinating exception is for those unwelcomed hormonal emotions that are released seemingly uncontrollably and periodically though they are acceptable even while often recognized as deplorable oversensitive female behavior. It is no wonder so many woman use it faithfully on a monthly basis. What an opportunity to express and or emotionally explode while feeling the right to act, as such, in anyway "it" so triggers. It is my opinion and my life-experience that those particular emotions are escapes and rebellions from suppressed emotions and has absolutely nothing to do with any biological chemical impact or hormonal imbalance. This is a default driven reaction prescribed by awkward manipulative unrealities that have been purchased and bought into by the massive population, especially woman. Society's defined female Premenstrual Syndrome (PMS) is a building block of a thriving commercial, nutritional, psychosocial and medical industry and is less significant than acknowledged to by the population ever wanting an excuse for emotional etiquette. The spirit of freedom is at work within what is known as PMS. I know better than to go there and attempt to convince anyone otherwise since it is ingrained into the social norm. However, in giving it less attention, while flowing in the nature of change, the experience will be more enlightening than symptomatic. The mention of this can bring the observer into the proximity to discover that appreciating the overwhelment of emotions periodically and appreciating the intelligent design of thoughts within the texture of the body, the availability to take back the charge of ones own emotional ride is only a thought away.

Likewise, there is an apparent dichotomy, that "desires" that other people want for society to have for them personally, are not selfish at all. That is a very convenient tilt. There is an acceptable favoritism there, meaning that it is only selfish to have desires if they are personal desires. There is an acceptable tolerance, meaning that any behavior is only too emotional if it is not an extreme emotion being exhibited and if it benefits the observer.

All this analyzing of self-thought and resulting self-emotions are disciplines in awareness that are not readily taught and are not intuitive until tried and tested. The results are amazing. In learning to embrace self, more and more choices for yourself are returned to you and your life is more deliberate. This is a reality course in responsibility.

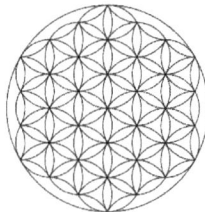

Chapter 9 - Peggy's Appreciations on Emotionally Appreciating Thoughts

- ❖ I appreciate knowing that my thoughts create the quality of my life experience.

- ❖ I appreciate thinking is manageable and creation can be deliberate.

- ❖ I appreciate learning better to focus on my intention and realizing my desires.

- ❖ I appreciate knowing that co-creation is the natural flow of relationships.

- ❖ I appreciate the intimacies of recognizing that we all are of one.

- ❖ I appreciate realizing the doubt lacks reason.

- ❖ I appreciate being a positive thinking and wanting to deliberately co-create with others.

- ❖ I appreciate intuition as an emotional guide and guard.

- ❖ I appreciate being responsible for paying attention to my emotions and my thoughts.

- ❖ I appreciate that emotions require notice.

Chapter 9 - Your Appreciations on Emotionally Appreciating Thoughts

I appreciate this about myself: _____

_____

I appreciate this about my life: _____

_____

I appreciate this about my future: _____

_____

I appreciate this about my Emotions: _____

_____

I appreciate _____

_____

I appreciate _____

_____

I appreciate _____

_____

I appreciate _____

_____

I appreciate _____

_____

It's Yours, so
GO FOR IT!

Chapter 10 Appreciating "Going for it!"

Whatever you can imagine, can be yours. Is that, "Imagine" as in "Desire" that whatever I fancy is a realized fulfillment? Imagine that! That is indeed a bold intriguing statement and clearly one I was not nurtured to consider, as I was growing up learning far too many of what others knew to be my limitations. Even worse, I believed them. This getting all I want granted is perhaps a big fish story or a fairy tale, but my "reality" and the apparent "reality" of my immediate ancestors, educators, acquaintances and caregivers did not divulge or even hint at it. I had heard the opposite more often, but I am not writing about that, I am writing about the possibilities of desire and imagination creating my dreams to come true. Wow, what a lovely soothing thought and one I am fascinated by more and more often and from more and more sources of confirmation.

What a flabbergasting fact that apparently every single one of my kin and relations, and, I, coming from a very large family, missed knowing or missed telling. Perhaps I just missed comprehending! How fortunate for me to be taking it so seriously now. I could otherwise have missed it too. Notably, as this cultural shock emerges within me a new enriched reality that is worth the chance for having taken it. It is an awareness of consciousness and it is a wonder to behold.

We are all thinking most of the time. It is a rare skill to halt thought. When we think on purpose our life has a known reason, which includes being happy with our life and living joy in our time. During the process of being happy it is time to imagine what we want to have, or do or be. I suppose that is another way of saying that we can benefit by deliberately thinking of what our aspirations actually are so that they can manifest and these thoughts are best to come when happiness is part of the experience. How great is that! Being happy creates better realities. Imagine that!

I for one, most of the time, enjoy knowing pretty much what I want. However, I am stumped about how I want to celebrate our upcoming wedding anniversary this year. What's more, Uri is feeling the same about this too. All we keep saying is that we want to be home. Perhaps we could go to the Inn of the Seventh Ray, which is a restaurant that we dined at during our honeymoon and is located not too far away in The Old Topanga Canyon. We are both in agreement with this simple plan. Neither of us want to travel off into some exotic land. We both want to just stay home.

Have we exhausted our imaginations? Are we forgetting the thrill and excitement of traveling away to a new place and being captured by the learning experience and the desire to expand? In all honesty, I think we know exactly what we want and we are less easily swayed by what others might want for us or for themselves.

I have met many people who are unclear about expressing to me or seemingly knowing for themselves what they desire and I have been there too. I tell you it is an uncomfortable place to be in, not knowing what you want. It is a blessing to reach within yourself and find out what you want. Some people may know their more current desires, such as being hungry and desiring to eat, feeling tired and wanting to sleep, being ill and desiring to be well, feeling lonely and wanting to share with someone etc., but many are uncertain about what, beyond this very moment or short span of time, they really want in clear well-defined terms. I believe, from my experiences, that the clearer and more concise I am to myself, and to others, about what I desire, and about as many things as possible to bring issue to, the happier I am and more of my desires are brought into fruition.

People without desires are pale and weaken by the low-baser tones of life. In comparison people with desires are vibrant. Do test that distinction. It is absolute truth. People who do not want for anything are muted with complacency. However, a desire for peace and quiet, calm and simple is a clear desire in itself. Really wanting to not do anything is a desire that brings truth and clarity as much as wanting for greater materialistic things. It's not the "things", it's the intensity of the wanting. Recognize that in the absence of desires what exists is a voiceless stagnation that unknowingly smothers passion into lifelessness. That is horrid! Some state that they have everything that they want, and in so doing, it is apparent that they appreciate desire or it would be untrue that they have everything that they want. One gets what they want from desiring it. These are not the ones without desires, not really. They may be somewhat unwilling to want for more openly, however, they want what they have already. They desire to maintain what they have. There is dissimilarity between not having desires and being enriched by fulfilled desires. These are living desires, the fulfilled ones. They are real. It is the appreciation of their wants actually materialized. Yet, once realized their fulfilled desires met, inevitably they begin to desire something new. Someone who states that they have everything and so have no real desires for more is occupied by their own success more than really not wanting for anything any longer. Abundance is having everything wanted when wanted. These people are truly in appreciation for what they have, abundance, and in that state of appreciation, more is a natural flow. I am not referring to those as the same people as the ones who are without desires. And of those people who say that they do not want to desire, well, is that not a desire? Desiring-people are alive with the wonder in hope of tomorrow. Even a vase desires to be filled with the water for the rose.

Desire's sparkles are analogous to brilliant night-stars pirouetting in a perfect effortless ballet through a dimension unseen but familiar in the heart. They are each crystal clear points-of-light and all contain multifaceted complexities that integrate precisely with ALL else. Desires are, of course, always personally agreed-upon thoughts and are collectively innumerable and immeasurable and reside in the incomprehensive shared-space of what is "total life". Vivacious thoughts of viewing these astronomically illuminated invisible collection of mankind's desires, if they could possibly be seen, from any place or depth, creates a sensation of pure simple beauty within a deep fulfilling breath of fresh cool life-giving air. It is the beauty that eyes do not see and hearts can feel. Yet, I can imagine seeing them, although I desire to only imagine, as this beauty is intended for the imagination alone, while there within this splendor is a very good and real feeling of inclusive pleasure. Desire clarifies the course of life with the thrill of creating.

In truth, there are many desires attached to most of us all of the time forming a vast array of components that some call dreams. Desires are vibrational emanations of strength and valor that populate our sight-invisible aura or persona and are responsible for definition and clarity of our path of life. Desires are always growing and ever glowing. There is no judgment from desires. Many they are independently chosen and, even in co-creation, personally born from the freedom of thought.

Desires are a frequency of continuous life-flow. That stream flows on and more so on, rather than just going on and on. The "more so on" portion of desire's growth makes it obvious that desires are a fantastic invisible crescendo of satisfying beauty, ever expanding and ever becoming. Desires accumulate and clarity becomes what converts them into manifested reality.

❁ ❁ ❁

What can you imagine to be? Anything is the answer. And what can you imagine to do? Again, anything is the answer. Ah, and what can you imagine to have? Right, anything it is! That is altogether amazing! Imagine that to be true. If you have the inclination to imagine it, the universe is prepared to yield whatever you really want. That is an eye-opening provision. Imaging is a casting of free desired-thought that enables actuality. That is worthwhile knowing. Postulating this out of the folklore and into a strong belief is the magic behind manifestation. The nuts and bolts of creating from imagination into reality is first desiring, then believing it to be true and finally trusting it to happen. In other words, Ask, Believe and Receive. Truly knowing that what you imagine transmutes your clarified-desires from a cherished suspended thought into real life is knowledge above education and wisdom at its birthplace.

Young people tend to believe easier, or more easily, that they can do or be or have anything they imagine, within their rearing-programmed reach of limitations, which is good to observe in young people. It is delightful to watch a young person realize that they want to "go for it", yet, this option, is intuitive to them mostly from a space of time rather than from a place of permitting. When this "science of the mind" message is absorbed and understood from a place of knowing then the clarity between youthful hopes and demonstrative manifesting becomes very apparent, albeit this enlightenment is not age dependent, it is a leading edge gift. Wisdom remains in the appreciation of grasping it. Young wisdom or old wisdom it matters not. If we were taught and if we taught our youth from birth to trust themselves and their greatness, changes could occur more often and faster and many the dream would come true sooner. Again, this focus of mankind's awareness of the power of their individual thought and their collective consciousness is what the Grand Transformation of Mankind is all about. This knowledge through wisdom is true power. It is more, much more, than having the time to achieve desires; it is the absolute power to create. A power we are noticing as individuals and sense defining changes throughout our world.

There is Magnificence "Within" you.

Let us presume that the Universe as a total singular collective living entity thriving in a form of omnipotent intelligence adores you and is completely aware of your essential spiritual existence and your higher capabilities, and in that it is possible that it also longs for you, as familiar love desires each other, yet with understanding and confident acceptance of what is. The Universe experiences other human qualities too. We are all interconnected so that is not surprising to connect to similarities. That is easy to appreciate if you can appreciate that you are a part of God. For example we humans are continuously expanding, evolving and growing and in our expansion the Universe also expands. With that in mind, if we can have the human quality of missing a loved one, can the Universe also desire for us when we have forgotten to be an integral part of it? Having been intentionally integrated from each other spiritually, rather than separated from each other, for time unknown to describe or quantify, it, the Universe, actually can miss you (as in desire), or rather misses the compete connectivity of you and the harmony of shared equaled acknowledgement of each, albeit the physical life experiences time differently than the essential non-physical consciousness of the Universe. Time must someway exist for the universal understanding of it in order for it to expand. And it does expand. In an analogous physical expression, you are basically a (kind of) departed family member, who has been co-creating deliberately with the Universe forever, yet now in physical form as such, you intrinsically are independent minded and often confused, especially before wisdom sets in. We come here in our physical forms and forget and are untaught about our total connection to All-that-is.

That is only a slight variation in thoughts from when we lose someone to death in the physical. We often miss and long for that person and we continue to love them, here among the living although they have departed and we feel detached permanently from them, or so we have been collectively thinking generally. We love our own people when they are alive and after they pass on. Likewise, we all are loved-ones of God and of the Universe and the Universe and God loves us so much even though we are physically here, in fact we are greatly love for having come here. In self-awareness of the existing Inner Being, each is more aware of God and the Universe. It waits for you to become awakened as in so being you are reconnected consciously with this love that always is. And so, in re-connecting up to your Inner Being, what will you create?

Your Inner Being can remind you of your joyous songs, your broadest intentions and your purposes. It can remind you that you are without limitations. It knows and you can remember. Listen and hear.

I wonder if the Universe mourns my birth and even as other humans, when I die, will mourn my death. I suppose not, as it is a part of the lovely unfolding of a life caused into purpose and with the ability to find joy. The Universe does not mourn. It is the same on either side and it is in our best interest to accept that we never really die, we just become physical for a course in life. Yet, no doubt we come with great intent.

Our intent becomes increasingly apparent, although we can only get it right, when we take charge of our own thoughts and enable the process of pure thoughts to attract onto us the pure intent of our desires regarding our coming forth into the physical experience, as Human Beings. Of course, the absolute intention is to enjoy the physical format we accept with much enthusiasm upon entry. It is a glorious trip we embark upon in coming forth as Humans. We come with clear visions of expanding this frame of living, this portion of time span, and this creative process with our desires to experience joy. We come forth with great intentions and we come forth realizing that we might well be confronted with discombobulation as to remembering our initial intent or rather our intent initially, as we know before we come forth that the contrasts are ever present on Earth. *We are totally empowered Masters of the Universe suffering from amnesia.*[5] We are not coming forth into physical form naïve of the ongoing growth mankind is promulgating, although that quantity changes with the span during life before awareness and so does purpose. We are very aware of this upon deciding our birth. It is only the un-training that brings us into having to experience so many different "things" before Wisdom sets in, before we come to realize that the Voice Within us is truth itself. Listen and hear, the Voice Within and find the Wisdom you came forth to recall and then create from.

I AM the Creator of what I alone determine to be the course of the life I want to experience. I so much appreciate that my thoughts are on a "journey" or a "way", as if a thruway, freeway or a speedway. We are moving-on and going-there. We are on a path of joy rather than only being in an emotion of joy. Joy is a way, a state of being, emotion and a place all at the same time. We get to decide what is joy for us. Some find joy to be "fun" as in laughing, joking and partying, being loud and being noticed. Others find joy in the sunset or the watching of a student absorbing teachings. Joy is a newborn baby's giggle or a flower come to bloom. There are many ways in which joy can be experienced and each of us has a unique path of Joy and each of us embrace all forms of joy, as appropriate. Furthermore, this creation of personal joy is evolved from the patterns of our own desired thoughts, our unique ways of thinking. So then, what do I want to experience is a good question to appreciate asking oneself and often. I AM unique, the only one like me, an individual, and at the same time I AM a part of the entirety of all that is and in that comes understanding that when I am seeking,

---

[5] Dining at the Cosmic Café. How to Be and Do and Have Whatever You Desire. Page 49. By Kate Corbin

finding, and living my "path of joy" it is then that all that is connected to me is also living their path of joy. We are all one.

All that explanation of the way of life feels so big for me to participate in sometimes and I find myself drifting out of phase, often without being totally aware of it at the time the shifting is taking place. Even out of sync, I am finding my way to joy. Sometimes by way of the slow boat from China, yet, it is uniquely mine and for that I respect this path and while knowing that my objective remains, joy. My goal is to appreciate that the journey is part of the joy as well; the way to the joy is joyful, hence the objective is the journey rather than the final destination, as there is no final destination, we are experiencing steps along the path that always is in the process of never becoming complete.

❋ ❋ ❋

We are all uniquely on our own paths and in a parking lot in San Diego I found a very valuable and personal lesson about the Law of Attraction and the power of my thoughts and my intentions. It was very joyful to experience and I want to share this story. Apparently, it was mine to allow and with allowing there is always joy. Yet, with all that I know to be, I remain timid about the allowing, ever wanting to learn how to allow more. I believe this longing is necessary to balance my life or it could easily be overrun by instant manifestations. It was time to grow in understanding allowing. It was not a turn; rather it was a time to allow. It is not my turn then yours. Abundance is always available. It exists for you and me all of the time, not in turn one than the other. I want to allow more. It is a goal for me. I want to reach for the understanding "Within" me that opens me easier and easier to allowing. Life is so good and allowing makes it more so. Allowing the way of the will to be is as easy as appreciating that it is always upon me. It is always available. I am allowing what is my perceived capability to allow. I want to allow more and more often and I can. It is bigger a feeling than merely saying to myself that I am allowing, for the evidence of allowing is in the surroundings of my life, and within the actual mood or emotions I am encountering. I am distinguishing between my allowing in awareness and my receiving in the default value. That day in San Diego I must have been more that self that can open up to allowing. It is valuable to reflect upon what I was experiencing then and form the experience I know very well that I want to experience more of it.

When I had studied the Law of Attraction for about a year and a half, during that process it was mentioned that one should attempt to play with its concepts of intention, so I did. I did not want to intend something easy for the Law of Attraction to prove itself. I wanted my test to be a hard one almost thinking it was a bit too silly to "thought-intend" something as a test. I had a lot to learn about the "ways" of the Law of Attraction. I was curious. I wanted to try it out.

I had heard of a man who wanted to prove the Law of Attraction by intending a cup of coffee and got it, or another had intended a parking space up front at the market and got it, and one person even wanted a feather to float down to the street in the middle of Manhattan and it did. I wanted to make it a hard test. One that would say to me that it was really working. I wanted to personalize my Law of Attraction test. So, I requested that no plain old feather would do, I wanted a Peacock Feather to come to me. I mean not seeing one in a store either. I wanted one to come out of the blue to me and present itself right in front of me. That had been perhaps three months ago and no Peacock Feather found me yet. I had nearly forgotten about it completely. Maybe the forgetting about it actually helped prompt it forward. Once in a while I would think that perhaps that was too hard a test, so I wasn't sure if I could believe it could happen. And then, it was in a parking lot where we sat down on the curb together, Uri and I, after receiving a cell phone call from our daughter who was skiing in Colorado that it happened. We were, of all places, sitting in a conference workshop with 400 others in the audience when the cell phone vibrated and Uri noticed a call coming in from Michelle. It was the middle of the winter and her college break had taken her and her boyfriend to Colorado to visit her sister, Tasha. Tasha is a great skier though Michelle is more the summer surfer. Having received this call, Uri quickly walked out of the conference room, so to not disturb anyone and since she was so far away and we knew that she was skiing that day with her sister and her boyfriend we both immediately wondered why she was calling. We did not expect to hear from her and intuitively we took the call. She was calling from a nursing station at the resort where some paramedics brought her in. That was questionably uncomfortable to hear, however and quickly, she let us know that she begged them to bring her in because she found herself too high on the mountain's surface and her inexperience in skiing had worn her out. She really wanted the ride off and down from the side of that mountain. She has a way of figuring out what she wants and what she wants materializes often for her. She was so happy to be off that mountain, apparently not really wanting to become an expert skier like her sister, nor like her sister apparently wanted.

We were appreciating her comical embarrassment when there it was! Yes, the Peacock Feather finally manifested right in the way I had requested in my intent. Sitting on the curb, I looked down and right in-between my feet, on the asphalt of the parking lot was the most beautiful perfect Peacock Feather ever looking as proud as can be up at me, it's eye touching my heart and soul instantly. I asked Uri if he had planted it there because it was so surrealistic to see. Uri and I had spoke of the desire of mine to manifest a Peacock Feather almost lightheartedly from time to time, less often more recently. And there it was in living color and in great glory. There was no breeze and the air was still and the environment was quiet and strangely mysteriously beautiful. How could it be that we were even sitting on a curb ever less having this feather manifest? It was especially amazing as we were attending a Law of Attraction Workshop. The first one we had ever gone to. What perfect timing. The Law of Attraction took such impressive measures to bring me to find this out.

It was clearly my own unique way. The way I could most learn from, the way I could learn to believe from, the way my beliefs could receive from. It was perfect for me. The Law of Attraction proved true to me many times including that moment in time. It was a perfect time to happen and it was a perfect time to get the phone call from our daughter that took us outside the conference room to sit on the curb in the parking lot. It was a very unlikely place to learn the strength of the truth of the Law of Attraction yet it was exactly the most likely place at the same time. I love testing the Law of Attraction! In that very conference we were told that it is as easy to manifest a button as a castle. Nice thoughts running in that circle.

I have asked for other equally absurd testing manifestations that I am still wanting for. One is most vivid in my minds-eye and I requested it on the same day I requested the Peacock Feather and yet it is still at large. It is a scarf. I want a light lavender opaque scarf to appear to me, like a ruffle in the wind. It sounds like an image I might see in a TV commercial. It is but a trinket, but I see it clearly. It is months now and I am still wanting for it. If you see it send it my way, yet I know that I can allow it any moment now. It is something for me to look forward to. I wonder sometimes how and when it will appear and satisfy my senses with wonder. I imagine looking outside at the sky and watching this illusive scarf drift from nothingness into my sight. It can happen any moment now and as I want for it and visualize it and sense its energies afloat and sailing towards me even at this very second I think, I hope I do not miss it. I hope I can really comprehend it. I want to welcome it into my experiences, yet I know also that it will appear when I am at a place in thought of accepting it as possible. It will feel appropriate. The Peacock Feather felt so appropriately placed when it happened.

I appreciate that I am on this way, which is the way I am required to go. I appreciate that sometimes it feels a bit longing. I appreciate that other times I find enough doubt to halt it's coming although I appreciate that doubt lacks reason. I appreciate that the waiting is connected to my wanting. Wanting out of the understanding-place where I believe it will be mine and that I will easily be able to allow it into my existence is a wonderful and comfortable feeling that time is independent of and is enjoyable. Wanting out of a place where I hold doubts that it can happen is an uncomfortable feeling that makes me experience waiting or reconsidering. Finding what I want is connected to finding what I trust and believe in that I can accept myself having and that feels very good. I appreciate the desire to allow. That seems simple enough; yet I wonder where the lavender scarf is and what possibly can I do to retrain my thought to allow this lovely gentle scarf into my sight, into my world and from my allowing. I see the color of the pale lavender scarf often and I can feel the touch of it, and I know it is only "me" holding it off a little longer and I appreciate the journey. I am holding it off until I can accept and receive it while I am appreciative of the wait itself. It started out being a trivial scarf perhaps I didn't even really want it so much and now it is rather than a test of the Law of Attraction, which I know is working one hundred percent of the time, it is my own test. I am testing myself to become an allower.

What then is it this joy of manifesting from allowing that makes me want so much to be a better allower? At the end of a hard working day or better yet a softly woven day what can one say to the things that accumulated around; "Goodnight sweet light, see you in the morning dear bed, sleep tight big TV set, or I love you closet of clothes." No, it is not things that bring living-joy; it is the appreciation of these desired manifestations that enlighten-up the space between having and applying, owning and using, wanting and getting.

There are vast differences in the impressions of materialism, yet, everyone seems to want possessions. However, most feel that possessions are a result of hard work, with the exception of those who inherit, win or steal theirs.
"Unless you are willing to drench yourself in your work beyond the capacity of the average man, you are just not cut out for positions at the top." So says J. C. Penny, who _was_ the top position in his company and he did not have to compete for it. What action is required of the person at the top? Yet, already knowing the answer, I wonder whom he said that quote to? Most would agree that it was his employees. After all, he had to take less action when his employees took more action. In that quote of his all I can

sense is that he is leveraging his own desires onto others. That makes perfect sense for him. Quite honestly, the required action for the person in the top position is only to get others to act on their behalf. Positive thoughts are influential.

There are gazillions of "work hard to succeed" quotes. I was personally raised on them from birth. Here is another one written by Charles Lazarus, the founder of Toys R Us (look for the similarity between Lazarus and Penny in more than their department store occupational success), *"Hard work is the key to success, so work diligently on any project you undertake. If you truly want to be successful, be prepared to give up your leisure time and work past 5 PM and on weekends. Also, have faith in yourself. If you come up with a new idea that you believe in, don't allow other people to discourage you from pursuing it."*

A closer look at these types of quotes that are handed down to us with the theme that "hard work brings financial and material rewards" finds that they are primarily from people who benefit the most from others hard work. We are actually being programmed from a very young age to do work for someone else and to work hard at it. These beliefs are without malicious intent by those whom are primarily teaching us these things, as they too have been taught in them and have worked hard for everything that they have. So it is not a bad person providing a bad message, it is however, untrue, yet it is so engrained into our society and into ourselves that we fear any other thought to the contrary for loss of the obtained. If you are reading this you have probably already invested a great deal of hard work into what you consider your success. Furthermore, to confuse the issue, it is hard to argue with the fact that action moves things and hard work does yield something, often beneficial and many times financially rewarding. Yet, there is so much more to the equation. I only wish I knew then, when I was being raised up, when I was 3 and 10, and 18 and 26 and 35 and on, what I know now. And yet, I tell you that it is not a lazy person who obtains their desires. It is the thinking person and it is the feeling person. It is someone who appreciates his or her Personal Freedom and wants to enjoy life.

The Law of Attraction takes a very different approach than to teach struggle into success in the form most reference as hard work. It is in the pursuit of Joy that one becomes active and that active state is an inspired state, and in inspiration come success. It is the hard work in realizing what you Love, what is of Joy to you, what you desire, and what makes you feel Good. That is the hard work that brings inspiration to the surface. For me inspiration in and of itself required a disciplined approach towards what many would see as hard work.

One of the most interesting aspects of the Law of Attraction regarding "hard work" is that if you feel good working hard then it is the inspiration you are made of. If you want to "play", which is defined herein as the opposite of "hard work" as commonly thought of, then play. Yet, if in your hard work you want to be playing then your hard work is harder. If in playing you feel you should be working hard then you are not playing properly either. Playing or working hard either way one should feel joy in the doing, and then there is created in the focus of that joy the manifestations of your desires, your possessions, and your material or financial rewards. Playing at hard work is the catalyst for abundance. What you feel appreciation for doing or thinking always provides you direction towards what is your inspiration. What you are feeling and thinking creates what you desire and what you desire is the incentive for the behavior to obtain the same.

It is all about the Law of Attraction on many levels that we are reaching for understanding about, including our action to take as it relates to the fulfilling of desires. Successful actions (ones that feel good and that benefit) and possessions to be obtained, collected and distributed (ones that we love and want to have), all have to be the results of our specific focus upon what is our personal definition of Joy.

❋ ❋ ❋

The Tao Te Ching[6] states that there are three things to teach: simplicity, patience, and compassion. It says that these three are your greatest treasures. With simple actions and thoughts, you return to the Source of Being. With patience with both friends and enemies, you will accord with the way things really are. And with compassion toward yourself, you reconcile all Beings in the world.

The Tao Te Ching has similar messages if one looks for them towards the Law of Attraction. What you think about you bring about. They both teach measures for measures. The Tao Te Ching, like so many other brilliant books tend to teach joy as the guiding light in the journey of simplicity, patience and compassion. What do we manifest if we are joyful through times of sorrows. They are both great gifts to accomplish tomorrow, knowing your way by the feelings acquired and attracting upon which is the flow of your heart's desire. This is the Law of Attraction.

I shall not desire a loss of a friend, yet it comes. Did I think wrong? Did I manifest this sorrow? One cannot care about things when there exists tears of sorrow that seem unreal to appreciate. It feels sad to lose a friend even knowing that the friend is returned to pure positive energies and is in heaven or wherever you think appropriate for them to be departed. What is manifested in such a loss? There is no hard work in feeling the loss of a friend or the sensation of sorrow. It is an empty feeling to invest in one who is gone from physical form now. So is it true to want for anything that one might desire and receive it without the power of wanting the living with longing, the choosing to have, the sensing it coming, the satisfaction in proclaiming or recognizing its manifestation? So without joy to wallow it's being what is the use of having more than your own Being? For in the appreciation of it all, only your heart will fill up with its joy. Being here and now is the place it belongs and neither time nor space can remove it alone. But death arrives

---

[6] According to tradition, it was written around the 6th century BC by the sage Laozi (or Lao Tzu, "Old Master"), a record-keeper at the Zhou Dynasty court, by whose name the text is known in China.

more slowing and confiscates the space you are in, with a senselessness of not understanding of a lose of correctly grasping all that one knows the Law of Attraction provides to each. Are we but doomed in this needing without the kindness to manifest a moment added to a life?

And then there is the friend who croaks and in so doing there seems great joy in my heart. Not for them really dying, but rather for the feelings that they were ready, they lived well and are available to go on. I do not spend time pondering away in sorrow for the soul that I sense appreciated life in a similar way I do. Why is that so? I am amazed to know. It is similar to why J.C.Penny advocates his employees to work hard. It was his selfish pursuits. And there in is the reason that I selfishly feel joy at the soul return of a well-lived happy person. People who have been filled with dramatic sadness, fears or any form of hopelessness, I feel more grief at their departure, as if they missed out on the vital lesson life yields at our desire. Even in death these departed ones leave their message of sadness behind for a while.

In our own volition we seek joy. Become Joy and more Joy is attracted to you. Appreciate what you have and more comes to you to be appreciated. Acknowledge something to appreciate and something appreciates you. Love harder rather than work harder today and tomorrow and you will have more love. All of what I do and obtain comes forth from my attention on Joy. Allowing joy is the hard work.

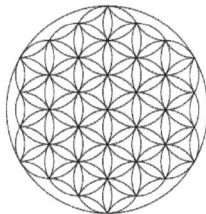

Chapter 10 - Peggy's Appreciations on Going for it!

- ❖ I appreciate being alive now and being a part of the awakening of my own thoughts in this time of great change.

- ❖ I appreciate that I get this Law of Attraction stuff.

- ❖ I appreciate the changes I make and will continue to make in my life by adapting to deliberate thoughts.

- ❖ I appreciate breaking the chain of dark default value thoughts that were handed down to me from generation to generation.

- ❖ I appreciate manifesting the simple and the huge and the wanting still to allow.

- ❖ I appreciate the magic of allowing.

- ❖ I appreciate leveraging joy into work of enjoyment.

- ❖ I appreciate that eternity hears my desires.

- ❖ I appreciate everything I experience.

- ❖ I appreciate that allowing joy is hard work.

Chapter 10 - Your Appreciations on Going for it!

I appreciate this about myself: _____

_____

I appreciate this about my life: _____

_____

I appreciate this about my future: _____

_____

I appreciate this about my Emotions: _____

_____

I appreciate _____

_____

I appreciate _____

_____

I appreciate _____

_____

I appreciate _____

_____

I appreciate _____

_____

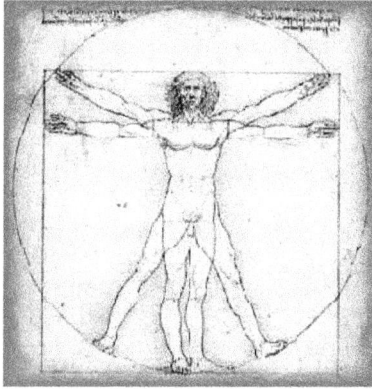

"When you're Dead you're Dead for a Long Time."

Uri Halevi

Chapter 11 Appreciating Death Everlasting Life

Today I heard that an old friend Joe has died. Two friends have died in as many weeks and as the Law of Attraction is working as it wills in my life, these deaths happened just as I was starting to write about the subject of appreciating the Death Experience. As a result, my instincts are now to combine the ideas of dying with the results of living in recognition of Everlasting Life

I was enjoying June. So far, the one word to bring me into focus with June this year is, "Juxtapositions", in which I find twin-contrasts can be duplicitous in nature and creates a new understanding of each being comparatively different than either looked alone. It was in this moment recalling that this is the Gemini time and I am experiencing two's of things, even seemingly connected contrasts.

Two friends "kicking the bucket" at the same time made me realize that there is twice as much to consider about the subject. Having either of them die was hard enough but, having them both go, this is more than rare. It is an absolute first experience for me. It was two years ago that my Aunt passed away and no one I knew of personally died since until these two decided to go, nearly simultaneously and from two different sides of the country. Seems more than an interesting coincidence to me. Apparently, I was having a double dose of appreciating death and acknowledging my belief in everlasting life.

Joe was 75 years old and I feel only happiness for him because, from my prospective, he must have been ready to die and we haven't been in contact for years and years, so it was less of an impact on my life, so it seemed at first. I cared for him, in fact I loved him and love never dies, so it was not unnoticed by my heart or soul. Interestingly enough, I am happy for him, as I do not recall him being especially fond of aging, as I am. I knew him well when I was in my early and very young 20ies and he was in his late 30ies and he already thought and spoke of himself as pretty old. He was attracted to youthfulness and new stuff. He did not appreciate antiques unless they were replicas like the brand new Cord he drove sometimes. He was a big NYC boss man and he was a good person to me.

He introduced me to the book "*How to Win Friends and Influence People*, by Dale Carnegie, and signed me up to take a class related to this book, which he thought would assist me, and it did. He taught me a great deal about life when I was like a sponge willing to absorb everything within reach. I was beautifully young and was interested in everything and everyone. Now, I am beautiful, much older and still interested in everything and everyone. Yet, as I mentioned, I rather enjoy getting older. Boy, did Joe feel differently about that subject.

He had a great attitude and was filled with confidence that he knew everything there was to know already before turning 40. It seemed to me he felt that life above 40 was just a deterioration process that took away and did not give as much back. I was on the other side of that thought, whereby, age seemed to not matter to me, then or now, and in fact I liked him because he was older than I was. His wisdom remained with me from that standpoint all of my life and I will forever see him as a little boy, a Peter Pan boy man, although he stood over 6 feet tall. I felt indifferent to age and time so I am young when I was supposed to be young and I am enjoying the process of change rather than aging. Now, if I had met Joe say four years ago instead, I do not think he could have influenced my life at all. And for that, I am so fortunate to hold a good memory-story of Joe. He was a special teacher to me and I forevermore will respect and honor him for the life experiences we shared. We were close friends for about 4 years, and strong acquaintances for about 6 years. I will not miss him. I will only continue to love him. I did not hang around with him in the past 30 plus years, though I loved him through them all. I never chatted with him recently or emailed him, like I did with Bob.

It strikes my interest that when they told me Bob was dead just last week, I cried and felt sad, for the entire week, although I do not feel so sad for his dying now. My grieving is over for Bob perhaps. And I will not, and cannot grieve for Joe. It is okay with me now that both have "kicked the bucket", not that I can do anything about it anyway. I knew Bob on and off over the past 30 years and the recent three years we have been communicating regularly through emails and rare phone calls. They are both dead as dead can be, not one more or less than the other.

I knew Joe and Joe knew me better in some ways than Bob and I did, yet longer ago then I knew Bob. Joe and Bob were very different individuals and yet, now, in common, they are dead, dead, dead, and within days of each other. Neither knew the other and I was probably the only person in the world who knew them both. If I had to identify the major differential between them, Joe was apparently outwardly happier while living, at least while I knew him well. He had more fun being alive then most people do and definitely more fun living then apparently Bob did. It is hard to compare them in relation to "happiness", because that is so subjective from the point of view I hold true, yet, when Joe was with me, he seemed to enjoyed life more as far as I knew them each. Joe had fun with living. He smiled a lot; in fact, my memory of him is in his smile and in the echoes of his snickering laughter, even after all these years. That's what I remember. Some people are happy, others not so. These two souls were clearly on different wavelengths as far as their expressing happiness and joy, yet they are equally happy now!

Bob might have been "happy" too, yet his form of happiness was very different then Joe's of that be certain. Bob found joy apparently in noticing and judging everything that was wrong with the world and then bringing it to your attention too. He especially noticed what were the weaknesses with other people who were different then he was in this worldly sense. He was "opinionated" with the burden of "cause and effect" as his purpose. He actually cared sometimes too much about the huge world around him and the impacts he and everyone else has upon this world. He discovered and carried the latest most obsolete intellectually unknown, yet somehow you knew to become tomorrow's trendy, causes to a near obsession. He loved to consider natural change to be a mass consciousness that just needed to be realized. He knew he saw it differently than did most others, and for that reason he always tried so hard to influence into society more considerate thoughts of nature and the gentleness of mankind's potential through his example. If you believed in his political party or the ideas in which he stood for, you were good, if not he did not think that much of you and might tell you so as he continuously attempted to convert you to his side, his awareness, whatever that meant, as I never quite figured that out. Bob could have won the debate team trophy on any of the opinions he held mightily. Joe would win a debate with his smile. Both always felt they were always right.

I wonder if I just got used to dealing a little better with death in-between the days of Bob's croaking and Joe's croaking. Perhaps that is why I do not cry for Joe. I had already cried for Bob. I liked them both the same if that could possibly be measured, so it wasn't that one was more important to me over a lifetime of knowing each of them. Strangest thing about them both is that I feel more connected individually to both of them in some ways more so now that they are dead, dead and gone. I feel towards both of them that in living, each was hard to really know well, especially over the more recent years. Like I said, I had no communications with Joe for years and Bob and I recovered our weakening friendship just a few years ago, although we have not seen each other in person for about 7 years. Bob and his family moved up Northern California. In Bob and Joe's dying I feel both are equally easy to know. They are both equally accessible to me too, and both equally dead.

Does death make us appreciate life more or does life make us appreciate death more? Death confuses me when I have to deal with it in any real sense. When death is not an issue in my life, it is easier to understand, but, when it comes close, I am confused by my feelings about it and I am perplexed by the inconsistency in those feelings.

It amazes me that I can feel in appreciation at one person's death and sorrow at another person's death. It is almost creepy that I feel like celebrating one person's death and celebrating another person's life. It is all so mysterious to me, although on a purely personal level, I am in less fear of death than ever before in my life. In fact, I am not afraid of my own death, as I was most of my life. Perhaps, that is so easy to say since I am a healthy person figuring to live a long time, yet I think there is much more to it and, additionally, I want to grow much older and wiser.

Being raised Catholic, or most any religion basically, believers are instructed that when one dies one goes to heaven or hell, depending upon the way one lived their life, the way the heart loved, the way others were treated by them, if they went to church, temple, or synagogue regularly, if the great 10 Commandments were kept and, of course, if one stayed away from sin, or repented for sin. That's all so "heavy". The way to death and heaven is taught in the most vague terms, as the rules seemed to stretch past the 10 Commandments and included other rules; such as the Golden Rule that states Love thy Neighbor as Thyself. Additionally, I was taught that merely believing with my whole heart and soul that Jesus is the only Son of God and my savior that I go to heaven, no problems. Loving Jesus as much as I love God and definitely more than myself was a sure ticket into heaven. Easy, right! Not so!

❋ ❋ ❋

All that is simply amazing to me, now. All the religious mumbo-jumbo teachings seem so contrived to me now, although, I admit, I respect and love others who are religious and I will remain "more than a Catholic". Religions seem so well planned out to control me, to keep and own me. To instill fear within me, or to create a fear of dying or, is that, a fear of living, it is a similar impact from a different direction. Religion seems so thought limiting now. I was taught that God decides my going to heaven or hell after I die and I should try to prepare to go to heaven by being obedient to God's rules. That's great, yet man has created and even altered some of these rules. I am not interested in finding fault in religion; I am interested in finding what is right with religion. The most wonderful thing about the religion I have lived with, being a Catholic, is that from it I arrive at where I am. Being a Catholic proved a spiritual stepping-stone to arrive at today, and today is a wondrous place to be.

I started to seriously re-evaluated what I considered about life and death when I began to take control of my own thoughts, although I was experiencing a life worthy my looking at, so changes were incremental on many levels which brought me to realize what my thoughts actually are. I challenged the concepts of what I was told of heaven and hell. In so doing, I became enlightened on this subject! It was a spiritual awakening. The voice "Within" me spoke. I started to emotionally feel aware that when I die I return to non-physical. That made so much sense because my soul therefore lives on just as I was taught as a Catholic. I also became aware that being non-physical wasn't a place against a backdrop of heaven, which was pleasant above imagination, or hell, which was the worse place to be one could ever imagine. I learnt and felt the understanding of through a growing Wisdom that I AM that when I die I return to what I still AM, pure good and positive energy, although I AM not the opposite while alive, I, like you, just forgot to what extent that is true. I AM, we are, just sometimes less aware that we are all pure good and positive energy. Dying into the non-physical is a good place to return. I exist and I cannot do anything about that. I AM. There is no hell for me any longer. I think Hell is a figment of man's imagination, along with the Easter Bunny. So in that regard it is all very real, yet, like Bob, I turn my head and see a different world then what most others see. I sense only a Source of Wellbeing. God is only good!

God did not invent Hell. Man invents Hell. God gives man the freedom to invent Hell. We invent it with our focus toward its existence. We have so much freedom that we can decide to live in limitation, even servitude, is what the Law of Attraction teaches. If we want we can imagine Hell. God enables us to imagine whatever we will to imagine. Why when hearing this or knowing this does anyone continue to acknowledge Hell? I can probably see that reason if I want to, yet even the answer is an imagination. In the religious story of the best place, Heaven, versus the worse place, Hell, was it no wonder that with those choices, I wanted to do all I was told that God wanted me to do, especially with the innocence of a child, which is when this stuff is taught. I like some of it, in fact, I still do live the best life I can and I always do want to please God. Yet, now it is not so planned out for me by others. I AM able to think about my thoughts on this matter. I AM able to realize what thoughts are actually mine and what thoughts have been told of me to believe. Every "thing" is now Every "think".

Before becoming aware, of course, doing the rules that God left in the Bible or at church was the only thing I knew. I apparently thought I had no choice. I was an adult before I even thought freely about how those rules got put into the Bible in the first place, by whom, when and more importantly, why. Yet, even as a child, I wondered about the way these rules sounded and the way some of them made me feel bad. They did not sound so sacred to me, but rather were ambiguous and only powerful in the fear leading up to them. The rules seemed so filled with words that completed their purpose instead of assisting my life. I was actually ignorantly in bliss before they were explained to me. And then I was amazed at these stories of good and evil, yet something never felt right to me about such a mean God! The loving God, I liked knowing, but this "vengeance is the Lord's" God, well, something just did not feel good about it all and it was very hard for me to focus on it for any length of time, although I always realized myself to be a very "spiritual" person. It, religion, struck me as a nasty fairy tale that I did not like listening to before falling asleep. As a child I always knew the difference in the storybooks filled with those "lessons", without mentioning it to the adults reading them to me. I did not feel a need to be told these rules that did not pertain to me or to anyone I knew. I knew good people, and I was a good person, a good child, and a good child of God's. All kids know that!

As I have grown to understand myself, to feel good about myself and to appreciate myself, I also grow to appreciate my physical self and my non-physical self, equally validating each self. I really appreciate that I am on-loan here in my physical body. I will die someday. We are all going to die someday. Just like I can create my life, I can decide more about dying than I have been taught. I just know it with the same gut instinct that I had as an innocent child of God's. I can greatly influence the way I die. I can decide to live and I can greatly influence the way I live. I feel more and more in control of my life and my death more and more often. I sense ramifications more from thoughts than from sin, although, I do not sin. I cannot sin. I know better and I do not desire any type of sin. Do you?

When Bob first got sick, he and his wife, Linda, who I have always felt was a really nice sister to me (you know the sister you always wanted), asked me for any information on alternative healing that I might have since they wanted to fight this disease off aggressively from all lines of attack. I knew the Law of Attraction had clear messages on wellbeing and I knew also that our thoughts create our quality of life. Our quality of life is our evidence of our wellbeing. Bob was not so willing to listen to my understanding of the Law of Attraction. I also knew that "fighting off" disease was an upstream action. Fighting is against the flow of the life God provides and enables us in our free will to hold and live. Fighting thoughts result in more fights. That is what Mother Teresa taught when she said;

"Don't invite me to an Anti-War Protest, invite me to a Peace Rally instead".

I knew that Bob's fight was pushing up against something and that in so doing he was growing more ill. What we think about we bring about and what we resist persists. Regardless and in a feeling of hope, I sent Bob a lot of information on the subject of health and wellness from the Law of Attraction's perspective.

I had known Bob was anti Law of Attraction person just by the lack of radiation he emanated and he didn't share my thoughts on the mind science of feeling good already, but since they asked for my opinion of measures to take to heal and recover into wellbeing, I started to compile emails with links to websites containing wonderful expressions of wellness from what I considered was "things" that Bob had forgotten out of his natural self. In my search there was a healing of all, if any, illness from me so the pursuit started to feel really good to me as a byproduct. I was hoping for a miracle and I continued to envision Bob well, totally well. It is not my thoughts that created Bob's illness; it was Bob's culmination of his life's thoughts and actions that had created his present status. I knew my thoughts could not change his thinking. We each only control our own wonderful thoughts; no one can control another's thoughts, although I kept feeding him this lifeline of love and support in my alternative fashion and in good will. It felt healing to be "maybe" reaching Bob with my Law of Attraction messages. I held firmly to that hope and perhaps it was that departure of hope when hearing of his death that made me grieve so hard at his surrender out of living.

During Bob's illness and return to non-physical, he was subjected to my periodic emails that contained links to spiritual wellness videos and websites, and I supported those messages with words of letting him know that I envisioned him totally well. It seemed the least I could do and it is exactly the way I do see him, curiously enough even now, I only see Bob as his healthy self, standing ready to take the next walk and social challenge. He never commented directly on my emails and just kept me informed of his demise. So when he died, I was sad that he didn't get it in time! Manifestations are like that. We keep working on them in what we do, how we think and feel.

I wished that he had heard the messages I sent to him as often as I could without intruding in his life, but he probably didn't. I loved also listening to these messages myself before I sent them off, as they are freeing and simple. They were great reminders and reflected upon the responsibility of oneself in the way one creates and accepts illness and disease or health and wellness. It is always a choice we have as individuals who are in control of our own thoughts. We chose to be here in these bodies and in this time-space-reality and with our thoughts we create all Wellness, or not.

We are supposed to feel good and wellbeing is naturally ours. Feeling good and searching and finding our own forms of joy and enjoyment are exactly the required ingredients in a life that enables and maintains good health. It is that very direction that healers should direct ill people. In so finding and obtaining happiness and joy, relief is realized. Relief, resolve and refocus are the proper responses of any and all illness. Relief from stress, resolve of fear, and refocus on better thoughts is the way to have good health. I now practice faithfully appreciating the sensations of relief, resolve and refocus. I feel relief finishing a chore, or fulfilling a promise, resolve in believing in myself, and refocus in shifting thoughts to wellness. I find relief in so many simple aspects of my life now that I am amazed at how good it feels to recognize another opportunity to find relief. I experience resolve in the confidence that I am worthy of controlling my desires. I refocus with a persuading desire to hold a better feeling thought. I feel and appreciate relief, resolve and refocus in the little events of the passing of a common day. For example, when the line is short at the post office. When the line is long at the Post Office, I stand aware among others who are a part of me. That is a simple way to embrace a feeling that is bringing health. I simply find relief, resolve and re-focus in all things in life. The more illness and worry about illness is thought about, the more illness is attracted. The more relief and resolve in focused thoughts about wellness, the more wellness is attracted. In discovering "contrasts" relief, resolve and refocus can be applied to satisfaction. Practicing this concept could change the direction of the medical industry.

To me, Bob left a residue of sadness behind at his passing forward and Joe did not. We can die, leave our bodies and ascend from them without having to experience illness, hardships or pain. That sounds good to me. As I think today about everything and anything the value of my life and my health, I feel a belief that my wellbeing is mostly in my thoughts. Thinking thoughts of joy will prolong life in health and wellness for a long time. Think thoughts that feel good and as a result you will design your life in wellness and on purpose, if you want to. It is a relief to know that. I create my life, I create the quality of my living, and I create the way in which I decide to die, and I create these things as a result of the way I am thinking and the way in which I am relieving.

Taking responsibility for thinking good of your weight or your choice of clothing this morning is a long way from taking responsibility for creating the way in which you die. I mean, what if someone kills you. Did you decide on that too? The answer, like it or not, is yes. You attracted that into your life, with your vibrations and in your focus. We do not always think we deliberately wanted what we attract, because we can attract negative stuff as easily as positive stuff, just by given either our thought attention. Intense thoughts create intense reactions to those thoughts. So thinking good thoughts is really twice as good as thinking stuff unwanted. It is in our vibrations and one doesn't even have to say a thought out loud, words are strong but they start from a thought. It is the biggest relief to not blame anyone else for anything that happens or not to me. The Law of Attraction states that you get what you think about if you like it or not. When we think what we don't want we are saying please give and send to me this what I do not want. When we think about what we do want, we are also saying give and send to me this that I do want.

It is in the realizing of your own ability to choose that we can do that. Even though it is our own choice, what happens after you die?

That's easy to answer. We are everlasting pure positive Life! Do you believe that? I do. Why do I believe that when there is no apparent evidence of this and I have been mostly instructed to believe otherwise, although there is no evidence to the alternative messages either? There is no apparently provable understanding as to what happens to you after you die. We do not understand it any more than we understand getting born. Really! Do you think you understand being born better than dying? Honestly! I think not. Further, I think it is similar in most ways just in another direction, a continuing direction, rather than in an opposite direction or an ending. Birth is a transition of the soul one experiences into the physical and death is another experience out from the physical. Death is the reconnection to the self, identified "Within". I think this to be true because, I can feel it to be true. That's enough for me.

I believe I am an everlasting entity. When I feel that I am connected to the Inner Being of me, the Source in which I am a part, especially through the "Art of Appreciation", I feel it is absolutely true. There is no evidence to the contrary, although I hear from "Within" it is true. I do not think anyone knows that the dead, as we know them, are less alive but are rather just in another dimension. It is all very subjective, yet, so many seem readily in belief that when you die you go to heaven or hell, or when you die you become reincarnated, or when you die you just cease or a number of other beliefs, yet, if all those beliefs are theoretically acknowledged, then I choose to believe in the one that makes me feel the best to believe in. Hence, without physical proof, I feel good about believing that I am going to live on after this physical body croaks, and it will. I also feel I have always been. I like the way that feels. It makes me feel good about my destiny and it makes me feel good about my life, here and now. It has to be better or easier or more relieving to live a physical life feeling better about what happens after you die, because we are all going to die, so far as I can tell. When believing that there is more, much more, then there is a whole lot less fear for dying, because dying is just the time to transition into a different dimension this wonderful soul that lives "Within" me.

I am happy to be alive, and I am going to be happy to die. I love and appreciate this wonderful feeling of Everlasting-Well-Being and Death-Everlasting-Life. I find that distinction, that I am everlasting, in my mindset of tremendous value as it settles several aspects of my being alive just as much as my dying. I do not fear Hell either, as I am sure that my soul communicates with a God that does not provide Hell an option to me. We, humans, are the only orchestrators of Hell, if we so choose. We can create our own Hells, however, God has created only goodness. Why would anyone think or teach that God would want anyone to be put to Hell ever! What a delight that we have free Will to believe and to think anything we want. Believe in Hell if you wish. I chose to believe differently.

Looking it up in twenty different versions of the Bible, Jesus doesn't spend time talking in those terms either; in fact I cannot find a single verse in the Bible where the name Jesus and the word hell are in the same sentence. The association of Jesus and hell is pretentious. Fear is the fundamental cornerstone of religions not of Jesus' teachings. Hell is a worthy proponent for both fear and religions, yet, neither for Jesus nor the other masters of the many religious beliefs on Earth. I do not hear that Jesus preaches hell at all. Do you? Why then does Christianity teach hell so fervently? What are they so angry about? Other religions teach hell, as well. I cannot buy into that any longer. I am feeling that there is an energetic inculcation of joy in thinking about that long and clear. There is only a Source of Wellbeing. There is no hell. That is something new to sing Hallelujah to. We can view life as a beautiful adventure of joyous interpretations of what we are capable of appreciating. "The Art of Appreciation" lifts up this concept and unites one to the Source "Within" that strengthens thought to connect to forever.

We are all a part of God and God doesn't want a part of him or her in hell. I do not think that if hell were like a fiery place, God wants for anyone to experience that! God wants to provide only goodness for us now and after now. I did not come form hell and I am not going to hell. I am pure positive energy. It matters little to me if you believe that, I believe that to be true. Furthermore, I believe you are also pure positive energy, whether you believe it or not. If anyone of us believes that they are less than love-energy it must make for a negative feeling about oneself. It is not God who is feeling negative, God loves you all of the time.

There is so much mental manipulation about this specific issue that religions mostly revolve around it. Sin is only the reality of your belief. If you believe that you sin, then you sin. I am no longer a sinner. I cannot sin. I am past sinning. I am more than Catholic. I am a believer in that I control my thoughts and I chose to think thoughts that are pure and loving, and I appreciate that option. There is an option to feel otherwise, yet, I cannot do that any longer. I am not going to die when I die; I am going to live some more. I am going to continue with my trusty old soul into where ever it goes, and I already know it is going to a perfectly wonderful place. I am unafraid of the wherewithal my soul travels inter-dimensionally. I've been around long enough to realize that it is all-good. But, you can believe whatever you want to believe. You can think what ever you want to think. It is all up to you what you choose. If you are happy with believing that you have reasons to fear dying for the sake of going to hell for something or other that you think God is angry for you about, then so be it. But, I have a feeling, a very good feeling, that you and I are going to laugh about this after we transition from this physical status into the marvelous continuation of life everlasting.

I am more than what I see in my physical body and I feel wiser and ancient, in fact. I have a wonderful understanding of Time and Time is always a comfortable place to put my thoughts and hence, it is a friend of mine and further more I feel like I actually can associate with the commencement of time, in the formidable sense of it's actualization. That, I must admit, feels grand. I become entwined within Time, a part of it, upon becoming physical. I have a good feeling of this, though it is impossible for me to bring anyone or myself evidence of this natural intuitive understanding and internal appreciation. Even the appreciation of eternity comes from Time. I ask people this question; "Do you believe that you are everlasting life?", when I can, without making them uncomfortable. Some say yes, of course. Others say they are unsure. And some people say no. I am always a bit sad for those who say no. I have hope for those who say maybe. I am in sync with those who say yes. I believe that we will all come to realize our forever-ness, it is just a matter of realizing it now while alive in this physical body, or realizing afterwards. It is just a matter of Time. It is certainly more enjoyable to live life believing in a glorious eternal afterlife.

In what most certainly feels to me as a heightened state of life and while experiencing "The Art of Appreciating" I brought to my Inner Being questions about Death and Everlasting Life, wanting to avail that insight into this book. I will describe the encounter by first mentioning that this reaching out and being in the connecting-space that I share with my Inner Being is mutually consented to, yet I am always excited about the space in which I enter into while the communications are returning from non-physical to physical. It is very enriching. I often sense being there in an altered time-space-reality and my senses are increased in many ways and simultaneously this absorbing slowed-down state can seemingly fog up my sight slightly and somewhat "animate" my penmanship. It is not spooky or anything. I definitely do not sense any possession of me. I allow connection. During this time I am equally inserted and not as an invader, into my Inner Being's space. It is a mutuality. It is a shared space of Appreciation.

In this communication I was bringing forth more in my vibrations than the words I used to frame a question, which I knew would commence a purposeful communication. And the answers are of more than the question, per say. I enjoy mental communications, however, I am truly appreciating written communications between my Inner Being and myself. Mentally, there is so much given to me at an instant that I am, although comprehending the messages, stunned with it all. I prefer that once the communication is commenced that I request that I write it down. This request is honored. I feel so much more comfortable in knowing that the messages will be parsed at the speed in which I can write, so I can absorb them better in comparison from the mental downloads that seem to flood me with a stillness from being almost frozen from the immensity of the thoughts that are provided, as if in huge blocks of comprehension.

I am a slow reader naturally and I enjoy reading slowly also. Words to me are so rich with meanings that as I create them slowly from my mind out or from written words in, either way, I love feeling that I understand the words and the placement of those words before me. The structure of a sentence is of interest to me and each word is to me an entity onto itself with space between them. So I read slowly so I can appreciate the meanings of these words strung together. My reading slowly allows me to comprehend words and sentences fully. I hardly ever, although sometimes do, move on to a new sentence while reading whereby I did not understand it completely. Although often, I re-read until I do understand. Some things I accept that I may not understand, yet, when I read and write slowly I follow thoughts better.

So when I asked a question of my Inner Being recently of what should I write to express better the concepts of Death and Everlasting Life it answered much more. I would like to share what I can of this experience with you because it is profoundly beautiful to me and I think it will assist, especially those who have a strong Christian or Catholic foundation.

I agreed to write the following words into this book:

"I am here holding us together in this "Now place" of this "Art of Appreciation". It is a Sacrament, as you understand those to be. They are beginnings. Are they not, to you? And they are a continuation. Are you hearing?

(This communication had to do with explaining our connection and also was starting to connect to my comprehension of Death and Everlasting Life.)

Be open to the news I bring: Be open here. We want you to hear!

Place a thought upon a thing.

(I did)

Ok, the tip of the pen does very well. It symbolizes the place in which at this very moment we connect to each other. Do you see that?

(I answered mentally, Yes.)

And do you feel that?

(Again, I answered Yes. And I did feel it. I felt the animation of my pen and a soft confidence in the flow of the penmanship, without personal intent. The words had a depth of meaning far greater than what they are as they appeared before me on the paper).

It is the same as in the experience you call death. Death is like the tip of our communications. It is the invisible connection between this dimension of physical humanity and the returning to Larger Self.

(I will note here that when the words 'invisible connection' were being written they were almost invisible to see. That is an example of the amazing multi-directional communications that I am encountering between the words being given and written.)

It (Death) *is not as you sometimes reflect in thought as the ending nor the beginning. It is rather the thru-way, the doorway, the "way" not the end or the beginning."*

I am sensing the desire for my Inner Being to clarify my growing understanding from these words brought to me to be placed into this book. In so doing, I first want to remind myself of what a Sacrament is. My favorite definition of a Sacrament is an outward signs of an inward Grace. That is exactly what I experience putting the Inward messages into outward practice. Sacraments are celebrations of God's gifts and gracious actions in our lives. Sacraments are chosen instruments of divine power. I sensed in the flood of perceptions that my Inner Being was telling me of, that it was a Sacrament that we were able to connect at the tip of a pen and that physical death itself is a Sacrament.

There is a revelation within me that both these experiences are Sacraments. The Catholic Encyclopedia says that Sacraments are "instituted by Christ for our sanctification" and surely I can believe that to be true. There are seven Sacraments in the Catholic Church and many Christian religions have similar equivalent Sacraments, perhaps by different names though, in fact, many forms of religions incorporated many similar conceptual signs and graces into their processes of participation. For the Catholics they are: Baptism, Reconciliation, Communion, Confirmation, Marriage, Holy Orders and The Anointing of the Sick. Each Sacrament is mightily filled with symbolic aspects often in ceremony and with community while silently and personally reflecting upon a variety of continuing measures of spirituality and self-awareness in agreed unity. Books are written on each and all of them; yet, herein I wish to focus on The Anointing of the Sick, or rather on its extended ritual, which are the Last Rights. The Last Rights are administered to the sick that are dying. The Last Rights, or the "Viaticum" figuratively derives from the ancient custom to make certain at a dedication last supper that the preparing traveler held all the provision for the journey of life and finally by metaphor, in the case of the Last Rights, the provisions for the passage out of this world into the next, which is still Eternity.

It is worthy to pay attention to the passage out of this world's perceptions of growth rather than the focus upon the ending of this physical experience. Be at Peace. It is ok to refute thoughts, actions and procedures that mindfully strive to follow a path already taken rather than to create a new way, or a "you" way. They still exist. Hear less the baser-tones while listening more intensely to a higher continuum. It, this being self, is a gleeful expression of fulfilling tomorrow's dreams in which you bring into creation from higher tones. Be willing to allow much and much will arrive. Appreciate and more things to appreciate come into your life.

In blessed appreciation, may you forever choose clarity while creating the colorful interwoven patterns that connect humanity.

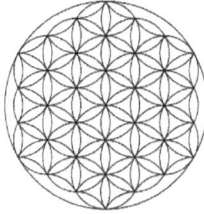

Chapter 11 - Peggy's Appreciations about Appreciating Death Everlasting Life

- ❖ I appreciate the stories of the loved ones of my life; those that touch my heart and help me sing my own song.

- ❖ I appreciate that the Law of Attraction provides me with the experiences I am ready to receive.

- ❖ I appreciate that I have everlasting life.

- ❖ I appreciate that I belong where I am and I am on a wonderful adventure.

- ❖ I appreciate you.

- ❖ I appreciate connection with my "Inner Being".

- ❖ I appreciate having enough Time.

- ❖ I appreciate sensing the Universal awareness of me.

- ❖ I appreciate my awareness of the Universe.

- ❖ I appreciate Life.

Chapter 11 - Your Appreciations of Death Everlasting Life

I appreciate this about myself: _____

_____

I appreciate this about my life: _____

_____

I appreciate this about my future: _____

_____

I appreciate this about Death: _____

_____

I appreciate _____

_____

I appreciate _____

_____

I appreciate _____

_____

I appreciate _____

_____

I appreciate _____

_____

APPENDIX A.

APPRECIATION LISTING

AND

CATEGORY CHART

CLASIFICATION

Appendix A List of Appreciations

This Appendix contains a collection of "Appreciations" submitted by friends and relatives. Each Appreciation sentence has been parsed and labeled with the categories that it associates best with from the Category Chart in Chapter 4. The collected results that follow the listing indicate that most "Appreciations" address outside-of-self focus.

Appreciation	Outside	Inside
1. I appreciate the life that appears through my windows.	Outside Self, Other Life, Thing	
2. I appreciate the humming bird drifting close to me.	Outside Self, Other Life, Places	
3. I appreciate the cat passing by with no apparent notice of me.	Outside Self, Other Life, Awareness	
4. I appreciate the neighbor passing by, perhaps seeing me when I did not see her, yet I appreciate that I felt her see me.	Outside Self, Other Life, Sense	
5. I appreciate the vibrations of sounds much like music beating the rhythm of now in time.	Outside Self, Sense, Present, Awareness	
6. I appreciate the continuous alignment of all I acknowledge and perceive.		Inside Self, Senses, Thoughts, Awareness
7. I appreciate writing thoughts and thinking about what I am thinking.		Inside Self, Action, Thoughts, Awareness
8. I appreciate visiting my parents yesterday and sensing their shared lives of better than survival feeling as I sense their wellbeing.	Outside Self, Other Life, Actions, Relationships, Awareness, Thoughts, Abundance	
9. I appreciate the light that is provided into my life today		Inside Self, Present

10. I appreciate the mood of flourishing into the flow today		Inside Self, Emotions, Abundance, Present
11. I appreciate the Law of Attraction	Inside Self/Outside Self, Experience, Emotions, Future, Thoughts	Inside Self/Outside Self, Experience, Emotions, Future, Thoughts
12. I appreciate stillness of thoughtfulness.		Inside Self, Sense, Thought, Spirit
13. I appreciate contrasts.	Outside Self, Emotions, Experiences	
14. I appreciate watching and learning from other people's experiences.	Inside Self/Outside Self, Other Life, Sense, Thought	Inside Self/Outside Self, Other Life, Sense, Thought
15. I appreciate the warmth of my home.	Outside Self, Sense, Place	
16. I appreciate my face and complexion.	Outside Self, Body	
17. I appreciate the visions I set into motion.		Inside Self, Sense, Action
18. I appreciate the great many times that things go well for me.	Inside Self/Outside Self, Allow, Abundance	Inside Self/Outside Self, Allow, Abundance
19. I appreciate my computer, the Internet and email.	Outside Self, Things	
20. I appreciate loving my family, my friends, my home, my clothes and myself.	Inside Self/Outside Self, Emotions, Relationships, Things	Inside Self/Outside Self, Emotions, Relationships, Things
21. I appreciate that we each have so much to offer each other and the world.	Inside Self/Outside Self, Relationship, Other Life, Abundance	Inside Self/Outside Self, Relationship, Other Life, Abundance
22. I appreciate and believe in myself.		Inside Self, Believe
23. I appreciate family and the honor it is to participate in my children's lives.	Outside Self, Relationships, Sense, Action	
24. I appreciate Sunday	Outside Self, Body	

Mornings and the freedom to rest.		
25. I appreciate the excitement I see my husband experience when opening a box containing something new in it.	Outside Self, Relationship, Action, Emotions	
26. I appreciate Wisdom; asking for it, and using it.		Inside Self, Spirit, ask, Action
27. I appreciate glass; the way you can see through it and the way is shines and the way it is used in so many pretty and useful things.	Outside Self, Sense, Thing, Action	
28. I appreciate my body and the way it works.		Inside Self, Body, Action
29. I appreciate Time for providing enough of it.	Outside Self, Thing, Abundance	
30. I appreciate Words and the way they transfer messages spoken, written or thought.	Outside Self, Thing, Senses, Thoughts	
31. I appreciate the tiny bird that is torso colored a beautiful orange and is playing with its mate outside the window in the gutter on the house.	Outside Self, Other Life, Sense, Thing	
32. I appreciate life and the world I live in.	Inside Self/Outside Self, Other Life, Abundance	Inside Self/Outside Self, Other Life, Abundance
33. I appreciate the way a smile feels.		Inside Self, Sense, Body, Emotions
34. I appreciate the way a twinkle in the eye feels.		Inside Self, Sense, Body, Emotions
35. I appreciate the cat walking by and stopping to see me.	Outside Self, Other Life	
36. I appreciate what happened, what is happening now and what happens next.	Outside Self, Past, Present, Future	
37. I appreciate Babies in stores.	Outside Self, Other Life, Places	
38. I appreciate shoes and clothes.	Outside Self, Things	
39. I appreciate the taste of food.	Outside Self, Sense, Thing	
40. I appreciate the day and the night.	Outside Self, Things	

41. I appreciate reading books.	Inside Self/Outside Self, Things, Action	Inside Self/Outside Self, Things, Action
42. I appreciate my neighbors as they come and go to and fro.	Outside Self, Other Life, Action	
43. I appreciate the green infused into this day.	Outside Self, Sense, Thing	
44. I appreciate words.	Outside Self, Things	
45. I appreciate hot and cold being a world apart within its similar nature.	Outside Self, Sense, Think	
46. I appreciate friends who link me to their thoughts.	Outside Self, Other Life, Relationships, Emotions, Thoughts	
47. I appreciate personalities of variety and people of similar minds.	Outside Self, Relationships, Thoughts, Abundance	
48. I appreciate the extraordinary, and the simple.	Outside Self, Things, Abundance	
49. I appreciate Federal Express packages.	Outside Self, Things	
50. I appreciate the roads and streets in our neighborhood that take us back and forth to the places we need to go to.	Outside Self, Things, Action	
51. I appreciate avoiding the dentist.	Outside Self, Other Life	
52. I appreciate growing plants, watching them grow and harvesting their fruits.	Outside Self, Other Life, Action, Senses, Things	
53. I appreciate having raised my children.		Inside Self, Relationships, Action
54. I appreciate being creative.		Inside Self, Thoughts
55. I appreciate telephones, cells, faxes, texting, instant messaging and the like.	Outside Self, Things, Abundance	
56. I appreciate my ability to care about others and myself.		Inside Self, Emotions, Other Life, Action
57. I appreciate the aromas of Christmas, the colors of	Outside Self, Sense, Things,	

Easter, the sounds of the 4th of July, the quiet of Veteran's Day, the food of Thanksgiving and the acknowledgement of my Birthday.	Abundance	
58. I appreciate the polite wrong number.	Outside Self, Thing, Other Life	
59. I appreciate Time to notice.	Outside Self, Experience, Awareness	
60. I appreciate change and finding my way along the new path it requires.	Outside Self, Place, Action, Thing	
61. I appreciate my alignment within my physical structure and within my spirit.		Inside Self, Body, Thought, Spirit
62. I appreciate a good night's sleep.		Inside Self, Body, Thought, Spirit, Thing
63. I appreciate someone saying "God Bless You" after a sneeze.	Outside Self, Sense, Other Life, Thing	
64. I appreciate taking a shower.	Outside Self, Action, Thing	
65. I appreciate getting sweaty and dirty in the garden.	Outside Self, Action, Thing	
66. I appreciate the feeling of knowing that what I am doing, the decisions I make and the ideas I have are all perfect.		Inside Self, Action, Thought, Things, Emotions, Abundance
67. I appreciate the smile I am wearing now.	Outside Self, Body, Action	
68. I appreciate the learning path I am on.	Outside Self, Thoughts, Experience	
69. I appreciate that the more I seek wisdom the more wisdom there is to see.	Outside Self, Thoughts, Sense, Abundance	
70. I appreciate my thoughts and my experiences.		Inside Self, Thoughts, Experience
71. I appreciate my husband and how special he is to me and how much I learn from him.	Outside Self, Other Life, Emotions, Action, Thought, Relationships	
72. I appreciate the future charging forth into my	Inside Self/Outside Self,	Inside Self/Outside

awareness.	Future, Present, Awareness, Action	Self, Future, Present, Awareness, Action
73. I appreciate the changes that occur so seemingly seamlessly.	Outside Self, Things, Experience, Action	
74. I appreciate my Well-Being and the energies that I yield.		Inside Self, Body, Spirit, Action
75. I appreciate all that I am attracting and wanting.	Inside Self/Outside Self, Abundance, Desires, Action	Inside Self/Outside Self, Abundance, Desires, Action
76. I appreciate old friends who seem to fade away ~ and new friends who are finding their way towards me.	Outside Self, Other Life, Sense, Relationships, Present, Future	
77. I appreciate TIME, especially NOW!	Outside Self, Thing, Present	
78. I appreciate helping my Mom out.	Outside Self, Relationship, Action	
79. I appreciate Face-book, and peeking-in.	Outside Self, Thing, Action	
80. I appreciate Neighbors who stop by for a chat.	Outside Self, Other Life, Sense, Action, Relationships	
81. I appreciate Family photos that continue to collect into years.	Outside Self, Relationship, Things, Action, Abundance	
82. I appreciate sleeping-in on Saturday mornings.	Outside Self, Action	
83. I appreciate listening to people talk to each other in another language.	Outside Self, Sense, Other Life, Abundance, Relationships	
84. I appreciate the cool fog.	Outside Self, Thing	
85. I appreciate the firemen in my town.	Outside Self, Other Life, Place	
86. I appreciate beautiful things.	Outside Self/Inside Self, Things	Outside Self/Inside Self, Things
87. I appreciate the Protestor of whom I can see that there is only joy in victory.	Outside Self, Other Life, Sense, Emotions, Action	
88. I appreciate that it		Inside Self,

behooves me to think for myself.		thoughts, Action, Spirit
89. I appreciate that all is going well for you.	Outside Self, Action, Abundance	
90. I appreciate your children.	Outside Self, Other Life, Relationship	
91. I appreciate that all is going well for me and my family too.	Inside Self/Outside Self, Relationship, Abundance, Action	
92. I appreciate the overcast cool morning and the song birds in the yard.	Outside Self, Sense, Thing, Action, Experiences	
93. I appreciate my future.		
94. I appreciate Breakfast, Lunch and Dinner.	Outside Self, Things, Abundance	
95. I appreciate that things are coming together so well and I am allowing much into my life.	Outside Self/Inside Self, Things, Abundance	
96. I appreciate clean clothes, the washer and dryer and the clean water that comes in the pipes into our house.	Outside Self, Things, Place, Action	
97. I appreciate the comforts of home.	Outside Self, Place, Sense	
98. I appreciate water.	Outside Self, Thing	
99. I appreciate seeing color.	Outside Self, Sense	
100. I appreciate the full moon.	Outside Self, Thing	
101. I appreciate what I see and what is incomprehensive to me.		
102. I appreciate you.		
103. I appreciate me.		Inside Self
104. I appreciate the high-pitched vibration I hear inside of me.		Inside Self, Sense, Experience
105. I appreciate good family morals and good choices for honor and happiness	Outside Self, Spirit, Thought, Action, Emotions, Relationships	
106. I appreciate the contrasts in my past and present and I		Inside Self, Past, Present, Sense,

love seeing from the results what was the path of least resistance.		Thoughts, Emotions, Experience
107. I appreciate not thinking about how things work out but rather finding joy in knowing that they do work out.	Outside Self, Thoughts, Thoughts, Action, Abundance, Emotions	
108. I appreciate being able to think for myself.		Inside Self, Thoughts
109. I appreciate God's love for me	Inside Self/Outside Self, God, Emotions, Relationships, Abundance	Inside Self/Outside Self, God, Emotions, Relationships, Abundance
110. I appreciate that the sun is brighter earlier today.	Outside Self, Thing, Abundance	
111. I appreciate that the flowers are rejoicing in bright fragrance today.	Outside Self, Thing, Emotions, Sense, Present, Other Life	
112. I appreciate time is "now-er" today.	Outside Self, Thing, Present	
113. I appreciate that my choices are clearer today.		Inside Self, Abundance, Present, Desires
114. I appreciate the awareness of spiritual growth.		Inside Self, Awareness, Spirit, Abundance
115. I appreciate answers to my questions.		Inside Self, things
116. I appreciate the sound of the sprinklers on the lawn.	Outside Self, Sense, Thing, Place	
117. I appreciate the gathering of clouds before my eyes.	Outside Self, Abundance, Thing, Sense, Present	
118. I appreciate that the finite is contained in it the infinite.	Outside Self, Thoughts, Abundance	
119. I appreciate this day.	Outside Self, Present	
120. I appreciate whirlwind plans.	Outside Self, Action, Thoughts	

This pie chart shows the appreciations percentage of

Inside (31%) and

Outside (69%)

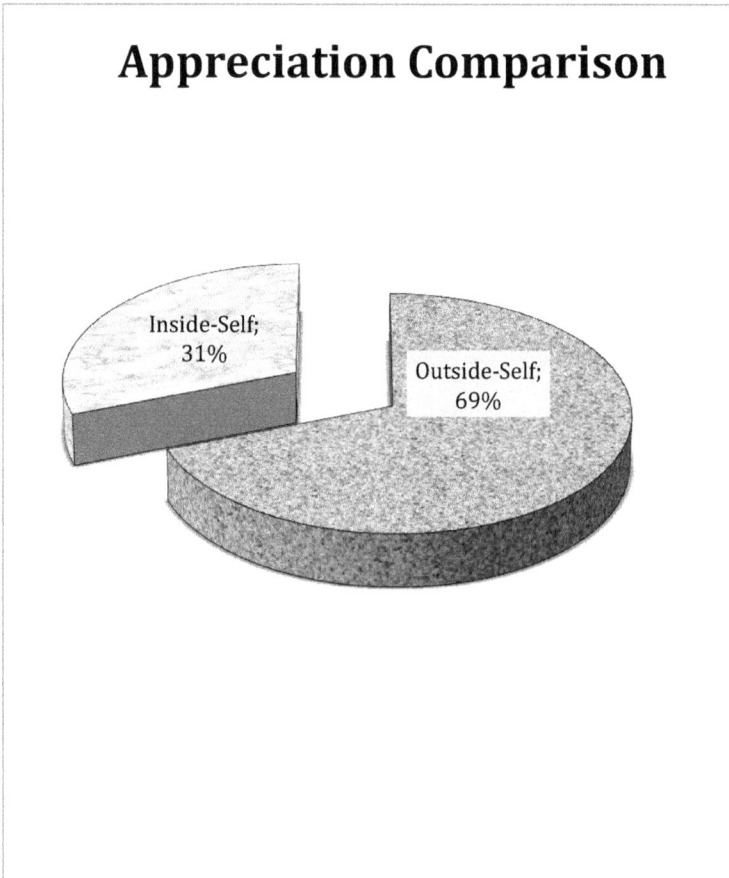

Appreciation Comparison

Inside-Self; 31%

Outside-Self; 69%

The bar chart shows the overall category distribution from Inside and Outside Self focuses.

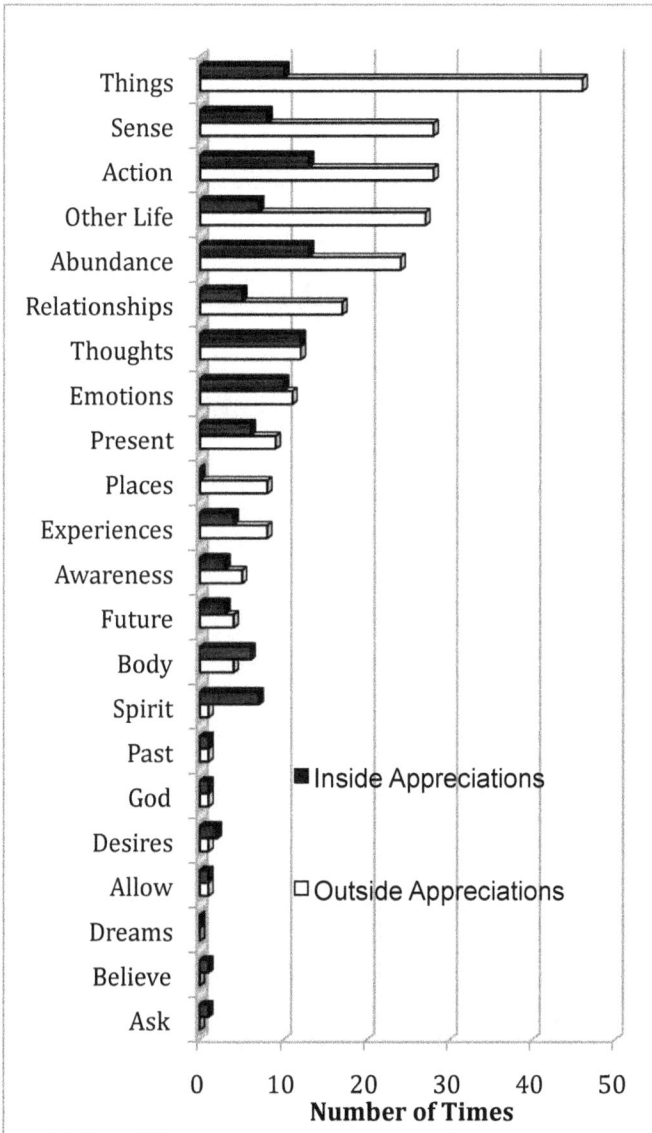

Note: The delimiter symbol used to emphasize thought-transition in the text of this book was miniaturized from a diagram of the Crop Circle reportedly discovered at Poirino (Torino) Italy. Reported the 13th of June 2010.

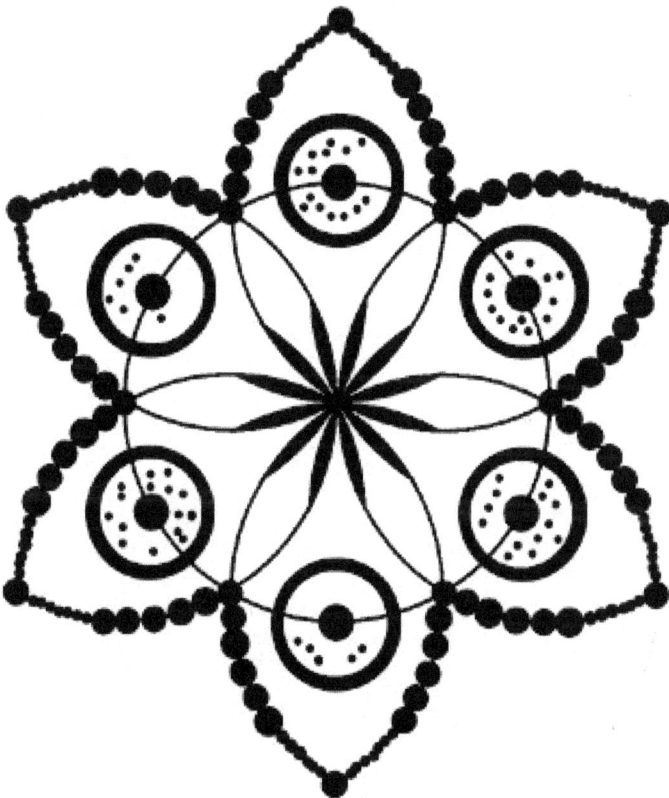

www.ingramcontent.com/pod-product-compliance
Lightning Source LLC
Chambersburg PA
CBHW051945090426
42741CB00008B/1271